PR
1807
.S5
1972

1-29519

3 9351 00054148 4

Date Due

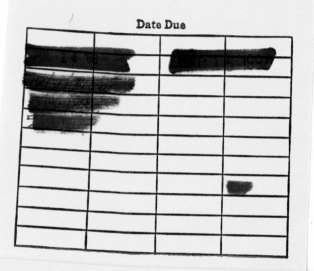

Tex...

Denton, Texas

BRO
DART   PRINTED IN U.S.A.   23-364-002

ANCRENE WISSE

OLD & MIDDLE ENGLISH TEXTS
General Editor G. L. Brook

Ancrene Wisse

PARTS
SIX and SEVEN

Edited by
GEOFFREY SHEPHERD

MANCHESTER UNIVERSITY PRESS

BARNES & NOBLE BOOKS · NEW YORK
(a division of Harper & Row Publishers, Inc.)

First issued 1959
by Thomas Nelson & Sons Ltd

This edition 1972
© Geoffrey Shepherd
issued by
MANCHESTER UNIVERSITY PRESS
316–324 Oxford Road
Manchester M13 9NR

ISBN 0 7190 0515 9

Published in the U.S.A. 1972 by
HARPER & ROW PUBLISHERS, INC.
BARNES & NOBLE IMPORT DIVISION

Printed in Great Britain
by Butler & Tanner Ltd
Frome and London

PR
1807
.D5
1972

CONTENTS

1-29519

ACKNOWLEDGMENT

Grateful acknowledgment is made to the Master and Fellows of Corpus Christi College, Cambridge, for permission to publish MS 402 in part ; and for help of various kinds to D. S. Brewer and E. G. Stanley, to Sister Ethelbert of St Paul's Convent, Birmingham, and to the Librarian and staff of the University Library, Birmingham.

ABBREVIATIONS

AB (dialect)—The common dialect of AW and texts in MS Bodley **34** (see Introduction, p. xiv)

ad Her.—*Rhetorica ad Herennium*, ed. Caplan

AN—Anglo-Norman

Ang.—Anglian

AR—*Ancrene Riwle*

AR N—*Ancrene Riwle*, ed. from Nero MS by M. Day

AR French—French text of *Ancrene Riwle*, ed. J. Herbert

AR Lat.—Latin text of *Ancrene Riwle*, ed. C. D'Evelyn

AW—*Ancrene Wisse*

BT (& Suppl.)—Bosworth and Toller, *Anglo-Saxon Dictionary* (and *Supplement*)

C—Cleopatra text of AR

DAC—*Dictionnaire d'archéologie chrétienne et de liturgie*, ed. Cabrol

de Ghellinck, *L'Essor*—J. de Ghellinck, *L'Essor de la littérature latine au XIIᵉ Siècle*

E&S—*Essays and Studies by Members of the English Association*

EETS—Early English Text Society

EGS—*English and Germanic Studies*

ELH—*Journal of English Literary History*

EME—Early Middle English

ESt—*Englische Studien*

G—Gonville and Caius MS of AR

Hall, EME—J. Hall, *Selections from Early Middle English* (2 vols.)

HM—*Hali Meiðhad*, ed. Colborn (with line reference to text)

JEGP—*Journal of English and Germanic Philology*

Jordan—*Handbuch der mittelenglischen Grammatik* (1934)

KG texts—Katherine Group texts (see Introduction, p. xiii)

Lat.—Latin

LMS—*London Medieval Studies*

LOE—Late Old English

LWS—Late West Saxon

MÆ—*Medium Ævum*

MDu—Middle Dutch

ME—Middle English

MED—*Middle English Dictionary*, ed. Kurath and Kuhn

Med. Lat.—Medieval Latin

MLR—Modern Language Review

MnE—Modern English

N—Nero text of AR

N&Q—Notes and Queries

NED—New (or *Oxford*) *English Dictionary*

OE—Old English

OE Hom I—*Old English Homilies*, ed. R. Morris (1st Series)

OFr—Old French

ON—Old Norse

PBB—Beiträge zur Geschichte der deutschen Sprachen und Literatur, ed. Paul and Braune

PG—Patrologia Graeca, ed. Migne, quoted by volume and column

PL—Patrologia Latina, ed. Migne, quoted by volume and column

PMLA—Publications of the Modern Language Association of America

QF—Quellen und Forschungen zur Sprach- und Kulturgeschichte der Germanischen Völker

RB—Revue Bénédictine

RES—Review of English Studies

RS—Rolls Series

Salu—*The Ancrene Riwle*, trans. by M. B. Salu (with page reference)

SJ—S. T. R. O. d'Ardenne's ed. of *Life of St Juliana* (with line reference to text)

SK—E. Einenkel's ed. of *Life of St Katherine* (with line reference to text)

SM—F. M. Mack's ed. of *Life of St Margaret* (with page and line reference to text)

SW—*Sawles Warde*, ed. Wilson (with line reference to text)

Stratmann-Bradley—*Middle English Dictionary*

T—Titus MS of AR

INTRODUCTION

NEARLY eight hundred years ago an anonymous cleric wrote by request a book for a small group of unknown women to whom he acted as spiritual director. These women had already shut themselves up for life within a small range of uncomfortable buildings. They were still young, it appears ; they had been well educated, and they remained highly respected in their neighbourhood. The book written for them to read in their separate cells is a lengthy exhortation to a life of prayer, privation, self-inflicted pain, self-analysis, and longing. Such a life, deliberately based on the cultivation of physical suffering, inhibitions and frustrations, may well seem strange and remote to us.

But the work is much more than a curious case-book. It shows—as does no other early writing in English—the temper and intensity of the noblest aspirations of English people in the twelfth century. At the same time in a vernacular mirror is reflected a whole complex of new spiritual ideas which belonged to Europe as well as to England.

Few English writers have commanded the wit, liveliness and sentiment of this unknown cleric. He writes with the simplicity of extreme sophistication. He was not the first of the great writers of English prose, but he is certainly not the least. His distinction was admitted for centuries, and the book was translated, copied and adapted down into Tudor times. Its continued influence gives it an added importance. For many highly gifted Englishwomen and Englishmen of the last medieval centuries, this book served not only as their manual of counsel. It remains for us the only earthly memorial of many holy lives.

MANUSCRIPTS

This rule of life for anchorites survives in Latin and French versions as well as in English. None of the existing texts in any of the three languages gives the work in its original form. The present edition of Parts 6 and 7 of the Rule is based upon one of the earliest English revisions, that in MS 402 of Corpus Christi College, Cambridge (CCCC MS 402).[1] The title *Ancrene Wisse*, ' Anchorites' Guide ' (AW), is reserved for this text of the Rule, and is provided by a rubric on f. 1r of the MS : ' I þe feaderes & i þe sunes & i þe hali gastes nome, her biginneð ancrene wisse.' The Rule as it appears in other MSS is usually referred to as the *Ancrene Riwle*.[2] The Early English Text Society has undertaken to print all existing texts of the Rule, and most have now appeared.

CCCC MS 402 consists of 4 + 114 folios. The first four folios are covered in sixteenth-century hand-writing. AW occupies the numbered folios 1 to 114*v* and is written in a firm, clear hand of the first third of the thirteenth century. At the foot of *f.* 1r a thirteenth-century inscription indicates that the volume was given to St James's church at Wigmore in Herefordshire by John Purcel, at the instance of the monk Walter of Ludlow.

The present edition of Parts 6 and 7 gives no more than a sixth of the whole rule. In preparing the text, MS contractions for English and Latin words have been silently expanded, corrections and insertions in contemporary hand-writings have also been silently admitted. Modern punctuation and capitalisation are employed, but the original paragraphs and, as far as intelligibility allows, the word divisions of the MS have been retained.

AW was written out by an intelligent scribe and there are few textual difficulties. But the fact that AW is one of several surviving revisions of the Rule makes it impossible to treat the text in complete isolation. The other English texts of the Rule are :

[1] See M. R. James, *A Descriptive Catalogue of the MSS in the Library of Corpus Christi College, Cambridge* (1912), II, 267 ; G. C. Macaulay, *MLR* 9 (1914), 145 ; N. R. Ker, Introduction to J. R. R. Tolkien's edition of CCCC MS 402, EETS 249 (1962).

[2] More anciently as *Ancren Riwle*. On title, see F. P. Magoun, *ELH* 4 (1937), 112–13.

1. Thirteenth century

(i) (N) British Museum Cotton MS Nero A.xiv. The best known text in as much as it provided the basis of Morton's original edition of the *Ancren Riwle* in 1853 : not the original text of the Rule, but some features of language and the inclusion of certain passages not found in AW suggest that N is closer in some respects to the original : see G. C. Macaulay, *MLR* 9 (1914), 149–50. N has been re-edited for EETS by M. Day (AR N). The last ten folios of the MS contain other material printed in OE Hom I, 200–17 : and see Table, p. xiv below.

(ii) (T) BM Cotton MS Titus D.xviii. The text (edited for EETS by F. M. Mack) is imperfect at the beginning and two folios later are missing. Following the Rule, *ff.* 105v–147v contain related material : see Table, p. xiv below.

(iii) (C) BM Cotton MS Cleopatra C.vi. Contains only the Rule on 196 folios. The margins carry thirteenth-century comments and additions, some from a text apparently similar to AW.

(iv) (G) Gonville and Caius College, Cambridge, MS 234/120. 93 folios contain lengthy extracts from the Rule in an order unrelated to that of any other MS. G has been edited for EETS by R. M. Wilson (1954).

2. Fourteenth century

(v) (V) Bodleian Library Vernon MS. The Rule was contained on *ff.* 271v–392v originally, but there are some losses of folios and some omissions of text.

(vi) (P) Magdalene College, Cambridge, Pepys MS 2498, 'Wicleef's Sermons'. A Wycliffite revision of the Rule (see E. Colledge, *RES* 15 (1939), 1–15, 129–45) occupies pp. 371–449. P was edited as *The Recluse* by J. Påhlsson, Lund (1911).

(vii) A MS of which only a folio remains, printed by A. Napier, *Journal of Germanic Philology* 2 (1898), 199–202.

Other English adaptations of material from the Rule are William Lichfield's *Treatise of the Five Senses* (fifteenth

century), edited from BM MS Royal 8 C.i for EETS by
A. C. Baugh (1956); the anonymous *Tretyse of Loue* (fifteenth
century), edited for EETS by J. H. Fisher (1951). Further
incorporations and borrowings from the Rule are indicated
by H. E. Allen, *MLR* 18 (1923), 1–8 and 24 (1929),
1–15.

There are French versions of the Rule : in BM Cotton
MS Vitellius F. vii, which has been edited for EETS by
J. A. Herbert (1944). A fragmentary French text also occurs
in Trinity College, Cambridge, MS 883, edited for EETS
by W. H. Trethewey (1958).

There are a number of Latin versions. C. D'Evelyn has
edited the Latin text for EETS from BM Cotton Vitellius
E.vii and Merton College, Oxford, MS 44 with variant
readings from other MSS (Magdalen College, Oxford, Latin
MS 67 and a sixteenth-century transcript, BM Royal MS
7 C.x). Several Latin Rules of the later medieval centuries
appear to draw directly or indirectly upon the English
Rule.

Until all the different texts of the Rule are available it
is scarcely possible to begin a full investigation of the
relationships between them and of many other problems
connected with the Rule. But there can be little doubt that
the Rule was written originally in English.[1] Moreover, it is
already clear that CCCC MS 402 provides the most readable
of the English texts, and it is likely that in points of detail
it often best preserves the meaning of the original. The
general modifications of tone and intention introduced by
the reviser responsible for AW are of little importance in
Parts 6 and 7.

There are several pieces of early English religious writing
—pious and didactic tracts, meditations, and saints' lives—
which show many correspondences, in vocabulary, style, and
theme, with the English texts of the Rule. They are pieces
which would provide highly suitable reading for women in
religion, such as those for whom AW was intended. CCCC

---

[1] See D. M. E. Dymes, *E&S* 9 (1924), 31–49 ; cp. M. L. Samuels.
MÆ 22 (1953), 3–6 ; H. Käsmann, *Anglia* 75 (1957), 134–56.

MS 402 contains nothing but AW. But two of the other MSS in which the Rule is found contain some of these pieces. Together all these pieces are usually referred to as the Katherine Group (KG) texts—taking the name from one of their number. The Katherine Group texts include : the lives of the virgin martyrs (i) St Katherine (SK) ; (ii) St Margaret (SM) ; (iii) St Juliana (SJ), all in alliterative prose. (iv) An alliterative prose tract *Holy Maidenhood* (*Hali Meiðhad*, HM), on the advantages of virginity. (v) A prose allegory, the *Guardian of the Soul* (*Sawles Warde*, SW), based on part of Hugh of St Victor's *De Anima*. (vi) *Hymn to our Lady* (*On Lofsong of Ure Lefdi*, HoLa), an alliterative prose paraphrase of a Latin verse prayer by Marbod of Rennes. (vii) *Orison to our Lady* (*On God Ureisun of Ure Lefdi*, OoLa) a rhapsodic address in 200 long alliterating lines. (viii) *Orison of our Lord* (*On ureisun of oure Lauerde*, OoLd), an alliterative, rhythmical address to Christ as the heavenly lover. (ix) *Hymn to our Lord* (*On Lofsong of Ure Lauerde*, HoLd), similar in style to OoLd but somewhat more penitential. (x) *The Wooing of our Lord* (*Þe Wohunge of Ure Lauerd*, WoLd), a lengthier piece in similar style exalting Christ's beauty, suffering and love.

To these texts should probably be added some of the Lambeth homilies in Lambeth Palace Library MS 487 (which also contains an imperfect copy of OoLd) ; see H. E. Allen, *PMLA* 44 (1929), 671-80. For editions of all these texts, the Bibliography should be consulted.

There is an important further link between AW and the KG texts. The spelling and language of the scribe of AW is remarkably consistent. Almost exactly the same system is used by another scribe in MS Bodley 34, which though not containing a text of the Rule, contains many of the KG texts. Of all the thirteenth-century MSS containing either the Rule or some of the KG texts, only MS Bodley 34 and CCCC MS 402 show the exceptionally intimate linguistic link, but British Museum Royal MS A.xxvii duplicates much of the material in MS Bodley 34. The following Table shows the agreement in content between a number of thirteenth-century MSS.

CCCC 402	Bodley 34	Royal 17 A. xxvii	Cotton Nero A.xiv	Cotton Titus D.xviii	Cotton Cleopatra C.vi
AW			AR	AR	AR
	SK	SK		SK	
	SM	SM			
	SJ	SJ			
	HM			HM	
	SW	SW		SW	
		HoLa	HoLa		
			OoLa		
			OoLd		
			HoLd		
				WoLd	

LANGUAGE

Much work has been done on the language of all these texts. Some of the most useful studies have been those stimulated by Professor Tolkien's work, particularly as represented in his subtle essay, ' " Ancrene Wisse " and " Hali Meiðhad " ', *E&S* **14** (1929), 104-26. The fullest account of the language of AW and of the texts of MS Bodley 34 (called by Tolkien ' the AB dialect ') is to be found in Professor d'Ardenne's edition of the legend of St Juliana. Her book provides an indispensable basis for the study of AW. In the present edition there is no call for more than a sketch of the linguistic character of the AW text.[1]

The dialect presented to the reader by the scribes of CCCC MS 402 and MS Bodley 34 is 'the written idiom of gentle and lettered people, with a knowledge in various degrees of French, written and spoken, and of Latin' (d'Ardenne, SJ, p. 177). Copied in the early thirteenth century, these MSS exhibit consistent and conservative scribal habits suited to a living literary language which retained many features of the traditional vocabulary, syntax and idiom of OE homiletic prose. Certain conventions of spelling (e.g. the spelling *Godd*, the invariable contracted forms *prof*, *pruppe*, etc., the distinguishing of pronoun *oþer* from the adjective and conjunction *oðer*) demonstrate the conscious acceptance of a scribal system. The AB language is probably best thought of as a standard but local literary dialect of Middle English.[2]

It is a western dialect, but some features of LWS are not represented (e.g. there are no forms showing LWS smoothing of *ie* to *y*). There are several words of Scandinavian origin. But the rare words *cader* (see **16,22** note); *genow*, SM 22/1 (see d'Ardenne, SJ, p. 179); *keis*, SW 37 (see J. Russell-Smith, *MÆ* **22** (1953), 104–10) are of Welsh origin. In short, the language of CCCC MS 402 and MS Bodley 34 appears to inherit the characteristics of the literary language of Wessex and yet to show significant variations and additions which suggest a localisation in an area somewhat to the north and certainly still westerly. Phonologically the OE dialect closest to this AB dialect is that variety of Mercian associated with the Vespasian Psalter. It seems probable that the AW was written out in some area of the West Midlands. The connection between West Mercia and Wessex was close from the time of Alfred. The vitality of OE life and habits in the West Midlands after the Conquest

---

[1] Other useful accounts of KG dialect in relation to particular texts are Mack, SM, *Introduction*, and Colborn, HM, pp. 47–110.

[2] See J. R. Hulbert, *JEGP* **45** (1946), 411–14 ; A. J. Bliss, *EGS* **6** (1952–3), 3–9.

is well known.[1] It is permissible to attempt even a more precise localisation. In view of the association of CCCC MS 402 with Wigmore in the thirteenth century, and later connections of MS Bodley 34 with Herefordshire, there is good reason for accepting the common belief that AW was written out in, or in an area adjacent to, Herefordshire.

(i) *Spelling*

The orthography of AW is based on OE scribal habits somewhat modified by process of time and French usage. Striking features are the frequent appearances of the letter *h* and of the combinations *ea* and *eo*.

OE *þ* and *ð* are retained without distinction of value (= *th*); *þ* is reserved for initial and occasional medial use, *ð* appears sometimes medially and in all final positions.

OE *ρ*, which appears commonly in MS with value of consonantal *w* or of vowel *u* in diphthongs, is replaced in this edition by *w*; MS *w* is rare.

h is used for OE *h* generally; as aspirate; in combinations *ht*, *hw*; and for OE spirantal *g* in medial or final positions. Initial spirantal OE *g* [j] is retained as *ȝ*. Continental *g* is used for stop and fricative.

c is usual for stop [k], but *k* is used before *e* or *i* and appears in group *ck*. Following French use, *c* sometimes appears for [s] before *e* and *i* and after consonant.

ch is used for OE front [č]; doubled, it appears as *cch*. *sch* is normal for OE *sc*; *sk* appears in ON and AN borrowings.

y (MS *ẏ*) is reserved almost exclusively for foreign words.

u is used for the vowel, but also consonantally, for voiced [v], sometimes initially, but commonly between vowels; but *f* is also used for this sound, initially and before a consonant. The *v* form (properly a capital letter form) is occasionally used instead of *u* for vowel, or instead of *u* or *f* for consonant.

---

[1] See W. Keller, *Die litterarischen Bestrebungen von Worcester in angelsächsischer Zeit*, QF 64 (1900); R. W. Chambers, *On the Continuity of English Prose*, Oxford (1932), p. lxxxiii; R. M. Wilson, *Early Middle English Literature*, London (1939), pp. 112ff.

(ii) *Phonology*

In AW the same symbols are used for both long and short vowels. The developments of native stressed vowels from OE into AW dialect are set out in the Table on pp. xviii, xix.

Vowels in unstressed syllables are usually reduced to *e* ; *tþ, dþ* are assimilated to *tt* ; final *d* is often unvoiced to *t* ; *ch w* are assimilated to *ch ch* in *ich chulle* ; final *n* is frequently dropped before consonant.

(iii) *Accidence*

Nouns are of two main types,
1. Strong nouns with plural in *-es* (chiefly strong masc. and neuter nouns in OE).
2. Weak nouns with plural in *-en* (chiefly fem. nouns and weak nouns in OE).

Type 1 has either no ending or *-e* in all cases of singular, except genitive in *-es* ; plural is also *-es*, with genitive plural *-e* or *-ene*. Frequently, however, in singular after preposition, *-e* is added to a noun which has no inflexion in nominative or accusative.

Type 2 has *-e* throughout singular ; in plural *-en*, genitive plural *-ene*.

But many nouns show variation from this system : *freond, þing, word* have uninflected plurals ; *cwen* is of Type 2, though without *e* in nominative ; *licome* (OE weak noun) falls into Type 1 ; *sunen* and *limen* assume Type 2 plurals. French nouns add *-s* for plural ; those ending in *t* show *z* (= *ts*).

Adjectives. The usual inflexion is *-e*, used to mark (i) plural ; (ii) weak declension, *viz.* after article, demonstrative and possessive adjectives, and in vocative use ; (iii) substantival use of adjective. There are anomalous uses of this inflexional *-e*.

Survivals of other OE adjectival inflexions are rare ; but *alre, tweire* (genitive plural), *summes, alles, reades* (genitive singular), occur.

Gender. The regular OE use of grammatical gender is lost ; but that a sense of it survives is occasionally shown in the use of pronouns.

	OE (WS)	OE (in Vespasian Psalter)	Development into EME (W. Midl.)	AW form	= MnE
OE a before 1	habbað	habbað		habbeð	'have'
" back consonant (but cf.)	eall	all		al	all
after palatal with back mutation	dagas (pl.)	dægas		dahes	days
	dæg (sg.)	deg		dei	day
	scearp	scearp		scharp	sharp
" shortening	fæder	feder (nom.), fedur (dat.)	*fedur	feader	father
	lǣssa	lǣssa	*lǣsse	leasse	less
Gmc. a WS æ with breaking	hwæt	hwæt hwæt		hwet fhweat	what
	hearm	hearm	*hærm	hearm	harm
OE ā	ān	ān		an	one
WS ǣ, Ang ē (Gmc. ǣ)	þǣr	þēr		þer	there
OE ǣ (Gmc. ai)	hǣlan	hǣlan		healen	heal
OE ēa smoothed before pal. with umlaut smoothed after pal.	dēad	dēad		dead	dead
	nēah	nēh		neh	nigh
	hīeran	-hēran		here(n)	hear
	scēawian	scēawian	*schāwin	schawin	show

OE					
e	hell	hell		helle	hell
with breaking	heorte	heorte		heorte	heart
after w	weorpan	weorpan	wurþan	wurðen	'become'
smoothed before pal.	weorc	werc		werc	work
with back mutation	heofon	heofen		heouene	heaven
ē *from ō by umlaut*	hēr	hēr		her	here
	cwēn	cwēn		cwen	queen
ēo	brēost	brēost	*brōst	breoste	breast
i + *h consonant*	bringan	bringan		bringen	bring
	riht	reht	riht	riht	right
ī	līf	lif		lif	life
o a/o + *nasal*	folc	folc		folc	folk
	man / mon	mon		mon	man
ō	gōd	gōd		god	good
u	lufian	lufian		luuien	love
ū	hū	hū		hu	how
y	cynn	cyn		cun(nes)	kin
	cyning	cyning	king	king	king
ȳ	fȳr	fȳr		fur	fire

Adverbs are often formed from adjectives by the addition of *-e*, and accordingly are distinguished from adjectives sometimes with difficulty.

Pronouns are the least stable feature of AW language (see d'Ardenne, SJ, p. 222ff). Often the context of meaning alone can suggest a distinction between the definite article and the demonstrative usage of *þe, þet*.

Verbs. The OE strong-verb system survives in the main. In using weak verbs, a new grouping was carefully observed by AB scribes. This grouping has been submitted to an examination, important for its general implications in matters of linguistic development, and of date and provenance of AW dialect, by J. R. R. Tolkien, *E&S* 14 (1929), 117–26.

Verbs in AW dialect are most conveniently classified according to the scheme provided by Professor d'Ardenne (SJ, p. 234), as follows.

(i) Strong verbs of all classes, e.g. *neomen*; (ii) weak verbs with long stem, e.g. *heren*; (iii) weak verbs with doubled medial consonant in infinitive, e.g. *sullen*; (iv) weak verbs (corresponding to OE Class II weak verbs with long or dissyllabic stem), ending in *-in*, e.g. *lokin*; (v) weak verbs (corresponding to OE Class II weak verbs with short stem), ending in *-ien*, e.g. *þolien*.

	(i)	(ii)	(iii)	(iv)	(v)
infin.	neom-en	her-en	sull-en	loki-n	þoli-en
1 *sg. pres.*	neom-e	her-e	sull-e	loki	þoli-e
pl. pres.	neom-eð	her-eð	sull-eð	loki-ð	þoli-eð
sg. pres. subj.	neom-e	her-e	sull-e	loki	þoli-e
pl. pres. subj.	neom-en	her-en	sull-en	loki-n	þoli-en
pres. part.	neom-inde	her-inde	sull-inde	loki-nde	þoli-ende
2 *sg. pres.*	nim-est	her-est	sule-st	loke-st	þole-st
3 *sg. pres.*	nim-eð	her-eð	sule-ð	loke-ð	þole-ð
sg. imper.	nim	her	sule	loke	þole
1 & 3 *sg. pret.*	nom	herde	salde	lokede	þolede
2 *sg. pret.*	nome	herdest	saldest	lokedest	þoledest
pl. pret. (& *subj.*)	nomen	herden	salden	lokeden	þoleden
sg. subj.	nome	herde	salde	lokede	þolede
past part.	inumen	iherd	isald	iloket	iþoled

The Glossary should be consulted for represented forms of ' anomalous ' verbs, i.e. for the ' preterite-present ' verbs *ah, con, dear, duhen, mei, most, schal, unnen, wat,* and also for *beon, don, dan, wulle.*

(iv) *Vocabulary*

KG texts have a number of characteristic forms and words, some of which are not found elsewhere in ME. Often, too, their usages recall the phraseology and vocabulary of OE. Attention is drawn to such words and forms in the Notes.

In AW there are many words of French origin[1] (well over a hundred in Parts 6 and 7). The Scandinavian element is much smaller and sometimes marked simply by a modification of a native form or meaning.

DATE AND AUTHORSHIP

CCCC MS 402 has been dated palaeographically as of the first third of the thirteenth century. In the insertions in AW (not found in N) are references to the Friars, to ' Vre freres prechours & ure freres meonurs ' on *f.* 16*v* (cp. also *f.* 112*v*). AW must then have been transcribed after 1224, the year in which a party of Franciscans (Friars Minor) first came to England. The Dominicans (Friars Preacher) had arrived in 1221. Both orders quickly attracted notice and spread rapidly.

Professor Tolkien, in his abstemiously linguistic discussion of the AB dialect, has argued convincingly that the stage of development represented in this dialect cannot ' be put back much before 1225, if as far ' (*E&S* 14 (1929), 120). We may assume that the Rule had been revised and transcribed into the volume which was to become CCCC MS 402 within ten years of the Friars' arrival—after 1225 and probably before 1235.

When and where the original Rule was written is not so easily settled. There have been several speculations. The most elaborate investigation is still that provided by Miss H. E. Allen, whose work on many aspects of the Rule has

---

[1] See O. Funke, *ESt* 55 (1921), 24.

been of first-rate importance. Unfortunately Miss Allen succumbed to the attraction of her own discovery of a curious parallel between the circumstances that seem to underlie the Rule and the history of three nobly born sisters, Emma, Christina, and Gunhilda, living as recluses. As early as the 1130s these ladies lived at the priory of Kilburn near London, a dependency of the abbey of Westminster, under the direction of a priest, Godwine. Miss Allen urged that this Godwine wrote the original Rule for these three sisters.[1] The general situations are indeed remarkably similar. In one of the passages peculiar to N (quoted in note on 7,17) the recluses of the Rule are spoken of as well-born and natural sisters, and the conditions of life and status implied throughout the Rule, and indeed even in AW (except in some of the inserted passages where there is the suggestion of a larger community), agree very well with what is known of this small community at Kilburn in the mid-twelfth century. But there are great and accumulating difficulties in accepting so early a date for a Rule approximating to AW as we have it.

There are a score of passages in AW which make close contact with writings available only in the second half of the twelfth century, not only with those writings of Bernard and Ailred to which R. W. Chambers (RES 1 (1925), 17ff) drew Miss Allen's attention, but with the work of such men as Adam the Scot, Peter of Blois, and of a number of Masters of the University of Paris. Miss Allen was able to believe that Ailred drew upon the Rule, not the Rule on Ailred; but it is impossible to ascribe all the correspondences to the influence of the Rule. Praise it though we may and should, it seems improbable that a vernacular Rule should have been common reading at the University of Paris before the year 1200. On the other hand, if all points of contact with writings later than the mid-twelfth century are to be explained as later interpolations into the original Rule, then we need not be much concerned with the original Rule, for it must

---

[1] See H. E. Allen, *PMLA* **33** (1918), 474–546; *PMLA* **44** (1929), 635–80 (both full of information about the eremitical life in general), *MLR* **16** (1921), 316; *PMLA* **50** (1935), 899–902.

have been completely recast and reformed. Our concern is bound to be with the Rule as we have it, which, despite variations, exhibits an unmistakeable homogeneity and unity. It reveals the devotional and social interests of the late twelfth century at the earliest.

The material of latest date as yet discovered which has been incorporated into the Rule is liturgical. AW *f.* 5r contains a salutation *Ave principium nostre creationis*, etc. This, according to Peter of Roissy, Chancellor of Chartres in the early thirteenth century, was a composition of *dominus P. Cancellarius Parisiensis* (see V. L. Kennedy, *Medieval Studies* 5 (1943), 9). This Lord P. would be either Peter of Poitiers, Chancellor of the University 1193–1204, or Praepositinus, Chancellor 1206–10. If the prayer is ascribed to the earlier Chancellor, though he was active in the learned world as early as 1175, it is unlikely that the prayer could have had wide diffusion long before the end of the century. But indeed the liturgical background of the Rule, altogether and in its details, cannot be earlier than the late twelfth century, and may well be that of the early thirteenth.

There are moreover several pieces of evidence even in Parts 6 and 7, slight in themselves, which taken together suggest a date for the Rule not earlier than the last decade of the twelfth century: the interest in and treatment of Greek fire (see **27,11ff** note); the question of the crucifix with three nails (see **22,13** note); and the slight but palpable hostility against the Jews (see **23,13f** note; **28,14**).

But if the author was knowledgeable about contemporary affairs, as he appears to have been, he would not have referred to the tournament as he has done (see **22,8** note) if he had been writing well into the thirteenth century. Moreover, his devotional interests belong to the twelfth rather than the thirteenth century. His treatment of confession, his apparent aversion from mysticism, his insistence on the usefulness of reading as against overmuch prayer, all point in the same direction. The Fourth Lateran Council of 1215 insisted upon a stricter ecclesiastical control of unattached religious, and it is reasonable to assume that the original Rule, even the Rule as presented in N, is somewhat less concerned with institutional religion than is AW, and considerably less concerned with it than the Lateran Council expected spiritual directors to be. Most of the insertions peculiar to AW attempt to inject into the Rule a slightly more formalistic spirit.

As far as present knowledge extends, it seems fair to conclude that the Rule which provided the basis of AW was written about the year 1200, and on the whole probably after, rather than before 1200.[1]

No version of the Rule in the vernacular gives any information about authorship. Nor is there any direct information about any of the authors, revisers, or scribes of any of the KG texts. Absence of knowledge often serves as a stimulus to speculation.

At the beginning of the Latin version of the Rule, Magdalen College, Oxford, Latin MS 67, is a note that the work was written by Simon of Ghent, Bishop of Salisbury (1297–1315) for his sisters, recluses at Tarrent in Dorset. The ascription could apply only to this Latin version, but, on the strength of this fourteenth-century association with Tarrent, Morton suggested that the original English Rule was composed by an earlier Bishop of Salisbury, Richard Poore, consecrated in 1217, translated to Durham in 1229, but buried at Tarrent on his death in 1237. No evidence of weight supports the ascription of authorship to Richard Poore.[2]

For many years the Dominican V. McNabb persisted in maintaining that the Rule was of Dominican origin, written as he thought probably by Robert Bacon (c. 1170–1248). The argument was early shown to be devoid of substance, though the discussion continued unprofitably.[3]

---

[1] E. J. Dobson, *Proceedings of British Academy* **52** (1967), 162–93, has some useful observations on the preceding paragraphs.

[2] *The Ancren Riwle*, ed. James Morton, Camden Society, LVII (1853), pp. xii–xv; but see R. W. Chambers, *RES* **1** (1925), 13–14.

[3] V. McNabb, *MLR* **11** (1916), 1–8; *MLR* **15** (1920), 406–9, etc.; cp. H. E. Allen, *PMLA* **33** (1918), 538–46, etc. C. Kirchberger, *Dominican Studies* **7** (1954), 215–38, reasserted this Dominican origin, but unconvincingly.

J. Hall, in EME II, 375–6 (and see his line notes), con-
cluded that there were two Englishmen in the twelfth century
capable of having written the Rule : Gilbert of Hoyland
(*d.* 1172, the continuator of St Bernard's Sermons on the
Song of Solomon), of whom Hall has little to say ; and
Gilbert of Sempringham (?1083–1189), the founder of the
Gilbertine order, a great spiritual director of women. Once
again, no positive evidence is brought forward to support
either suggestion. Both are unlikely.

It is possible that the author of the Rule will be identified
in the future. But much more information about the
religious life and literature of the late twelfth and early
thirteenth centuries in England must be collected before a
considerable measure of luck makes the identification at all
likely.

But the book tells us something about the man who wrote
it if we do not ask too much. The author of the Rule was
a scholar. We can observe something of his interests and
something of his range of reading from an examination of his
book. The Rule is in many respects a compilation of
commonplaces, but they are commonplaces of an uncommon
mind. Like Walter Map or Adam the Scot, he would have
shrunk from the thought of being considered an original.
Like Ailred's *On the Anchorite Life*, the Rule is advisedly put
together out of other men's counsels. In the Rule there is
scarcely a turn of thought which cannot be closely paralleled
in books with which its author may well have been acquainted.
One of the purposes of the Notes in this edition is to show
how representative is the Rule of the devotional and homiletic interests of its time. If we cannot distinguish the
author's features, we can at least recognise some of the
furniture of his mind.

The author's reading

The Bible provides most of the material of the Rule—the
medieval Bible, a vast indivisible unity, but perceived only
by glimpses. The author knows the Bible well (from a text
usually recognisable as the Vulgate), but he appears to know

it primarily as it was interpreted for moral and devotional purposes, and also in its use in the services of the Church (see 7,7 note, 9,12 note, etc.). Often his approach to the text is through the crust of traditional commentary, at times bizarre enough to the modern mind. On several occasions he refers to a gloss (see 7,29 note). Often it is a gloss which leads him to the scriptural text, not an initial memory of Scripture which prompts him to interpretation (cp. 6,36, 8,28, etc.). Often, of course, his use of Scripture depends on the use made of it by the author he is following, as for example in his adaptation of Bernard's sermon at the beginning of Part 6.

To the author, as to all men of all orders in the Middle Ages, the Psalms is the most familiar book. But he draws on Genesis and Exodus often, also on Isaiah. The so-called Sapiential books, Proverbs, Ecclesiastes, and Ecclesiasticus, are well known ; in a clerical education they were studied early. His use of the Song of Solomon reflects twelfth-century interest (see 15,38 note). In his use of the New Testament the author also conforms with the habits of his time. St Matthew and the Pauline Epistles provide most of the material ; only to a limited extent (in Parts 6 and 7) is the Book of Revelation drawn upon.

His use of the Bible is in the main moralistic—that is to say, he follows the older fashion of exegesis which aimed at drawing out moral and spiritual counsel. The newer method, particularly as promoted by the scholars of the abbey of St Victor in France, was to examine the text for its literal meaning. On some occasions the author of the Rule, although still in fact using the Bible moralistically, appears acquainted with the new methods of study. In his etymologising (6,26, 14,9ff), in his dissection and comparison of texts (6,18ff, 15,34ff, 30,1ff) and in his allegorising we may believe he made use of some of the new aids which were being devised to promote Biblical studies. Not only was the gloss being systematised, but learned clerks were producing alphabetic handbooks (*Distinctiones*) of keywords 'from A to Zyma' with moral and symbolic meanings, dictionaries of interpretations of names, collections of

synonyms or of allegories, classified handbooks of birds and
beasts and flowers and precious stones and numbers (each
with a moral meaning attached). The output of compilations
of this sort was large in the late twelfth century.[1] The
author of the Rule made judicious use of them.

As with the Bible, so with other writers to whom he
refers, it is often difficult to tell whether the author of the
Rule is making a direct use of originals entire, or whether
he is not rather using some of the collections of authorities
(*Sententiae*), or current anthologies (*Florilegia*), which would
be available in any library by the beginning of the thirteenth
century. However, considering the Rule as a whole, we
must recognise that the range of scriptural reference or contact
with a variety of extra-scriptural writings is wide.

From the Latin collection of the *Lives of the Fathers*,
already well known in OE times, he draws several anecdotes.
Their ascetic character suited his theme. He adapts what
was a fairly familiar passage from Cassian at the beginning
of Part 7 (see 19,15ff note), and takes another story from
Cassian at f. 114v. But the basis of his moral and ascetic
theology is Augustinian. This was ordinary enough. But
some of Augustine's writings exercised a special attraction
for devotional writers of the twelfth century, for Augustine's
insistence on the knowledge of self which is implicit in the
knowledge of God, had the power of a new revelation in this
later age. Many devotional manuals of the twelfth century
incorporate or echo passages from Augustine's *Confessions* or
Soliloquies. Such manuals the author of the Rule certainly
knew and used. But how much of Augustine he knew at
first hand cannot be shown. There are nearly a score of
borrowings in the Rule from a range of Augustine's works,
and in addition there are several correspondences with works,
old and new, which in the twelfth century were mistakenly
attributed to Augustine.

But many of the more general Augustinian ideas come to
the author as they had come to his predecessors through
Gregory the Great, the practical populariser of Augustine's

---

[1] De Ghellinck, *L'Essor*, pp. 76ff.

theology. From Gregory the Rule makes nearly forty direct quotations, nearly half of them from the *Morals*. Several passages in earlier parts of the Rule run for paragraphs as free adaptations of a Gregorian exposition of Scripture.

The author also knew and used the influential *Book of Prayers and Meditations* (*PL* 158, cols. 709–1016), collected during the twelfth century under Anselm's name. The temper of heart and mind cultivated in the Archbishop's circle at Canterbury in the early years of the twelfth century, as portrayed in Eadmer's *Life* and in the collection of Anselm's *Similitudes*, lived long in the religion of the English. An attitude of spirit very like Anselm's, intense but refined, self-accusing, almost abject, but still self-controlled and courteous, pervades the Rule. It owes more to Anselmian piety than the half-dozen quotations might suggest.

But all late medieval devotional writings submit to the influence of Bernard of Clairvaux (see p. xxxii below). The Rule is something other than a mere product of Cistercian piety in the vernacular, but nevertheless its debt to Bernard and his disciples is declared on page after page. The author knows the pious tales of the order (see 12,35ff note). He knows also, and intimately, a variety of Bernard's writings and quotes from them more accurately than is his wont with other writers. He knows, too, some of the esoteric formulas of Cistercian piety (see 20,2 note). We must assume his acquaintance with other Cistercian authors, with the Cistercian Archbishop of Canterbury, Baldwin of Ford, with Geoffrey of Auxerre and Alcher of Clairvaux ; to Ailred of Rievaulx he owes a particular debt (see p. xxxvi below and Notes *passim*).

Naturally enough, in view of his theme and his audience, we gain but little idea of this author's more general reading. In earlier Parts of the Rule he quotes Ovid and Seneca, but the quotations are commonplace. He appears to have been acquainted with Geoffrey of Monmouth's *History* (see 22,8 note), and possibly with writings of John of Salisbury and Alexander Neckam.

There seems little doubt that the author of the Rule must be associated with a number of lively and scholarly English-

men at the end of the twelfth century who catch the tone
of, and indeed in many cases contributed to the eminence
of, the University of Paris at that time. The principal
teacher of this group had been the Frenchman Peter the
Cantor, lecturing at Paris from 1169 (bishop of Paris in
1196, died 1197). Among his English disciples are Robert
Curzon, who became Chancellor of the University, William
of the Mounts (or of Lincoln), and greatest of them all,
Stephen Langton. Apart from the Bible, no writing affords
more points of contact with the Rule in themes, development
of themes, and in common quotations than does the *Verbum
Abbreviatum* of Peter the Cantor. The author of the Rule
shares with him and his famous disciples their practical
moral interests ; he seeks similar forms of easy and lively
expression, avoiding theological technicalities, drawing upon
the contingences of everyday life. These men, together with
others of a very similar style of thinking, men such as Walter
Map, Gerald the Welshman, and especially Peter of Blois,
occupy an important area in English intellectual and literary
history which has never been adequately surveyed.

If we must have an image of the author of the Rule we
must seek it in his book. It seems unlikely that he was
a monk. His book owes scarcely anything to the Benedictine
Rule. In his liturgical recommendations he is decidedly
eclectic. If he is to be thought of as himself living under
a Rule, we should perhaps think of him as a member of the
least regimented orders, the Canons of Augustine. He may
well have been a secular clerk, a domestic chaplain, or a parish
priest.[1] He was certainly no ecclesiastical rigorist save in his
demands on conduct. Plainly he had had much pastoral
experience. He knew the English scene well, he was at home
among gentles that still lived close to the land and the market
town. His intellectual interests were wide. Part 7 certainly
suggests his acquaintance with French romance and his
interest in the visual arts. He was fond of medical imagery

[1] See Salu, *Introduction* by G. Sitwell, p. xxi ; C. H. Talbot, *Neophilologus* **40** (1956), 50 ; D. S. Brewer, *N&Q* (New Series) **3** (1956),
232–6.

and his terms are somewhat technical (see **9**,1ff, **10**,2off, **13**,3ff, etc.). He was probably a travelled man, to Paris at least, perhaps also to Rome. The recluses who received the first copy of the Rule could never have felt entirely remote from the experience of a wide and exciting world.

THE EREMITICAL LIFE

Among Christians the first large-scale movement away from society took the form of an individual flight by men and women of the fourth century into the deserts of Asia Minor and North Africa. There, in the following centuries, the so-called Desert Fathers led their solitary lives, though these were often passed physically within the confines of a loosely organised communal settlement. A monasticism of this type became familiar in Celtic lands later, and also in England. Solitaries are common enough figures in Bede's *Ecclesiastical History of the English* and in later OE records. But the norm of Western monasticism, as established by Benedict of Nursia (*c*.480–*c*.547) and set out in the Benedictine Rule, conceived of the monastic life as essentially corporate. Monks lived in community, their way of life was strictly regulated, and their devotions were highly organised. And this is the ideal which dominated English religious life in the centuries following the Benedictine reform of the tenth century.

But in northern Italy in the eleventh century arose a new but loosely defined movement, spreading northwards and westwards to attract many of the noblest, liveliest minds of twelfth-century Europe. This movement is marked by the vocation, once again, for the solitary life of contemplation. It is usual and convenient to distinguish as 'hermits' those who responded to this call by a life of devotion in geographical isolation, from 'recluses', those who lived in strict physical confinement. The life of the recluse was obviously particularly suitable for women.

The new attractiveness of the solitary life initiates and sustains a change in the character of religious feeling. There developed a new, intense, often savage concern with personal sinfulness and personal salvation. Old communal values in religion as in other social relations were crumbling. Hermits and recluses in great number ventured into a personal isolation, towards a fuller knowledge of self and a more intimate knowledge of God. Some were tempted to estimate their spiritual progress by measuring it on their own pulses. Pain, love, uncontrolled sentiment were all put to use. Often the psychological impetus appears aesthetic rather than moral. Religion with some of them became a life to be experienced rather than duties to be performed. The eremitical movement at this time is part of a tremendous shift in Western intellectual history. If we still assume the validity of Jacob Burckhardt's belief that a European Renaissance at the close of the Middle Ages is marked by the emergence of individual, freely-operating consciousness, then these hermits and recluses of the eleventh and twelfth centuries must be accounted its harbingers. Their habits of introspection, their techniques for the control of thought, their attempts to clutch at the irreducible core of personality—at the very ' spark of the soul '—and their struggles for adequate expression have given a stamp and character to the mentality of Europeans. Not only had they their own souls to save ; they were colonising kingdoms of the mind not yet constituted.

People of all sorts acknowledged and responded to the attraction of the new ideal in different ways. Anselm, driven over the Alps by the desire for a more austere, intenser religious life, ended his career as Archbishop of Canterbury. Godric, in his youth a sea captain, probably pirate as much as merchant, spent his last sixty years in retreat at Finchale, Co. Durham. William, a knight of the de Lacys, left their armed service to offer as a recluse at Llanthony armed service to God (see **18,11ff** note). But the beginnings of the great movement can now be studied best, not in biography, but in the devotional writings of such men as Peter Damian, John of Fécamp, John the Man of God, and of Anselm himself.

The spirit of the new movement affected the monastic world, and to accommodate it reformed orders of the Benedictines were established. Above all other orders, the

Cistercians, guided by the genius of Bernard of Clairvaux, gave character to the new spirituality. Bernard (1091–1153), of noble Burgundian birth, after an intensive education, joined the monastery at Cîteaux in 1113, and in 1115 became abbot-founder of the new monastery of Clairvaux. His own life gave the example of austerity, grace, and tranquil intensity of spirit which marked Cistercianism in its early history. But the tranquillity was won by the conquest of pride and desire, and with Bernard the intensity often broke into flame. From Clairvaux he exhorted and reproved kings and princes, he made and controlled prelates, he launched a Crusade, he put down Abelard, the most brilliant thinker of a brilliant century. Yet he was neither statesman, nor theologian, nor philosopher; as a preacher irresistible, he nevertheless acknowledged a greater thing than preaching. Prayer was the substance of his life; he was at home only in the cloister. He wrote tirelessly—letters, sermons, tracts. His Latin prose is highly sophisticated, energetic, witty, antithetical, bright with verbal figures and astonishing imagery, consciously designed to achieve effects of sentiment, pathos, anger, reproach, or delight.

Most of Bernard's writings were occasional pieces, but nearly everything he wrote can be used out of context for devotional purposes as matter for meditation. The popularity and influence of his writings in later medieval times is immense. He feeds the roots of pre-Reformation spirituality. Though he wrote as a monk and chiefly for monastic audiences, he spoke to the minds and affections and aspirations of all men in later times. St Francis of Assisi proclaimed before the world what St Bernard of Clairvaux had intended for the cloister.

For what had started with men as a compulsive vocation to solitude could not always be accommodated even in these new religious orders—the Cistercians, Premonstratensians, Savignacs, Grandmontines, Gilbertines, Carthusians, and so on—that flourished during the twelfth century, all in one way or other dedicated to the new ideal of a stricter, more intense spiritual life. Furthermore, the practical results of the reforms associated with Hildebrand (Pope Gregory VII,

1073–85), and the growing insistence within the Church on the power of the priesthood and the efficacy of sacraments to be administered solely by the priesthood—these developments left even less scope for the free workings of the spirit. Eventually solitary vocations were brought under ecclesiastical control, but during the twelfth century they were astonishingly numerous and varied. Many recluses or hermits were in more or less remote dependence on a particular monastery, or a particular priest, either monastic or parochial. Some appear to have considered themselves almost entirely self-sufficient. The degree of isolation from the world varied. Some lived in and on the world as beggars. Some lived in temporary retreats, or in small groups, some completely apart from men and the visible Church. To any of a variety of lives such as these, a call to the religious life might lead a layman or a laywoman of the twelfth century.

No people in Europe seem to have been more drawn to the eremitical life than the English. Probably the old call of the solitary life, which had been strong wherever the Celtic church had been established, never lost its appeal. At any rate in the twelfth century the recluses of Kilburn were three among many. At Ely, for example, there were several female recluses during the course of the century. A woman called Lucy was enclosed at Bury St Edmunds, one Matilda at Wareham in Dorset, another at Belchford (Lincs), a Basilia at Oxford, an Ælfwine at Flamstead (Herts). There survives a life of Christina, recluse of Markyate, St Albans (ed. C. H. Talbot, 1959). From the late eleventh century comes the strange story of Eve, a nun of royal blood at Wilton, who went oversea to live as recluse under the direction of a monk at Vendôme. More than a century later, about 1222, another great lady, Loretta the Countess of Leicester, became a recluse at Hackington near Canterbury and lived there for over forty years. She was well provided for, kept a small train of servants, and aided and encouraged the work of the friars. The list of recorded names of recluses could be extended. We must, moreover, believe that most left no record. The congregation of recluses of which AW f. 69r appears to suggest that there are already communities in London, at Oxford, Shrewsbury, and Chester is now quite forgotten.[1]

Inclusion

According to his biographer John of Ford, Wulfric of Hasel-bury about the year 1125, ' without any appointment of the bishop, with no solemnity of benediction, but by the author-ity of the Holy Ghost . . . buried himself with Christ in a cell close to the church '. But it was usually expected and was later required that anchorites should first be tested and approved before withdrawing from the world. The Rule certainly suggests that the anchoresses to whom it was addressed were under episcopal control (*f.* 1*v* (Salu 3)), and had taken solemn vows of obedience, chastity, and stability. These vows were presumably taken upon inclusion.

A Pontifical of the twelfth century (BM Cotton MS Vespasian D.xv) provides the order of service for the en-closing of an anchorite.[2] It is a simple service in this form (often much elaborated in later time), constructed about the ceremony at the entrance to the cell as an extension of the mass of the Holy Ghost. In other service books this mass is replaced by the mass of the dead, and this substitution emphasises a main motif of the service even in the Vespasian Pontifical. The recluse was to live as one dead; her in-clusion was a burial; and not only is the rite symbolic. According to the Vespasian Pontifical, at this time of her shutting up from the world she was being given those last rites, which perhaps could not be provided afterwards. After the mass at the service of inclusion, the anchorite walked into the cell singing the antiphon of the burial service, ' This shall be my rest forever: here will I dwell, for I have a delight therein ', while outside the rest of this funeral psalm, *Memento*

---

[1] For this paragraph (and for further information) see R. M. Clay, *The Hermits and Anchorites of England*, London (1914) ; D. Knowles, *The Monastic Order in England*, Cambridge (1949) ; Sir F. M. Powicke, *Christian Life in the Middle Ages*, Oxford (1935), pp. 148–67 ; A. Wil-mart, *RB* 46 (1934), 414–38, and *RB* 50 (1938), 58–83.

[2] In *The Pontifical of Magdalen College*, ed. H. A. Wilson, Henry Bradshaw Society, XXXIX (1910), *Appendix*, pp. 245–6

domine (Ps. 132), was sung. Earth was then cast upon the anchorite and she was prayed for as over a corpse. The door was finally shut and sometimes sealed. It was a solemn service, and it provides the basis for understanding much of the anchorite life. ' What is the anchor-house but the grave of the anchoress ? ' (AW *f. 29r* (Salu 47)).

The Rule of Life

Daily routine varied from one anchor-house to another. But the basis of the timetable is invariably the monastic day. Part 1 of the Rule offers an elaboration which assumes that some monastic scheme was known and kept. It is unlikely that the three sisters were very proficient in silent prayer or wordless meditation. Hence the need supplied in Part 1 for an abundance of formulas of prayer. With most recluses psalm singing was a constant occupation. But reading of English or French books is recommended (*f. 11r* (Salu 19)). The sisters were indeed urged to pray less so that they should have time to read more (*f. 78r* (Salu 127)). But for long periods of the day silence was required. Then presumably work was to be done with the hands, according to the Rule the plainer sorts of needlework (*f. 114r* (Salu 187)).

Domestic arrangements would again vary greatly among recluses. The Rule provides a fairly clear picture, incidentally throughout, but fairly methodically in Part 8. Here the author prescribes on frequency of communion, on diet, on the reception of visitors. That the author thinks it necessary to continue with counsels against keeping animals, conducting of trade, and the use of the cell as an inn, shows the uncertain discipline which obtained in some contemporary anchor-houses. Recluses had already earned the reputation for being the local gossips (*f. 23r* (Salu 39)). The author also gives advice on clothing and on permissible employments and on hygiene. Finally comes advice on the management and behaviour of the recluses' servants. Throughout the Rule the apparent discrepancy between the rigour of many of the prescriptions and the laxity with which the author seems to assume such precepts are commonly interpreted in anchor-houses need cause no surprise. The author was

wise in his generation. From our point of view medieval
people lacked not resolution of purpose but steadiness in
behaviour.

There are several medieval anchorite rules in existence,
written like the English Rule by a spiritual adviser for the
benefit of his charge or charges. The earliest appears to be
that of Grimlaic of Metz (*c*.900, *PL* 103, cols. 573–661),
but a dozen or so of various sorts are of a date earlier than
the thirteenth century. Usually these rules are no more
than a daunting set of paragraphs on outward observances.
The spirituality that informed the life to be led is not made
apparent. As far as our English Rule is concerned the only
important early rule is that composed by Ailred of Rievaulx
(see **12**,9 note) for his sister, *On the Anchorite Life*.[1]

Ailred recalls the requests he has had for a rule and now
proposes to supply one out of ancient authorities. First the
recluse should recollect the aim of her inclusion. Let her
be no lady of a household, no gossip, no schoolmistress, let
her live by her own work if possible. Let her speak as little
as she need, take an old wise priest as her confessor, and always
busy herself with work, reading, and prayer. Pray briefly,
sing psalms, read often. Instruction is provided on fasting
and in choice of food and clothes. She should be always
dead to the world. Solitude is essential for the careful pre-
servation of holy virginity. Beware of seductive talk, never
feel secure against temptation. But let moderation rule
austerities. Beware of pride and vanity which can run to
the decoration of the cell. Let her do nothing for others
but pray for them. Ailred's treatise concludes with several
chapters providing the substance of the recluse's meditations.
Let her meditate on the past, the present, and the future,
and on the life and passion of Christ.

The author of the Rule knew this work. He makes some
direct borrowings from it. Furthermore, it looks as if

---

[1] *De vita eremitica, PL* 32, cols. 1451–74 (incomplete), is used for
reference in this edition. C. H. Talbot, *Analecta sac. ord. Cisterciensis* 7
(1951), 167–217, gives full text ; ME translation printed by C. Horstmann, *ESt* 7 (1884), 304–44. A list of early Rules for recluses is given
by L. Gougaud, *Ermites et Reclus*, Ligugé (1928), pp. 62–5.

Ailred's work provided him with the frame, not of the structure of the Rule as a treatise, but of the concept of the anchorite life which he had in mind.

Ailred's book provides more than an Outer Rule, but at the same time it is much more directly didactic than the vernacular Rule. It is the treatment of the Inner Rule that distinguishes the English work. It is much more exploratory and discursive, much less peremptory and dogmatic than earlier Rules. It is also, in so far as comparisons are worth making between works in different languages, much better written than any other Rule. The English Rule recalls some of the letters of counsel, such as were written by Peter the Venerable and Peter of Celles, but is much more comprehensive than these. In its organisation, in its matter and tone it draws near to some of the great devotional Latin treatises of the century, to Bernard's *On the Love of God*, or *The Steps of Humility*, or to William of St Thierry's *Golden Epistle*, and to a number of other pieces in that great mine of twelfth-century spirituality, volume 184 in Migne's *Patrologia Latina*. But we must not exaggerate. To the subtlety and advanced analysis of the spiritual life found in such writers as Bernard and William of St Thierry, the English author did not rise, nor sought to. He is writing in the vernacular, which still lacked the resources of Latin, because it had never encountered the need which was being fully met by Latin. His audience is lay not monastic. The sisters are beginners in the spiritual life. But it is important to realise that we have in the Rule a rule which is more than the usual rule. It does proclaim and release the quality of spirit which the bare rules were formed to serve.

Ancrene Wisse

An exact summary of AW is not provided here; but some indication of the scope, arrangement of material, and development of theme is necessary for an understanding of Parts 6 and 7.

AW opens with an assertion of the need for rules as much in spiritual matters as in other arts and sciences. ' We can speak of what is right in Grammar or Geometry, and each of these studies has its own rules. Here we are concerned with what is theologically right. The rules are two : the Inner Rule and the Outer. The righteous are those who live by rule . . . ; and you, my dear sisters, have often asked me for a rule ' (*f.* 1*r* (Salu 1)). In this reduction of the spiritual life to a regular art the author must have deliberately recalled a type of treatment in vogue at Paris in the 1190s, when Alan of Lille and his disciples Nicholas of Amiens and Simon of Tournai, urging that ' all *scientia* depends on rules ', made religion itself *scientia* and sought to exhibit faith as a construction of Euclidean character.[1]

The Inner Rule, according to AW, must be kept inviolably and invariably. The Outer Rule can be varied on the advice of the director and is to be kept for the sake of the Inner. Let the recluse make few solemn vows. Outward things are a matter of choice. ' But charity, that is love, humility, and patience, fidelity in the keeping of the Commandments, confession, penance . . . these are the commands of God ' —these must be strictly kept (*f.* 2*v* (Salu 3)). If anyone ask ' to what order you belong ' say ' to the order of St James ' in as much as you are trying to do good and ' to keep yourselves unspotted from the world ' (James 1:27).

The author announces that the rest of the book is to be divided into eight *distinctiones* (a University word), which ' you call Parts ' (*dalen*).

PART 1 : on Devotions (*f.* 4*v*–*f.* 12*r* (Salu 7–20))
This, the first section of the Outer Rule, gives advice on the occasion of, the posture for, the recitation of the offices of the Virgin and the dead. The author provides special devotions to the Trinity, the Five Wounds, the Holy Ghost, prayers for the forgiveness of sins, in honour of saints, for benefactors, for the dead, for the afflicted, prayers for use at mass and devotions on the Passion, on the MARIA psalms, and the hours of the Holy Ghost, graces, and night-prayers. This Part is a collection of current devotional practices and formulas.

[1] De Ghellinck, *L'Essor*, pp. 84–5.

PART 2: on the Custody of the Senses (*f.* 12r–*f.* 32r (Salu 21–52))

Here begins the Inner Rule which is concerned first with the control of the senses. Sight is treated at some length; so are speech and hearing, with a recommendation of all the virtues of silence, and a warning against the dangers that attend ill-considered speech. After a recapitulation of teaching on the control of eyes, ears, and lips, the author deals more briefly with smell, which is allegorised somewhat, and finally with touch. All is interposed with counsels on behaviour.

PART 3: on the Custody of the Heart (*f.* 32r–*f.* 47v (Salu 53–77))

The author shows how best to control the feelings and emotions. Comparisons of the anchoress with the pelican and with other birds are sustained through much of this Part, which stresses the need for the elimination of angry thoughts, the need for humility, patience, lovingkindness, and indicates the blessings of solitude and of inner tranquillity.

PART 4: on Temptations (*f.* 47v–*f.* 81r (Salu 78–132))

Even if the senses and the heart are controlled, temptation will still be encountered. There are of temptation (as of most things with this author) two sorts—inner temptations and outer. But all temptations must be resisted and turned into occasions of good and a source of strength. Particular defences against temptation are suggested, notably meditation on the Passion of Christ. The variety of inner temptations is dealt with in an account of the Seven Deadly Sins. Against each remedies are proposed.

PART 5: on Confession (*f.* 81r–*f.* 94r (Salu 133–53))

But confession is the best of all remedies against the evil of sin. First briefly is indicated the profitableness of confession, then at greater length the characteristics of a good confession. This part of the work was no doubt useful to the anchoresses, but it provides, as the author admits, a general treatment of the subject without particular regard to his immediate audience. Indeed the whole resembles one of the *Summae Confessionis* which were produced in great number at the end of the twelfth century.[1]

PART 6 : on Penance (*f.* 94*r–f.* 103*v* (Salu 154–69))

Unlike Part 5, the treatment of penance is not technical. The whole hard manner of life of the anchoresses is penitential. Physical pain and humiliation of spirit are justified ; they propitiate God ; are able to refashion the recluse in the likeness of God. Out of bitterness comes the sweetness of love.

PART 7 : on Love (*f.* 104*r–f.* 111*r* (Salu 170–81))

The heart, now cleansed by pain and humiliation, can come to see God and love God. It can learn to make the proper responses towards God's own offer of Love. The author proceeds to show why and how God should be loved. The proper end of the religious life is in the loving response to the love God bears for us.

PART 8 : on the Outer Rule (*f.* 111*r–f.* 117*v* (Salu 182–92))

Some account of the practical instructions of this Part has been given already (see p. xxxv above). The author ends with a recommendation that the anchoresses should read a portion of his book each day. He hopes they will find it useful, else he has wasted his time. 'I would rather undertake the journey to Rome than start writing it again.' The scribe of CCCC MS 402 adds finally a request for the prayers of those who use the book.

It is plain that Parts 6 and 7 are the culmination of the whole : Part 6 as a general account of the essential character of the anchorite life ; Part 7 as a statement of its aspiration and final end.

THEMES IN ANCRENE WISSE PARTS 6 AND 7

The argument of AW or of any of its Parts is not easily summarised, nor does a synopsis do justice to the flexible and wavering line of advance. The following paragraphs

[1] See full treatment by P. Anciaux, *La théologie du sacrement de pénitence au XII*e *siècle*, Louvain (1949), particularly pp. 248ff ; cp. Salu, *Introduction* by G. Sitwell, pp. xix–xxi.

seek to do no more than isolate and solidify certain themes upon which the author relies in Parts 6 and 7 or to which he adverts in his exposition.

(i) *The Penitential Life*

At the basis of the penitential life is the Christian realisation of sin, general to mankind through Adam's fall (**9,28, 20,26**), but renewed in all men daily through countless acts of self-regard. Christian's lamentable cry, 'What shall I do?' has received many answers, but, recurrently, forms of asceticism, exercises in self-denial and mortification have been considered to offer the most satisfactory method of eradicating guilt and of readjustment. In the eleventh and twelfth centuries the eremitical life could provide a career of expiation. The soul was to be purged by hurting the body, in which the first motions towards sin were made. Underlying the twelfth-century ideal of ascetic holiness was a conception of the soul as a kind of insertion into the envelope of flesh. Flesh and spirit were of different stuff, sharply opposed one to the other. Taken to an extreme this opposition gave new life to the old Manichean heresy. The Catharism of the Albigensian heretics is a symptom of the age. Despite the formal assertions of orthodoxy that a loving and inextricable bond knit body and soul (see **23,6ff** note), at the heart of many an ascetic and mystic, then as later, of Peter Damian certainly, of Ailred even, of Pusey and Aldous Huxley no less, lies a horror at the beastly fascination of the flesh.

The denial of the body is given its sharpest point in the doctrine of the evil in sexuality after the Fall. It is in its sexuality that the body's proneness to sin is most evident. Most of the KG texts are concerned, directly or indirectly, with this issue. Virginity is their grand theme. *Holy Maidenhood*, in particular, states openly, often it has been thought, crudely and ignominiously, what the author of the Rule assumes. He never avoids the opportunity of emphasising the worth of virginity and its demands (**12,7ff, 23,35ff, 25,11ff**). It is a matter which does not admit of moderate counsels. The author of the Rule, who was certainly a wise and experienced guide, can see only shame and corruption as the outcome of any physical contact between the recluses and people in the outer world. 'Touching with the hands or any other touching between a man and an anchoress is a thing so disgusting, an act so shameful, and so naked a sin, and so horrible to all the world, and so great a scandal, that there is no need to speak or write against it ; . . . I would much sooner see all three of you, . . . my dearest sisters, hang on a gibbet in order to avoid the sin, than see one of you giving a single kiss in the way I mean to any man on earth. . . . Simply putting the hand out [of the window] except in case of need, is courting God's anger and inviting His wrath. Looking at her own white hands does harm to many an anchoress who keeps them too fair through idleness. They should be scraping up each day the earth out of the pit in which they shall rot ' (AW *f.* 31*v* (Salu 51)).

It must be conceded that whatever may be the real and positive grounds in terms of human psychology, or in terms of religion, for this exaltation of virginity, they are never made plain in any of these writings, nor for that matter in medieval writings as a whole. In KG texts the argument for virginity is by types and shadows, by analogies and from authority ; but above all by the strong appeal of its practical advantages. Sex was troublesome as well as nasty and insistent. Medieval lust, we may believe, was a thing to be avoided and a thing not easily avoided in medieval society. Medieval reactions, we may believe, were faster than ours, and the lusts of the flesh could be held in check often only by the sharpest and most intense contempt and control of the flesh which engendered them.

In matters of sexuality and of sense response, of laughter, of eating and drinking, an active, angry puritanism represents the medieval monastic ideal. The instinctive responses of the body had to be tamed to facilitate the ardent desires of the soul. And the object of these desires was quite clearly defined. It was eternal life and eternal joy : *þe blisse of heouene riche.* In KG texts, as in most ME texts, virtue is not convincingly recommended for its own sake. The author of the Rule finds it somewhat peculiar that the holy man of his acquaintance should have been able to think of loving God in hell (**18**,20ff). The notion of disinterested love is developed among the Franciscans and not until much later does St Francis Xavier's hymn,

> My God, I love thee not because
> I hope for heaven thereby,
> Nor yet because who love thee not
> Are lost eternally,

express a commonly acceptable desire. In AW the good life is recommended because it brings great rewards (**5**,33, **7**,22ff, **28**,28ff). An argument for virtue can start from self-interest (**11**,33ff) and appear to offer bliss as a market commodity (**9**,17ff, **29**,22ff).

Nor was this matter-of-fact basis of thought unreasonable. These men knew what they were dealing with. The character of heaven was no more doubtful than the character of hell. Anselm, in conference at Cluny, provided a famous account of the joys of heaven. He starts with the question, ' What sort of things do you want on earth ? Beauty, wealth, honour, strength, and so forth ? ' And he provides the comfortable answer : ' All these things you will have in heaven, but raised to a higher degree ' (*PL* 159, col. 965 ; see **25**,23ff note). Hell was similarly real, near, excruciatingly but intelligibly dreadful. ' If there were something the very shadow of which you could not feel without pain, would not the thing be very terrible ? Know for a certainty that all the suffering of this world is but a shadow of the suffering of hell ' (AW *f.* 51*r* (Salu 83)). All the pain possible in this world is but ball-play beside those eternal, terrible pains : no more than a drop of dew compared with the broad sea and all the world's waters (*f.* 49*r* (Salu 80)).

Considering then the nature of man, born in sin, a child of wrath, set momentarily between these motionless eternities of heaven and hell, redeemed by an insulted and tortured Christ who, remembering His wounds and shame, should come again to be our Judge, stern and strict and merciless, a reflective and prudent man would decide that these circum-

stances demanded an effort of self-control, which might seem
in other circumstances—our own for example—fantastic or
outrageously heroic. ' Were you not made out of foul
slime ? Are you not now a bag of excrement ? Are you
not going to be food for worms ? ' (AW *f.* 75*v* (Salu 123)).
The flesh should be tried to the utmost so that the spirit
could escape this mortality and live. On medieval premisses,
logic was certainly on the side of the ascetic.

(ii) *Ascesis*

The characteristic external austerities of the penitential life
as practised in England during the twelfth century, are well
set out in AW **12,**10-12. The penitential life required
' bodily pain, with fasts, vigils, scourgings, harsh clothes,
rough lodging, disease, with hard physical work '. The
author urges moderation and a golden mean in these things ;
but it is his golden mean, not ours. He certainly did not
envisage the harshest austerities, the self-mutilations, the cold
water immersions on winter nights, the living crucifixions
which were used by some English ascetics of his time.
Nevertheless the life he is taking for granted is harsh indeed,
an airless, colourless, comfortless life, with a minimum of
food, warmth, and sleep. The recluses were deliberately to
avoid sight of another human face. Often they were to
whip themselves thoroughly (see **11,**16 note). Their thoughts
were to be full of death and blood and pain and humiliation.
Hourly they were to contemplate the figure of Christ crucified,
the stripes, the nakedness, the thirst, the languor, all the
careful arrangement of pain that the cross provided, to
savour the blood that came from the five great wounds and
from the great veins that bled in His head. It required
judicious direction by a spiritual guide to ensure that mental
interests such as these, working on the effect of sleeplessness
and deficiencies of diet should not have alarming mental and
physical consequences.

By the twelfth century asceticism had a long history. The
justifications of bodily and mental austerities had acquired
many forms and the Rule reflects some of these complexities.
In part the harsh life is simply an attempt to make a settle-

ment for sin, both original and actual. The pain and humiliation is punishment—retaliatory punishment accepted for
a wrong committed, personally and through Adam, against
a stern, just God. AW recognises this aspect (**6**,22ff, **10**,29ff).

But further the pain and humiliation are conceived as
providing a training—*ascesis* in the strict sense—training in
self-control and the fuller use of the higher powers. The
crown of everlasting life was to be won by those who went
into strict training. Many a holy man in medieval times is
called *athleta* or *agonista Dei*. The author of the Rule usually
presents the eremitical life not as a state of acquired grace,
but as a progress towards sanctification. The anchoresses
are only young saplings in God's orchard (**16**,36): they can
expect to be weathered by unremitting temptation. It is
a long process which can transform their little hills into the
mountains of holy life (**17**,28).

Still further the ascetic life was thought of as a life of
service, particularly military service. From earliest times
monks were said to compose the *militia Christi*. Frequently
Benedict used military metaphors to describe the monastic
life; so does Bernard, in the Lenten sermon, for instance,
from which the Rule borrows at the beginning of Part 6.
Yet, though we speak of metaphor, for many recluses their
single combat against the principalities and powers of darkness was real enough. The *Life* of Godric, for example, tells
stories of spiritual conflict which left actual marks of violence
on his body. The coats of mail some hermits (*loricati*)
wore, seem to have been put on first, not so much as a burden
to the flesh, but to serve as a defence against the physical
assaults of the devil (see **18**,11ff note). In the twelfth century,
moreover, the old ideal of the *militia Christi* was reactualised
in the new military orders, the Templars and the Knights
of the Hospital of St John of Jerusalem. The images of
military feudalism in AW should be given this double force:
there is a lively reference to the social system of the day;
there is also an adaptation of a traditional account of the
spiritual reality. There are flashes of the Crusader spirit
in our author.

And finally the ascetic life is a martyrdom (**3**,6). Once

the great age of persecution in the fourth century was over, martyrdom in will or intention was recognised as a substitute for martyrdom in deed. This notion, particularly attractive to the Celtic church, was much employed in eulogies of saints and holy men. AW recognises that disease and pain can be accepted as a martyrdom; they can offer a means of expiation, can test our patience, keep us humble, increase our reward. Bodily sickness can be health to the soul. It raises the patient sufferer to the level of the martyr (*f.49r* (Salu 80)). The example of the early martyrs is repeatedly held up to stir the spirit of emulation in the pious of the twelfth century (see **9**,23ff note). For Adam the Scot the first historic epoch of Christian perfection was that age of the early martyrs. The last, succeeding the age of the monasteries, was to be the age when hermits and recluses, true heirs to the martyrs, multiplied (*PL* 198, col. 742).

(iii) *The Vision of God*

At the beginning of Part 7, the author justifies austerity by the end to which it is directed. In the old saying of St Irenaeus, *vita hominis, visio Dei*, the end of human life is the beatific vision enjoyed by the saints. Seeing God has always been very closely linked with loving God, for example in 1 John 3:2, 4:12,15, and by St Paul, 1 Cor. 13. Though knowledge may fail, charity shall not, and in the perfected love of God we shall see face to face. To see God is to come to know God through love. The propositions are reversible. ' To see God or to know God is to be like God, and to be like Him is to see or know Him ' (*PL* 180, col. 393). For only like can know like. To know God, then, it becomes necessary to recover the likeness of God in ourselves. ' The perfection of man is the likeness of God ' (*PL* 184, col. 348). The method of recovery recommended in the Rule is by humility, by the realignment of the will (see particularly **5**,33ff). In his Rule, chap. vii, Benedict had set out this standard teaching on humility as the ascent of a ladder of twelve steps. ' Having therefore ascended all these degrees of humility, the monk will presently arrive at

that love of God which, being perfect, casteth out fear.'
Thus by replacing self-will by God's will, we recover God's
likeness. It is this rectification of the will by acts of humility,
by voluntary suffering and by conscious humiliation, that
is the subject of Part 6. This is the rendering of satisfaction
deadbote, with which the author is here concerned.

(iv) *Purity of Heart*

After the penitential approach to the vision of God in Part 6,
the section on love opens with an insistence on the need for
purity of heart as the condition for the love of God. Purity
of heart is God's love alone (**20,10**). None may love God
unless he acquire virgin purity (**25,11**).

Such teaching comes of an ancient line, followed most
consistently in the Eastern Church. Thus Gregory of Nyssa,
writing on the sixth beatitude, taught that the soul purged
from evil desire and perturbation, becomes like enough to
God to see Him as He is. Purity induces a sort of deification
(*PG* 44, cols. 1263–78). Similar ideas are found in the West
with John Cassian (see **19,15ff** note), in his treatment of the
incessant war between flesh and spirit. With Cassian the
enemy is identified as the lustful will, but spiritual training
is directed, not as in Benedictine theory to the rectification
of the will, but instead towards its eradication, in fact towards
the evacuation of all thoughts and desires, towards an apathy.
This is the condition AW speaks of as a death (**5,3f,8ff**).
This teaching grows almost insensibly out of and into the
idea of the anchorite's life as a dying unto Christ (**4,38ff, 5,6**).

The Eastern equation of purity of heart with the love of
God is explicitly stated in AW (**20,10**). On the other hand,
and it is typical of the way in which the author juxtaposes
varied elements of twelfth-century thought, he can speak of
purity being the effect as well as the cause of love. Purity
of heart is God's love alone ; but also it is love that purifies
and brightens the heart (**18,33, 19,3**).

In AW, what may be called these traces of Eastern theory
are no more than nuances, which may have existed even in
the traditions handed down from the Anglo-Saxon Church,
or they may have been reflected into AW from the recovery

of the guiding ideas of Eastern asceticism effected in the
twelth century by such men as William of St Thierry and
by the Carthusians. But in the main the author of the Rule
conforms to the Western and Benedictine tradition, according
to which it is the attachment to God which recreates the soul
of man in its original purity.

(v) *The Love of God*

The treatment of love in the Rule is not simple. The bases
of the discussion are always assumed rather than declared.
But that is what is to be expected in a vernacular treatise on
this, the great theme of so much twelfth-century writing. No
comprehensive study of this debate on love, divine and
profane, which continued over generations, has yet been
made. The Rule provides in Part 7 a brief recapitulation
without much argument of many of the themes drawn out
at length in a great number of contemporary writers. Like
most of the discussions, it is a tissue of persuasive enthy-
memes. It is assumed without much question, as we might
expect, that love is a very fine thing and that loving is a
supremely satisfying activity. Throughout, appearing in
many forms and in many perspectives, the grand argument
for love and loving turns on gratitude, primarily in return
for love that has been given us, and secondarily for benefits
we have received.

'We love Him because He first loved us' (1 John 4:19).
This is the motive for the response to the appeal of Christ
as wooer (**20**,36ff) and for the valuing of Christ's love, since
it exceeds all others (**23**,9ff). The initiative in love belongs
to Christ (**21**,11). And this proffer of love is the ground
of His appeal for love. 'Now beseech I thee, for the love
that I have shown thee, that thou love me' (**21**,34).

Bernard's treatise *On the Love of God*, which, it would
seem, the author of the Rule knew, makes the succession and
range of thought clearer. God should be loved by us in as
much as He loved us first. Our return of love should be
as measureless as our finite natures allow, in response to
this love of His which like Himself is measureless and infinite.
We are by our natures bound to love God for our own good,

and God is not loved without reward, though He is to be loved without consideration of reward. To love and to be loved is reward in itself. There is a sweetness which accompanies the activity of loving and makes the progress upward through the grades of love pleasant and compelling.

In the Rule the idea that love is the only fitting return of love is usually enwrapped in nuptial imagery. In part, this use is a product of that characteristically medieval mental habit which insisted on expanding the human to measure the divine. Christ is recommended to young maidens as the lover *par excellence* in many medieval writings. The convention is exploited systematically in KG texts, and on the whole is managed in AW with discretion. But the use of such analogies has a history older than that of sex relationships in a feudal society. In the Old Testament, the Chosen People is regarded as the destined Bride of God (Hosea 1:14–20). Of this mystery had St Paul spoken, and following St Paul, the Church in the early Christian centuries was regarded as the Bride. This interpretation never died out entirely and still appears in the chapter summaries of the AV and in the Marriage Service of the *Book of Common Prayer*. In AW on occasion the Bride is still the Church (20,34).

But during the late Middle Ages, when the Church became more of a political institution and less an ideal of society, these nuptial analogies were modified. They come to provide conscious metaphors, either in application to the Virgin Mary, or to the individual soul. As often, a shift in consciousness is reflected by a shift in doctrine. Bernard is influential in this development. Bernard still formally explains the Bride as the Church, but in his eighty-six sermons on the Song of Solomon, his last, unfinished, and probably most impressive compositions, he provides an elaborate commentary on the relationship between the devout soul and Christ, invariably in nuptial terms. The devotional and mystical writers of later times use this new terminology with even less reserve. AW does not go so far as Bernard. The author gives both interpretations (24,35), but he will sometimes assume simply the identification of the soul with the Bride (23,32).

In the main, Cistercian devotion concentrated upon the experience of the love of God through an attachment to the humanity of Christ. A more speculative school of devotion was associated with the Augustinian Canons of the abbey of St Victor in France, and particularly with the German, Hugh of St Victor (c.1096–1141) and the Scot, Richard of St Victor (d. 1173), who made their characteristic schemes of meditation depend in the first place upon the contemplation of the harmony of the universe. God is to be loved for His gifts and benefits. Man has been placed at the apex of the natural creation and all creation has been designed to provide insight which can lead men to the love of God.

> What does thy Bridegroom give to thee, my soul ? . . . Observe this universal frame and see if there is anything therein which does not serve thee. . . . Thou receivest the benefit and knowest not the source. The gift is visible, the giver hid. And yet reason itself must doubt that this is not thy desert but a gift from another. Therefore whosoever he be, much should he be loved who could give thee so much, and whosoever wished to give thee so much, much indeed he loved. So loving then and so lovable he is shown to be by his gift, that not only would it be foolish not to desire the love of one so powerful, but sacrilegious and perverse not to love in return him who loves thee so much (Hugh of St Victor, *Soliloquy on the Pledge of the Soul*, PL 176, col. 955).

This type of theme is touched on by the author of the Rule at 20,22ff, but he does not press it and passes to consideration of other benefits received, more attractive perhaps to his feminine audience. But this theme of the argument—' Why God is to be loved ' (20,22–23,8)—is to be found in numerous twelfth-century treatments : so Bernard in Chapter 2 of *On the Love of God*, or Ailred in the series of Meditations written for his sister (*PL* 158, cols. 784–98), or Baldwin of Ford in his third Tractate (*PL* 204, cols. 417–30), where the love of God is urged in respect of benefits received, promises made, judgments to be passed and precepts given.

In AW the question, ' Why God is to be loved ', is answered
in a similar fashion, but the scaffolding of the scheme is
removed. The argument is turned into parables. In much
the same fashion the author explains ' How God is to
be loved ' (**23**,9–26,29). Again there is the scheme of
classification of loves such as is found in a great number
of twelfth-century works (see **23**,9ff note). The author
knows the accepted lines of argument and analysis in current
treatments of love—indeed they suggest his own treatment
—but he does not rely upon them for the effects he wants
to produce.

(vi) *Memoria Jesu Christi*

It is plain, however, that in the Rule the love of God is
treated essentially as a passionate attachment to the person
of Christ. This approach enables the author to fuse many of
the traditional themes. The attempt to make the person
of Christ vivid provides a characteristically medieval version
of the Vision of God. The imitation of Christ in His bodily
suffering suggests a means of becoming like God. Purity
of heart becomes the condition and result of this imitation.
Towards Christ is felt the gratitude for a wooer making
promises, for a benefactor and protector, and for a bridegroom. Throughout Part 7, God as the object and subject
of love is presented to the spirit of devotion almost entirely
as the incarnate Christ. This concentration on the humanity
of Christ is of immense importance in the history of medieval
culture, and is often associated particularly with the Franciscans of the thirteenth century. In the monastic world to
which the eremitical movement was attached it comes earlier.
It is anticipated in Anselm and elaborated in Bernard. It
is prominent throughout AW and had an obvious appeal to
a feminine audience which might be literate, but which was
certainly unlearned, averagely sentimental, and intellectually
unsophisticated.

Bernard, who put this attachment to the person of Christ
at the centre of Cistercian devotion, looked upon the sensitive
affection for His person as no more than an early step upon
the ladder of spiritual love. He calls this step a spiritual

love, but still a ' carnal ' spiritual love—the first-fruits of our
response to the Incarnation.

> I think the chief reason why God wished to be seen in
> the flesh and converse as man with man, was that He
> could thereby draw away at first all the affections of men
> (who, in as much as they are carnal, cannot love other
> than carnally) towards the saving love of His body, and
> so gradually lead them on into spiritual love (*PL* 183,
> col. 870).

The author of the AW may appear to aim for his charges
at little more than this ' carnal ' spiritual love. In his feudal
parables and analogies, of Christ as king and man of war
with His royal household, embassies, and siege-trains, of
Christ the lover with His infinite charm, His love letters
and kisses, of Christ the wretch on the cross, each of these
memories of Christ is designed to appeal to the senses and
sensibilities, often, it would seem, to stimulate an emotional,
almost physical, response. That holy things are treated with
even greater sensuous insistence in later times, should not
dull our perception of the novel and peculiar character of
this treatment in the twelfth century. Never had day-dreams
been put to more exalted use than in this concern with the
human interest of the Gospels and of apocryphal stories, in
the tearful lingering over sentiment, in the hypnotic repeti-
tions of names and phrases and in the often morbid identification of rôles. Out of this vivid imagining was to spring
a consciousness of the presence of Christ.

Many passages of KG texts recall this mood of piety.
Nowhere is it expressed more decorously, or more passionately, than in the Latin of the famous Bernardine song of
joy, *Jesu dulcis memoria* (the basis of the English hymn,
' Jesu, the very thought of thee ').

(vii) *The nature of love*

In medieval psychology, love was considered to be one of the
four fundamental dispositions (*affectus*) of the mind—love,
fear, joy, and sadness. From these four dispositions it was

held, all states of mind were compounded. *Affectus* is not an exact equivalent of the modern ' emotion ', if we think of emotion as a spontaneous, instinctive reaction to sensations of pleasure or pain, isolated from mental activities such as thinking and willing. Love as one of the *affectus* is itself ' an appetite of the will ', the directing of the whole self to what is desired. Hugh of St Victor defines ' to love ' briefly as *habere velle,* ' to want to have ' (*PL* 176, col. 529). Love was not merely a passion or a reflex, it was also the product of the conscious will. Man could love God if he would.

But it is clear that men ' want to have ' a great number of other things too. In what way is the wanting to have God to be related to the desire for other things ? By the twelfth century three general schemes of relationship can be distinguished. And it is characteristic of AW that all three are to some extent represented there.

First there was the idea that there were essentially two kinds of love, one good, one bad. This simple diagnosis was well known in Christian tradition (cp. 1 John 2:15). According to Origen (*c.*185–*c.*254), whose thought was strongly dualistic, there is one love coming from Satan, another love of the spirit with its source in God ; and no man can be possessed by both loves (*PG* 13, col. 47). This division becomes commonplace (see **29**,13ff note). In AW there is this opposition between carnal love, false, foul, stinking, fleshly love (**18**,8, **27**,29, **28**,37), and true and ghostly love (**18**,9, **29**,13ff). The author repeats that a true spiritual love for Christ was impossible for even the disciples until the physical presence of Christ had been withdrawn (**29**,1ff). A true love is entirely spiritual.

But this opposition between a good love and a bad was too simple. So, according to a second analysis of love, it was argued that all love is of a kind, but that its aims must be distinguished. Such a scheme had already been provided by Augustine. The most fundamental need of man, according to Augustine, is a need to love. But in itself this need is neutral, neither good nor bad. It is the objects upon which love is set that make loving good or evil. The love of God and of our neighbour is *caritas,* the love of this world, *cupiditas*. Love transforms a man into the likeness of the object of his love : if *caritas*, he grows into the likeness of God ; if *cupiditas*, he is deformed, corrupted, bowed down—*curvatus*. Obviously only God is the real and satisfying object of man's desire. Only God is to be loved for His own sake (for enjoyment) ; all other things are to be loved for the sake of something other than themselves— for their usefulness in bringing us to God (cp. **20**,3ff). Only God can be loved freely, without second thoughts, with abandon. Other things are to be loved and used only as a means towards this love for God. The love for God therefore provides a rule for loving. Love guides and directs the heart (**30**,29). Love is a discipline, requiring order and measure.

But the measure of our love for God is still that it should be measureless. Love should be given entirely (**25**,3ff). As a result, love is often spoken of in the language of excess. Love is violent, extreme, a fire (**26**,3, **26**,25ff). It is only at the summit of this measureless, ordered, willed love of God that Augustine's famous precept can be applied, ' Love and do what you like ' (**19**,35).

The treatment of love in AW can in general be called Augustinian. Its adherence can be illustrated in its treatment of the two great commandments to love in Matt. 22:37–9. According to AW these two commandments fall into one (**19**,23ff). The fusion is Augustinian and remained a medieval commonplace. Love to our neighbour is only a special instance of love towards God. A limit is set to this love for our neighbour by putting a literal emphasis on the words that we should love our neighbour *as ourself*. The extent of the love to self is of course strictly defined. Many forms of self-love are extremely sinful. Love of self extends only to the love of the self's best interests. We love our neighbour then, not for himself, but for his own good. His ultimate good like ours is God. Such an attitude could, and perhaps did, have harsh and cruel consequences, but it must be remembered that, living so closely in community, these men of the Middle Ages could have little awareness of what our own century has called ' social conscience '. In the twelfth century it was still all too easy to think as other men ; the heroic task was to lift oneself out of community and reach for personal salvation.

This Augustinian analysis is refashioned during the twelfth century somewhat nearer to an antique ideal of love and friendship such as was being found in Cicero's moral treatises. Now there emerges the outline of a third theory—a naturalistic theory of love. No doubt the rise of this new synthesis was, on a theological level, the result in part of a reaction against the violent dualism of the Catharist heresy, which insisted in its crude way on two loves, one spiritual and good, one physical and bad. At the same time, renewed speculation about love is prompted by the strength and exaltation during this century of the claims asserted by ordinary human affections, including sexual love. What we call ' courtly love ' the author of the Rule condemned outright (cp. **19**,7ff, **29**,9ff), and yet with his effective mastery of inconsistency he can still make use of some of the ' courtly ' arguments in love (**21**,1ff, **25**,4ff). Romantic love, which is indeed none other than stinking fleshly love, affords him brighter imagery than rigorous asceticism. The devotion of *memoria Christi* is itself a signal of the need religion found to come to terms with the new social ideals. Bernard and other writers of the twelfth century provided something of a theoretical basis for this accommodation.

All love sprang from the single *affectus* ; but instead of seeing, like Augustine, an immediate duality in the objects of love (God or the world), Bernard perceived a progression. Since human nature is frail, man is compelled to serve himself first. This is the carnal love by which a man loves himself for his own sake. Then when he considers his own unaided helplessness, he begins to love God for the use he can make of Him. When God continually renews His kindnesses towards us, and particularly when our familiarity with God increases, love grows less self-centred and eventually God is loved for His sake, not ours. There is a fourth step, rarely attained in this life, according to Bernard, wherein the soul entirely forgets itself and loves itself only in God (*On the Love of God*, chaps. viii–xi, *PL* 182, cols.

987–95). Thus self-love can be and should be gradually transformed into a pure love of God.

Ailred of Rievaulx puts forward similar ideas in his book, much influenced by Cicero, *On Spiritual Friendship*. The rational mind seeks with desire for something and longs to possess and enjoy it. Even in inanimate, irrational nature there is a movement towards union and rest which can be considered an image or shadow of love. So all human love, truly considered, is grounded in Christ and should proceed towards Christ. The relishing of a human affection can lead almost insensibly towards this higher love (*PL* 195, cols. 659–702).

Probably some such belief in the slow transformation of human experience into love of God lies at the heart of the Rule. Some formal acknowledgments of a naturalistic theory appear in Part 7. When the four chief loves of this world are classified (23,9ff), Christ's love is not distinguished from these in kind, but only in degree. The love of Christ subsumes all other loves (24,34ff). Love is a single force, it binds God as well as binding man (30,5ff). Love acquires the status and unity of a personality (29,19,36ff, 30,16). It is God's equal, nay, God's master, His counsellor and spouse. What is planted as a seed in bitterness on earth grows to overtop heaven.

(viii) *Relation to mysticism*

AW does not treat of mystical experience in Part 7. Writing on love at any time during the Middle Ages after the mid-thirteenth century, the author could have scarcely avoided it, for mystical experience came to be represented as the earthly consummation of a perfected love of God. In an earlier passage of AW, however, the author does approach the theme, but cautiously and in what were already old-fashioned terms. Through love of God the sight of contemplation is given, he is arguing.

> And then you shall see how all the world is nought and its comfort false. . . . You shall see sometimes the pain of hell. . . . You shall see spiritually the bliss of heaven.

. . . You shall see, as in a mirror, our Lady with her maidens and all the host of angels and Him above all that blesseth them all. . . . This sight, dear sisters, shall comfort you more than might any earthly sight. Holy men know well who have experienced it that every earthly joy is worthless in comparison. . . . It is a holy mystery that none may know that has not tasted thereof; and this knowledge comes of spiritual sight (*f. 24r* and *v* (Salu 40f)).

This is a much more discreet and hesitant account of rapture than writers of the thirteenth and fourteenth centuries would have provided.

There is little point in speaking of AW as a mystical work. Though the work of men like Richard Rolle and Walter Hilton may indeed owe something in matter as well as form to the Rule, they are cut off from it by a reversal in spirituality. The Rule is not concerned with the experience of union with God. It shows no trace of the teaching of the so-called Dionysius the Areopagite, who was being rediscovered at the beginning of the thirteenth century. It follows instead the earlier Western tradition which regarded the highest type of life as an intellectual life which yet acknowledged the calls and interruptions of practical business and acts of social duty and charity. Augustine, Gregory, even Bernard reserve the palm for this ' mixed life ', which is neither a strictly ' active ' nor a purely ' contemplative ' life.[1] It seems that the author of the Rule agreed. His teaching on contemplation is pre-scholastic and pre-Dionysian. Throughout Part 7 love is thought of as a humble, creaturely communion with God, the outcome of the fulfilment of duty and obligations. Union with God in this life —the goal of the mystic—is never mentioned in terms which are to be taken otherwise than as metaphors. The author will not even follow Bernard's account of St Paul's flight to the third heaven (see 5,14 note).

In the light of later developments in English piety, to which the Rule itself made a notable contribution, we may think that an ideal of the ' mixed ' life was not particularly

[1] See C. Butler, *Western Mysticism*, 2nd ed., London (1927).

suitable for anchoresses. In being shut up in their cells, they had renounced some of their social duties. But the author does not change his ideal to suit their condition. He does not exalt the life of pure contemplation. It is a life of penitence he urges throughout. He was fearful of the consequences of a deliberate pursuit of spiritual graces and spiritual favours. He counsels against extreme mortifications. He warns against visions and voices. He suggests no techniques of illumination. What 'contemplation' could mean among religious women of the twelfth century he probably knew and distrusted. The excesses that sometimes accompanied the deliberate cultivation of the 'angelic life' were never exhibited more horribly than in the barbarous scandal of the nun of Watton, a Gilbertine house of York-shire, a scandal in which earlier in the twelfth century Ailred had found himself involved (see *PL* 195, cols. 789–96).

An analysis of the terms and assumptions of AW is quite unprofitable, indeed altogether falsifying, if it should lead to the conclusion that the author did not know what he was talking about. Of course he did not know in any ultimate sense. Only the most superficial moralist can drive his tidy arguments straight through life and death. But he did know many things about the value of suffering and the nature of love. And he does reflect many topics current in religious debate at the end of the twelfth century (see **9,28, 22,26ff, 23,35** notes). Without an investigation of the complex assumptions which an author such as this one was justified in making, much of AW remains indistinct.

Nobody reading AW as it was meant to be read can be much troubled by the inconsistencies of the intellectual schemes worked into it, for their elements as they appear there do not exist apart from the use to which they were put. To those who believe that prose should be only a vehicle for notions and cannot be itself a triumphal progress, the author may well appear as a shameless opportunist and a confusing manipulator of other men's ideas. But his early readers did not count him so. They were not unconvinced by his arguments, for it is likely they agreed with his propositions before ever they started to read him. But in reading, their conviction was sustained and quickened by what we can still admire, what we shall baldly call the art of composition.

THE ART OF COMPOSITION

No doubt the author would have been gratified to find us praising the simplicity and naïvety of his work. In that case he has beguiled us very successfully. The structure and style of AW are highly artificial and carefully calculated.

AW falls within the genre of medieval sermon, a literary kind, distinct and recognisable, which was to develop a characteristic technique of its own.[1] *Artes praedicandi* become numerous only from the thirteenth century, and AW was written before the theory of sermon construction had become rigid, nor obviously could it conform exactly with the requirements of a pulpit piece. But the general principles of sermon-writing were already established, and may be illustrated from the work of Alan of Lille (*d.* 1202), *doctor universalis,* poet, humanist, theologian, teacher at the University of Paris, who wrote an early *Art of Preaching* (*PL* 210, cols. 109–98). According to Alan, a sermon may be delivered by word of mouth, or as a letter (the Pauline Epistles were models), or exemplified in action. He furnishes also a number of useful hints. The preacher should capture the good-will of his hearers, he should promise to edify and not go on too long. He should avoid excessive ornament and a parade of learning and should never descend to clowning. His words should be fully persuasive—*verba commotiva.* Above all he must preach to the condition of his audience, which is always a particular audience. Alan provides several specimen sermons directed to different sorts of congregation.

There is nothing startling in Alan's prescriptions. He is

---

[1] See T. M. Charland, *Artes Praedicandi*, Ottawa-Paris (1925), with edition of two late-medieval treatises and account of theory ; for twelfth-century Latin preaching, see de Ghellinck, *L'Essor,* pp. 206–30.

providing no more than a simple systematisation of parts of
On Christian Doctrine by Augustine. There is no reason to
think that the author of the Rule stood in much need of,
or ever studied, Alan's instruction. But AW does exemplify,
as far as a vernacular treatise can, the aims, tone, manner
of address, and the verbal devices generally approved in
sermon writing at the beginning of the thirteenth century.

The author's prime concern is, as has already been
suggested, not to prove but to move. Even in his use of the
forms of logical proof, his aim is to persuade, not to demonstrate a truth. He is not writing a theological or psychological
treatise, not even an analytical devotional manual. He and
his audience have their beliefs in common. He does not
seek at bottom to explain penance and love, nor to prove
them good things, but to stimulate and control acts of
penance and love in daily life. He aims beyond mere assent
to his propositions. He wants action, the exercise of penitence, virtue, and love. AW is thus written with a practical
end in view. Its words are intended to be fully *commotiva*.
It is always concerned with the striking power of its exposition rather than with its logic or accuracy of terms. The
fourfold classification of loves (**23**,9ff) is not intended to be
scientific—a piece of medieval lore. The author simply
puts together four kinds of love which he considers will be
of particular appeal to his women readers. In an analysis
of his argument, it is usual, as we have seen, to be puzzled
by what the author has put in and by what he has left out.
In Part 7, God's love for man is never carefully distinguished
from man's love for God. Formal arrangements are never
his prime concern, although he seeks to impart authority
and gain effectiveness by their use. It is difficult, for example,
to discover the second item which should precede the heading
Eft þe þridde reisun (**22**,36).

Structure of argument

Granting then that the general character of his writing is
plausibility, and his aim moving to action, we must recognise
that the materials the author turns to these uses have at
least the semblance of rational arguments.

The development of thought is elaborate. Even a first reading of the whole of AW will show how an argument appears, disappears, reappears, with many a reference backwards and forwards.[1] Frequently the author, like the pilgrim of Part 6, seems drawn aside by what he sees or hears by the way. Nevertheless, there can be no doubt that the work was planned as a whole, and that the parts were adapted and fitted to form a unified treatise. ' Notice ', we are bidden, ' how each Part leads on to the next ' (*f.* 81r (Salu 132)).

All skilled medieval writers attached particular importance to the divisions of their work. At the end of his Introduction the author indicated how the work was to be arranged—in eight *distinctiones*. ' Each part has a different subject, and while there is no mixing of subjects yet the parts are consecutive and follow properly upon the one before ' (*f.* 4r (Salu 6)). A consideration of the last two pages of Part 6 will show how gradually and carefully the theme of Part 7 is introduced. Part 6 reaches no further than to the idea that love is the sweet fruit of suffering. In Part 7 love itself is the power which makes the heart clean. Part 7 looks back to penance, but now bodily suffering is justified only as it leads to love. Across the division of Part 6 from Part 7 the author has changed his point of survey. The treatment in the two Parts is distinct, but as the author has promised, their matters fall inextricably together.

A more particular example of his careful transitions can be shown within Part 6, where the argument emerges from its dependence on Bernard's Lenten sermon and then goes on to use the *Declamations* (5,24ff). Following Bernard he groups the elect in three classes. In considering the third class, Bernard had spoken of the true contemplative caught up to the third heaven. This reference to mystical experience the author of AW omits (cp. p. lvii above). Instead he makes promise to this third class of an exceeding great reward (5,33). Straightway now he introduces the theme of the passage he is to adapt from the *Declamations*. By the

---

[1] See e.g. notes on **9**,1ff, **14**,34, **17**,16, **18**,29, **26**,23 ; cp. H. E. Allen, *PMLA* 44 (1929), 678.

time he begins a new section with the borrowed *Vilitas &
asperitas* (6,12), this distinction between bodily suffering and
mental humiliation is well established. He has already
spoken of *sum wa oðer sum scheome* (5,35), *scheome & teone*
(5,37); referred back to the third class of the elect *ahonget
sariliche & scheomeliche* on the cross (6,1); marked the need
for living *i scheome & i wa* (6,7). By the end of the paragraph a careful disjunction between humiliation and physical
pain has been made in terms which seemed to be no more
than casually conjoined when the author turned from
Bernard's sermon. Indeed further links could be explored
in this passage of transition : the theme of reward (5,33),
taken up at 7,20ff; the theme of exile running through
5,25ff, reappearing 7,24ff. And the end of this paragraph
(8,2ff) provides an excellent example of the way in which
a practised preacher pulled his themes together with a
scriptural reference, an appeal to an authority, followed by
a sentence of summary—the device of *unitio*, ' the bringing
together within a period of all the ideas that have been
developed '.[1]

Such methods of developing a theme, by anticipation, by
accumulation, and by recapitulation, give a curious spiral
quality to the structure of AW. Often in this book there is
recurrence to the same idea but with a different purpose and
in a different context of thought. Of course this characteristic is observed most impressively when any Part of the
work is read carefully in conjunction with the whole.

In the presentation of his arguments the author follows
the preacher's methods. In a sermon, the development of
argument, upon which persuasion depended, was of three
main sorts : (*a*) by the manipulation of authorities ; (*b*) by
drawing out and elaborating what an authority provided ;
(*c*) by the exemplification of a truth in a narrative.[2]

The first method is simply illustrated by the author's
method of showing that love is God's master (29,37–30,17).
He proves it ' by God's own words ' ; no other authority
could be needed. The proof is established by a simple

---

[1] T. M. Charland, *Artes Praedicandi*, p. 217.   [2] *Ibid.*, pp. 194–211.

juxtaposition of scriptural texts. With this method, we may think, violence is sometimes offered to Scripture as well as to reason. But a certain amount of modification of a text was permissible. Scriptural texts had of course a peculiar character. Other writings were made up of words, but the Scripture, through words, made a direct contact with things. Thus scriptural texts could be used somewhat as nowadays we use mathematical tables. You could abstract from them, rearrange them, but the truth to which any extract gave access remained unchanged in all circumstances. When you argued by means of Scripture you argued with constants. A text in or out of context had the timeless validity of the whole Bible.

The second method of advancing proof also starts with Scripture, but relies upon drawing arguments out of it by ordinary logical means. The validity of the Biblical text is of course quite unassailable, but it is permissible to make use of the full variety of meanings which traditional exegesis had accorded to any particular text, or to the words of any particular text. Frequently this method permits of that enumeration beloved by our author: the three sorts of pilgrim, the two wheels of the chariot, the three baths, etc. Or it can suggest commentary based on etymology (14,10), or on the equivocal value of a word (11,16). In choosing texts to provide matter for elaboration there would be inevitably a tendency to prefer the metaphorical (9,34, 10,3, 15,34, etc.), or at least a text which could be given a metaphorical turn (4,31ff).

Or the author could examine the concepts logically embodied in the text. This necessitated disengaging the essence and qualities of the thing to be dealt with. But there is never an escape from the actual wording. Sometimes the structure of the writer's argument appears to be imposed unwarrantably on the text: so, for instance, *Vide humilitatem meam et laborem meam* (6,18-19) is taken to provide the sharp distinction between shame and pain that the author requires (cp. also 17,17ff). Indeed the Bible may often seem to have been used in a way made familiar by our modern explicators of poetry: all that could be wrung out of a text was assumed to be there. Again, in this manner of use, syntax is made declarative of meaning (**9,12**) ; so is the precedence of words (**7,7ff, 16,2**). Or it is possible to incorporate meanings acquired in other contexts of the use of a word or concept (as with myrrh, **13,32–16,10**).

The Scripture either by reference or allusion provides the initiative for the main debate. To a limitèd extent the writings of the Fathers are used in a similar way. So are common maxims and proverbs (**6,32, 7,35, 8,34**). Sometimes arguments proceed from premisses provided by a general notion, such as fortitude (**7,32ff**), honour and social prestige (**8,2ff**), loyalty (**8,31ff**). The objections raised and answered on **10** and **11** are arguments of prudence, justice, and self-interest.

The third method of development is by the use of the *exemplum*. In the old rhetoric, which always lies close under the new art of preaching, the *exemplum* had a limited scope, as an interpolated anecdote from history offering a model of conduct for imitation. In popular preaching of late medieval times the *exemplum* becomes little less than the sum and substance of the sermon. This development was promoted by the lively preaching of the friars, but the *exemplum* was coming into use in the general revival of preaching at the end of the twelfth century. ' More are taught by *exemplum* than by precept ', observed Jacques of Vitry, the first systematic exponent of the method, and a preacher and confessor very closely concerned with pastoral work among pious women in France and the Low Countries. In English, AW provides some of the earliest uses of the *exemplum* : of the man absent from his wife awhile (**11,33ff**), of the fastidious monk (**12,35ff**) ; the story of the austere holy man (**18,11ff**) ; most famous of all, the royal wooing of Christ (**21,9ff**). But there are several rudimentary *exempla* : **7,32, 9,26, 10,9, 11,17, 23,13, 24,5**. In this use of parables the author is extending the methods of Anselm, who, according to Eadmer, used this device of teaching at Canterbury with great success. For the author of the Rule, the *exemplum* often serves as a temporary stabilisation of his continuously allegorical habits of mind.

Manner of address

The author's presupposition that his work was to be read aloud governs the style of AW. Most medieval writing is so controlled, but in AW the conditions and requirements imposed by oral delivery are nearer to the surface, or perhaps it should be granted at once that the author of AW is much more skilful in the management of his medium. The claim does not of course imply that AW exhibits the slackness of unrehearsed conversation; but rather that the syntax, the verbal effects, and the choice and arrangements of words are designed to satisfy first the ear of our mind and the brain that depends on the ear.

AW is written for that kind of formal delivery which the old rhetoricians called (appropriately enough) *sermo* (*ad Herennium*, III, xiii, 23), 'the tone of conversation'; and the old teaching on *sermo* is well exemplified in AW. It is a stylisation of serious conversation. In the main the tone should be dignified and restrained. Passages of explanation are to be kept to a matter-of-fact level. Narrative passages are simpler, less organised, requiring a range of intonation. The difference in style between passages of explanation and narrative can be clearly seen in AW. Some of the *exempla* are slackly written. The facetious tone, as a characteristic of *sermo*, is not employed in Parts 6 and 7, but the author is quick to exploit incongruities, and the syntax—and we may be sure the intonation too—is required to point these passages. Always it is important to hear mentally the voice of the reader—to expect him, as Augustine had advised, to speak smoothly and sweetly and levelly when the matter is love and devotion, in round, full, extended phrasing; the terror of death, hell, and judgment will require of him a sharper, more incisive accent.

If we attempt to read AW aloud nowadays (and it is difficult to think of a suitable occasion), we must rely upon our subjective judgment in choice of pitch and intonation. But to recognise that AW was written to be read aloud expressively is no subjective opinion. Contemporary theory expected it, and many of the verbal devices in AW declare it. Often an argument has been reinforced by the neat, satisfying sound of the phrases. Some of the devices have less elegance in print, but are perfectly acceptable to the ear. Among such devices which become immediately and effectively intelligible if cunningly read aloud, are the frequent use of parenthesis, involving a variation in pitch, used for a number of purposes, for instance, to sharpen focus (8,19), to refine meaning (4,22)—sometimes even as if such a modification of meaning were coming to mind in the act of speaking (5,27); the use of asseverations or expostulations for emphasis, or of the frequent calls to attention (4,29, 5,20, 8,33, etc.); sudden breakings off (25,14); changes of person, which can mark a withdrawal from, or entry into, participation in the argument (4,7, 6,20). With the conditions of oral delivery can be connected also the use of dialogue (10,16, 29, 28,29, etc.), and the use of question (and answer) (4,25ff, 9,1ff, etc.). Particularly serviceable too is asyndeton, or instead, sometimes of necessity, the repetition of subject, or a use of recapitulatory pronouns in organising longer sentences (4,26, 7,19, 8,2, etc.), or even the use of tautologies for emphasis (8,9, 10,1, 11,3, etc.). Any careful reader will be able to collect further and other examples of ways in which the author exploits the resources as well as admits the limitations of his medium.

Verbal composition

Any reader moreover, furnished with a handbook, can pick out and label a great number and variety of the old traditional figures of thought and speech. There is no doubt that the author of AW was trained in the art of rhetoric. He uses the terms *anto(no)masice* (*f. 1r*) and *hypallage* (*f. 20r*). His English prose style suggests he has applied wherever possible the ornaments and devices of the Latin rhetoricians. The art of rhetoric, first systematised by the Greeks, adopted by the Romans, readapted by men of the Middle Ages, had a long, unbroken history by the twelfth century. It had been assimilated early and almost imperceptibly into Christian learning. What had been designed originally as a systemisation of verbal persuasion for use in the courts of law and government was modified to provide the persuasive art of preaching. The *Artes Praedicandi* owe as much to traditional rhetoric as do the twelfth-century Arts of Poetry.[1] It is not surprising that a scholarly cleric in the twelfth century should have sought to apply the art of rhetoric to his Latin sermons ; he could not have done otherwise. What is surprising is the success with which the author of AW applies the rules of the art to composition in English. It should be recalled that Chaucer's technical achievement in poetry, at least in the eyes of his contemporaries and successors, was precisely this. He exploited in the vernacular with complete mastery the traditional art of rhetoric. And yet nearly two centuries earlier the author of the Rule was doing much the same thing, in a more limited and better prepared field it is true, but in what is often considered a more sophisticated medium than verse—in artificial prose. Across the sharp, but apparently quite narrow gulf, which cut the vernacular off from the language of the learned in the twelfth century, our author links hands with those great writers of his time, essentially literary men, such as John of Salisbury, Walter Map, and Peter of Blois. Like them the author of AW is a man with a natural flair for words, and one who has been carefully trained in elaborate ways of using them.

His favourite figures are figures of repetition ; and they are so common in AW that we must conclude that symmetry, parallelism, and antithesis are habits of his thought. We can acknowledge that he inhabited a symmetrical universe in which thinking was instinctively dialectical, with a result that many of his figures are functional to a degree beyond our immediate recognition. Much of the effectiveness of AW rises from the juxtaposition of contraries (' The discipline of contraries is one and the same ', *f.* 20*v*) : of heaven and hell, light and dark, woe and bliss, inner and outer, etc., etc. And much of the brilliance of the writing depends upon the superimposition of apparent contradictories : for example, the saints presented as naughty children (9,26) ; the love of God as a devastating weapon of war (27,13).

[1] See Harry Caplan, *Classical Philology* 28 (1933), 73–96.

Structural repetition is inherent in the management of the argument, as shown in the preceding section. But it is even more noticeable in the details of verbal composition. Some of these may be listed.[1]

(a) repetition of initial words in successive clauses (*anaphora*) : 4,24, 10,18,22,23, 25,4,5,6,9, etc. ; repetition with double-elements : 3,4–6, 25,23–4, 29,18–20, etc.

(b) repetition of final words (*conversio*) : 3,14–16, 5,23–4, 10,30,35,36, etc.

(c) repetition of a word within the same phrase (*polyptoton*), as *hure ouer hure, fel for felle, god of ure god,* etc.

(d) repetition of the final word at the beginning of the next clause (*anadiplosis*) : 14,12, 24,11, 29,33, etc.

(e) abrupt repetition for emphasis (*epanados*), often in passages of interpretation : 5,9, 7,33, 16,17, etc.

(f) repetition of stem with variation in inflexion, prefix, suffix, tense, or part of speech, etc. (*paregmenon*), as *sontes . . . sein . . . isonted,* 4,12ff ; *deade,* as adj. and noun *deað,* 4,37ff, etc. The figure is effective and often unobtrusive ; many examples can be collected from every page.

(g) use of homonyms (*paronomasia*) : 6,28,35, 9,6, 21,6, 23,14.

(h) conjunction of synonyms (or antonyms) in pairs often with alliteration as *wa ne wunne, sariliche & scheomeliche, i sar & i sorhe, irudet & ireadet,* etc.

(i) common but unsystematic use of alliteration to reinforce meaning or to indicate logical connection or to add an emotional tone : 4,7ff, 5,19,25ff, 7,4ff, 8,6ff, 9,14ff, etc.

Imagery

What we now call simile (*imago*) is no commoner in AW than it is in other early English writings. The basis of the modern simile is usually a likeness disclosed to sense perception. The author of AW is not sufficiently interested in appearances to explore these likenesses. But comparison (*similitudo*)

---

[1] The analysis of Morton's text by Sister Agnes Margaret Humbert, *Verbal Repetition in the AR,* Washington (1944), can be usually transferred to AW. In the present edition, here and elsewhere, references are exemplary, not exhaustive.

as an element in argument is much commoner (**5,19**, **6,35**, **11,19**). So **19,18**ff would be accounted by the rhetoricians a *similitudo* by negation for the purpose of proof.

If simile is rare, metaphor, both in its earlier, more specific sense and in its general, extended modern sense, is a condition of the thought and expression of this writer. Thus not only, following the rhetorical formula, does he use metaphor to make discourse vivid (**17,3**), to magnify or emphasise (**30,17**), to avoid obscenity (**12,21**), or simply to adorn, but a metaphorical cast of thinking underlies all the amplification and interpretation.

What we nowadays call rather loosely an author's imagery, i.e. the metaphorical references in his writings to what the modern reader will take to be the interests, the experiences, the physical, intellectual, and emotional environment of the writer as a man, the old theory of rhetoric dealt with not as part of style, but under the head of invention. We tend to assume that what has happened to a man will somehow or other get into his writings, modified and transformed perhaps, but still accessible. The old theory instead expected a writer to select such material from his own experience and knowledge as he thought should be useful for the matter in hand. His material was relevant to his argument, not to himself. The more comprehensive his coverage the more effective his arguments. Probably the modern reader should be gratified as much by the ' imagery ' of AW as the medieval reader would admire the richness of invention. Parts 6 and 7 of AW disclose to us now a feudal world of thralls and gentlemen, knights and clerks, of menials and officers of the household and hired men in the fields, of lovers and angry fathers, compassionate mothers and naughty children, of people with headaches and indigestion : outside the cell is a busy world where men live in cots and castles, haunt shrines and markets, beg, haggle, pawn, fight, pray, marry, feast ; a world full of material objects—pots, dishes, kitchen fires, cradles, hard beds, kirtles, girdles, leather aprons, laced shoes, ladders, spades, ploughs, thorn fences, shields, swords, banners, love-letters, and crucifixes. Out of these old actualities the author draws some of his analogies.

Much of what we should call imagery is prompted by the Bible, or by familiar exegesis of the Bible taken from Augustine or Gregory. The day-spring, the Body of Christ, the Bride of God, the fire of love, these are grand metaphors to which the author often returns. In this sort of treatment the radical metaphor is thoroughly traditional, and AW often provides a judicious arrangement or brilliant embellishment of ecclesiastical commonplaces.

But some of these metaphors acquire a peculiar significance out of a fusion of learning, observation, usefulness, and experience. It involves a process of sustained and complicated allusion which the authors of the *Artes Praedicandi* call *inculcatio*. Bernard was celebrated as a master of this use of metaphor. Certain words often repeated in his writing take on a substance of their own—they recur, as some words do in Yeats's poetry, as symbols with fixed but complex meanings. With Bernard, *speculum, misericordia, osculum, umbra* have this character.[1] A somewhat similar power attaches to certain words in AW, to *dunes, schadewe, schild*, and *spus*. The passage on the Beloved leaping over the hills (**17,16ff**) shows the difficulties which can result from *inculcatio*. For the modern reader here metaphor defeats meaning. But nowhere else does AW rely upon pre-conditioned symbols so heavily. Much more often, meanings are accumulated in the evolution of the argument. As is not unusual with the greater English writers, the particularity of the words as they come often seems to determine the process of thought. As in many highly powered passages in the later writing of Shakespeare, so in many passages of AW, it is scarcely possible to explicate the shift, slide, association, divergence, and resolution of linked words. But it is always worth attempting.

It is illuminating to follow the fortunes of the symbol of shield through **22,9–23,8**, not in itself perhaps a particularly memorable passage. Christ proving His prowess had His shield pierced (**22,10**). The shield which concealed (the verb has a double meaning) His Godhead was His body (**11**).

---

[1] See I. Valléry-Radot in *Bernard of Clairvaux*, Commission d'histoire de l'ordre de Cîteaux, III (1953), pp. 457–60.

A knight fights within the covering of a shield, so God fought for us within the covering of flesh. The physical shape of the crucified Christ resembles the shape of a shield (12–14). That this shield had cut-away sides indicates that the original disciples forsook him (14–18), a crime particularly associated with a battlefield. But the material representation of the Passion—that is, the crucifix in the cell of the recluse —is an actual shield to be used against temptation ; in this sense a crucifix as a shield is more than a metaphor (see 23, 2 note). Then by working in part of a psalm verse (22,21), the author can represent the shield not only as our defence but also as the means of our exaltation. It is perhaps worth remembering the Germanic custom of raising conquering heroes on shields.

This shield was voluntarily interposed on our behalf. The psalm phrase (21) points to one of the theological debates of the twelfth century, namely, to what extent did Christ suffer of His own free will ? Here Isaiah is invoked to settle the issue quickly (25), but the one scholastic debate introduces another and a related one : could Christ have saved us in any other way than He did ? In replying to this objection to penance, the author returns the usual answer (see 22,26ff note), and backs it with a proverbial maxim (30). Christ paid on our behalf the most precious thing of all—His heart's blood—a precious scutage indeed. He paid with the blood that was shed in having the shield of His body pierced in the battle of the Cross. And so the author returns to these concepts again. The shield which Christ provided was made of the wood of the Cross, ' the leather of God's body ' was stretched out on it, and the blood made there such a blazon as a knight wears on his shield in tournament (33–6). For Christ is of course the knight as well as the knight's shield. The crucifix in the recluse's cell, which is an actual defence against temptation, and looks like a material shield, can serve as a perpetual reminder of the Christ-knight's achievement, and so it fulfils the function of an earthly shield after a knight's death (22,37–23,4).

Throughout this passage the use of figured language should be remarked : the repetition and emphatic positioning of the

word *scheld* in *anaphora* (22,11,14,18,20) ; with *epanados*, 23 ;
with *paregmenon*, 20. Alliteration is added, apparently, to
supply the desired emotional tone to some phrases : *leoue
licome* (11); on *s* and *f* through 14 to 17 ; in 30,35,37,
23,2–3). *Paregmenon* appears elsewhere : *cruneð, icrunet*
(21, 23), *wil, willes* (24), *bohte, buð, bohte* (30, 31). Words are
repeated for emphasis or to link thought : *siden* (15, 16) ; *wil*
(23, 24) ; *lihtliche* (28, 30). Other common devices appear :
emphatic parenthesis (31), use of direct speech (22ff),
imaginary dialogue (26ff), and the classification (*distributio*)
of 23ff. The rhythm, basically trochaic, with a tendency
to mark two-stress phrases, is varying, nor do the cadences
seem to conform to a few recognisable types.[1]

What is perhaps worth lingering upon is the cunning of
the conclusion (23,4–8), a remarkable instance of the proper
way to exploit *unitio*, the binding together of themes at the
end. Many of the keywords have been anticipated : *hu he
bohte hire luue* (5, cp. 22,29f), *lette þurlin his scheld* (5, cp.
22,10), *openin his side* (5, cp. 22,14f), *to ofdrahen hire heorte*
(6–7, cp. 22, 31–2). The relationship of the clauses depends
upon a careful involved symmetry (the modified use of
isocola and *parison*).
Thus :

His leofmon bihalde þron

hu he {bohte hire luue
    {lette

        {þurlin his scheld,
        {openin his side

            { {to schawin hire
            { {to schawin hire {his heorte
            {
            {   {openliche
            {   hu {inwardliche he luuede hire
            to ofdrahen {hire heorte

And this arrangement is knit with alliteration on *h*, *l*, and *s*,
by the play on pronoun and possessive, *hire* and *his*, by the

---

[1] An excellent introduction to the study of EME prose rhythm is
provided by Margaret Schlauch, *PMLA* 65 (1950), 568–89.

fall of like endings of the infinitives and adverbs; and sustained towards the end by the opposition of *openliche* and *inwardliche* (with its slight turn of meaning). Finally there is a weighting of devotional content. The passage accumulates as well as recapitulates meaning. What started with the topical reference to the knight's shield in tournament, ends with a recommendation to contemplation of the mystery of the Wound in the Side, one of the earliest references to the pious practice which developed into the modern Roman Catholic devotion of the Sacred Heart.

Much of AW will sustain as elaborate analysis as this. It is astonishing prose. We are tempted to ask, as Jeffrey asked of the young Macaulay, where he got so early in time a style thus brilliant and assured. There is no doubt that the author of AW worked in the OE homiletic tradition; there can be no doubt either that he worked out beyond it. In some of his verbal devices, particularly in his reliance upon figures of repetition, he recalls Wulfstan, but he is infinitely more varied, and his thought incomparably richer. In his wit and grace, he may recall Ælfric, but his words are much more fully *commotiva*. Whatever its basis, the style of the author of AW is a style adapted to the needs and conforming with the intellectual habits of a time later than the Anglo-Saxon, of a time which was, as Walter Map indicated, quite conscious of its modernity.

Ancrene Wisse

Parts
Six and Seven

Efter schrift falleð to speoken of penitence, þet is, dead
bote ; ant swa we habbeð inʒong ut of þis fifte dale in
to þe seste.

[ON PENANCE]

AL is penitence ant strong penitence þet ʒe eauer
dreheð, mine leoue sustren ; al þet ʒe eauer doð 5
of god, al þet ʒe þolieð, is ow martirdom i se
derf ordre, for ʒe beoð niht & dei up o Godes
rode. Bliðe mahe ʒe beon þrof, for as seinte Pawel seið,
Si compatimur, conregnabimus : as ʒe scottið wið him of
his pine on eorðe, ʒe schule scotti wið him of his blisse 10
in heouene ; for þi seið seinte Pawel, *Mihi absit gloriari,
nisi in cruce domini mei Iesu Christi* ; ant hali chirche
singeð, *Nos opportet gloriari in cruce domini nostri Iesu
Christi* : al ure blisse mot beon i Iesu Cristes rode. Þis
word nomeliche limpeð to recluses, hwas blisse ah to 15
beon allunge i Godes rode. Ich chulle biginnen herre
& lihten swa herto. Neomeð nu gode ʒeme, for almeast
is sein Beornardes sentence.

PREO manere men of Godes icorene liuieð on eorðe :
þe / ane mahe beon to gode pilegrimes ieuenet; þe oþre *f. 94v*
to deade ; þe þridde to ihongede wið hare gode wil o 21
Iesuse rode. Þe forme beoð gode, þe oþre beoð betere,
þe þridde best of alle.

TO þe forme gredeð seinte Peter inwardliche, *Obsecro
uos tanquam aduenas & peregrinos ut abstineatis uos* 25
a carnalibus desideriis, que militant aduersus animam. Ich
halsi ow, he seið, as elþeodie & pilegrimes, þet ʒe wiðhalden ow from fleschliche lustes þe weorrið aʒein þe
sawle. Þe gode pilegrim halt eauer his rihte wei forðward.
Þah he seo oðer here idele gomenes & wũndres bi þe 30
weie, he ne edstont nawt, as foles doð, ah halt forð his
rute & hiheð toward his giste. He ne bereð na gersum

3

bute his speonse gnedeliche, ne claðes bute ane þeo þet
him to neodeð. Þis beoð hali men þe, þah ha beon i
þe world, ha beoð þrin as pilegrimes, & gað wið god
liflade toward te riche of heouene, & seggeð wið þe
5 apostle, *Non habemus hic manentem ciuitatem sed futuram
inquirimus* : þet is, nabbe we na wununge her, ah we
secheð oþer—beoð bi þe leaste þet ha mahen, ne ne
haldeð na tale of na worltlich froure, þah ha beon i
worltlich wei, as ich seide of pilegrim ; ah habbeð hare
10 heorte eauer toward heouene—& ahen wel to habben.
For oðer pilegrimes gað [*wið*] muche swinc to sechen
ane sontes banes, as sein James oðer sein Giles, ah þeo
pilegrimes, þe gað toward heouene, ha gað to beon
isontet & to finden Godd seolf & alle his hali halhen
15 liuiende i blisse, & schulen liuien wið him i wunne buten
ende. Ha ifindeð iwis sein Julienes in, þe weifearinde
men ȝeornliche bisecheð.

NV beoð þeose gode ah ȝet beoð þe oþre betere ; for
allegate pilegrimes, as ich ear seide, al gan / ha eauer
20 forðward, ne bicumen burhmen i þe worldes burh, ham
þuncheð, sum chearre, god of þet ha seoð bi weie, ant
edstuteð sumdeal—þah ha ne don mid alle—& moni
þing ham falleð to, hwer þurh ha beoð ilette, swa þet
mare hearm is—sum kimeð leate ham, sum neauer mare.
25 Hwa is þenne skerre & mare ut of þe world þen pilegrimes ?
—þet is to seggen, þen þeo men þe habbeð worltlich
þing & ne luuieð hit nawt, ah ȝeoueð hit as hit kimeð
ham, & gað untrusset lihte as pilegrimes doð toward
heouene ? Hwa beoð betere þene þeos ? Godd wat
30 þeo beoð betere þe þe apostle spekeð to & seið in his
epistle, *Mortui estis & vita uestra abscondita est cum
Christo in deo. Cum autem apparuerit uita uestra, tunc
& uos apparebitis cum ipso in gloria.* Ȝe beoð deade &
ower lif is ihud mid Criste. Hwen he þet is ower lif
35 eadeaweð & springeð as þe dahunge efter nihtes þeosternesse, ant ȝe schulen wið him springen schenre þen þe
sunne in to eche blisse. Þe nu beoð þus deade, hare
liflade is herre. For pilegrim eileð monihwet. Þe deade

nis noht of þah he ligge unburiet & rotie buuen eorðe—
preise him, laste him, do him scheome, sei him scheome,
al him is iliche leof. Þis is a seli deað þet makeð cwic
mon þus, oðer cwic wummon, ut of þe worlde; ah
sikerliche hwa se is þus dead in hire seoluen, Godd liueð 5
in hire heorte, for þis is þet te apostle seið, *Viuo ego, iam
non ego : viuit autem in me Christus* : ich liuie, nawt ich,
ah Crist liueð in me þurh his inwuniende grace ; & is as
þah he seide, worltlich speche, worltlich sihðe & euch
worltlich þing ifindeð me deade ; ah þet te limpeð to 10
Crist, þet ich seo & here & wurche i cwicnesse. Þus
riht is euch religius dead to þe worlde & cwic þah to Criste.
Þis is an heh steire, ah ȝet is þah / an herre. Ant hwa *f. 95ᵛ*
stod eauer þrin ? Godd wat þe þe seide, *Mihi absit
gloriari, nisi in cruce domini mei Iesu Christi : per quem* 15
mihi mundus crucifixus est, & ego mundo : þis is þet ich
seide þruppe, Crist me schilde forte habben eani blisse
i þis world bute i Iesu Cristes rode mi lauerd, þurh hwam
þe world is me unwurð ant ich am unwurð hire, as weari
þe is ahonget. A lauerd, hehe stod he þe spec o þisse 20
wise. Ant þis is ancre steire þet ha þus segge, *Mihi*
autem absit gloriari, & cetera : i na þing ne blissi ich me
bute i Godes rode, þet ich þolie nu wa & am itald unwurð
as Godd wes o rode. Lokið, leoue sustren, hu þis steire
is herre þen eani beo of þe oþre. Þe pilegrim i þe wor[l]des 25
wei þah he ga forðward toward te ham of heouene, he
sið & hereð unnet—& spekeð umbehwile—, wreaðeð him
for weohes ; & moni þing mei letten him of his jurnee.
Þe deade nis namare of scheome þen of menske, of heard
þen of nesche, for he ne feleð nowðer; & for þi ne 30
ofearneð he nowðer wa ne wunne ; ah þe þe is o rode
& haueð blisse þrof, he wendeð scheome to menske &
wa in to wunne, & ofearneð for þi hure ouer hure. Þis
beoð þeo þe neauer ne beoð gleade iheortet bute hwen
ha þolieð sum wa oðer sum scheome wið Iesu on his 35
rode. For þis is þe selhðe on eorðe, hwa se mei for
Godes luue habben scheome & teone. Þus lo, rihte
ancres ne beoð nawt ane pilegrimes, ne ȝet nawt ane
deade, ah beoð of þeos þridde : for al hare blisse is

forte beon ahonget sariliche & scheomeliche wið Iesu
on his rode. Þeos mahe bliðe wið hali chirche singen,
Nos opportet gloriari & cetera : þet is, as ich seide ear,
hwet se beo of oþre þe habbeð hare blisse, summe i
f. 96r fleschcs licunge, summe i worldes / dweole, summe in
6 oþres uuel, we mote nede blissin us i Iesu Cristes rode,
þet is, i scheome & i wa þet he droh o rode. Moni
walde summes weis þolien flesches heardschipe, ah beon
itald unwurð ne scheome ne mahte he þolien ; ah he
10 nis bute halflunge up o Godes rode, ȝef he nis igreiðet
to þolien ham baðe.

*V*ILITAS & asperitas, vilte & asprete, þeos twa,
scheome & pine, as sein Beornard seið, beoð þe twa
leaddre steolen þe beoð up iriht to heouene ; & bitweone
15 þeose steolen, beoð cf alle gode þeawes þe tindes ifestnet,
bi hwucche me climbeð to þe blisse of heouene. For þi
þet Dauið hefde þe twa steolen of þis leaddre, þah he king
were, he clomb uppard & seide baldeliche to ure lauerd, *Vide
humilitatem meam, & laborem meum : & dimitte uniuersa*
20 *delicta mea.* Bihald, quoð he, & sih min eadmodnesse &
mi swinc, & forȝef me mine sunnen alle to gederes.
Notið wel þes twa word þe Dauið feieð somet, swinc
& eadmodnesse : swinc, i pine & i wa, i sar & i sorhe ;
eadmodnesse, aȝein woh of scheome þet mon dreheð þe
25 is itald unwurð. Ba þeos bihald in me, quoð Dauið,
Godes deorling, ich habbe þeos twa leaddre steolen.
Dimitte uniuersa delicta mea : leaf, quoð he, bihinde
me & warp awei from me alle mine gultes, þet ich, ilihtet
of hare heuinesse, lihtliche stihe up to heouene bi þeos
30 leaddre. Þeose twa þinges, þet is, wa & scheome ifeiet
to gederes, beoð Helyes hweoles þe weren furene, hit
teleð, & beren him up to parais þer he liueð ȝetten. Fur
is hat & read. I þe heate is understonden euch wa
þet eileð flesch ; scheome bi þe reade, ah wel mei duhen.
35 Ha beoð her hweolinde, ase hweoles ouerturneð sone
ne leasteð nane hwile. Þis ilke is ec bitacnet bi cherubines
f. 96v sweord / biuore paraise ȝeten, þe wes of lei & hweolinde

4 oþre] ordre

& turninde abuten. Ne kimeð nan in to parais bute þurh
þis leitinde sweord þe wes hat & read, & in Helyes furene
hweoles, þet is, þurh sar & þurh scheome þe ouerturneð
tidliche ant agað sone. Ant nes Godes rode wið his
deorewurðe blod irudet & ireadet forte schawin on him 5
seolf þet pine & sorhe & sar schulden wið scheome beon
iheowet? Nis hit iwriten bi him seolf, *Factus est obediens
patri usque ad mortem, mortem autem crucis* : þet is, he
wes buhsuṃ his feader nawt ane to deað, ah to deað
o rode? Þurh þet he seide earst ' deað ', is pine under- 10
stonden ; þurh þet he þrefter seið ' deað o þe rode ',
is schendlac bitacnet ; for swuch wes Godes deað o þe
deore rode, pinful & schentful ouer alle oþre. Hwa se
eauer deieð ine Godd & o Godes rode, þeos twa ha mot
þolien, scheome for him & pine. Scheome ich cleopie 15
eauer her beon itald unwurð & beggin as an hearlot, ȝef
neod is, hire liueneð & beon oþres beodes mon, as ȝe
beoð, leoue sustren, & þolieð ofte danger of swuch
oðerhwile þe mahte beon ower þreal—þis is þet eadi
scheome þet ich of talie. Pine ne trukeð ow nawt. I þeos 20
ilke twa þing þet al penitence is in, blissið ow & gleadieð
for aȝein þeos twa ow beoð twafald blissen iȝarket :
aȝein scheome, menske ; aȝein pine, delit & reste buten
ende. *Ysaias : In terra, inquit, sua duplicia possidebunt* :
ha schulen, seið Ysaie, in hare ahne lond wealden 25
twauald blisse aȝein twauald wa þet ha her dreheð,—in
hare ahne lond, seið Ysaie, for alswa as þe vuele nabbeð
na lot in heouene, ne þe gode nabbeð na lot in eorðe :
*super epistolam Iacobi : Mali nichil habent in celo, boni
uero nichil in terra.* In hare ahne lond / ha schulen *f. 97ᵛ*
wealden blisse, twafald cunne mede aȝein twauald sorhe, 31
as þah he seide, Ne þunche ham na feorlich, þah ha her
þolien, as in uncuð lond & in uncuð eard bituhhen
unþeode, scheome ba & sorhe ; for swa deð moni gentil
mon þe is uncuð in uncuððe. Me mot ute swinken, ed 35
hame me schal resten ; ant nis he a cang cniht þe secheð
reste i þe feht & eise i þe place ? *Milicia est vita hominis
super terram* : al þis lif is a feht, as Job witneð ; ah efter

28 þe] þe þe

þis feht her, ȝef we wel fehteð, menske & reste abit us
ed hame in ure ahne lond, þet is, heoueriche. Lokið nu
hu witerliche ure lauerd seolf hit witneð : *Cum sederit
filius hominis in sede maiestatis sue, sedebitis & uos iudicantes*
5 *& cetera ; Bernardus : In sedibus, quies imperturbata,
in iudicio, honoris eminencia commendatur* : hwen ich sitte
forte demen, seið ure lauerd, ȝe schulen sitten wið me
& deme wið me al þe world þet schal beon idemet,
kinges & keisers, cnihtes & clearkes ; i þe sete is reste
10 & eise bitacnet aȝein þe swinc þet her is ; i þe menske
of þe dom þet ha schulen demen is hehschipe menskeful
ouer alle understonden aȝein scheome & lahschipe þet
ha her for Godes luue mildeliche þoleden.

NIS þer nu þenne bute þolien gleadliche, for bi Godd
15 seolf is iwriten, *Quod per penam ignominiose passionis,
peruenit ad gloriam resurrectionis* : þet is, þurh schentful
pine he com to gloire of blisful ariste. Nis na selcuð
þenne ȝef we wrecche sunfule þolien her pine, ȝef we
wulleð o domes dei blisfule arisen—ant þet we mahen
20 þurh his grace, ȝef we us seolf wulleð. *Quoniam si
complantati fuerimus similitudini mortis eius, simul &
resurrectionis erimus*— seinte Paweles sahe, þe seið se
f. 97ᵛ wel eauer : / ȝef we beoð i-impet to þe ilicnesse of Godes
deað, we schulen of his ariste : þet is to seggen, ȝef we
25 libbeð i scheome & i pine for his luue, i hwucche twa he
deide, we schulen beon iliche his blisful ariste, ure bodi
briht as his is, world buten ende, as seinte Pawel witneð :
*Saluatorem expectamus, qui reformabit corpus humilitatis
nostre configuratum corpori claritatis sue.* Let oþre acemin
30 hare bodi þe eorneð biuoren hond ; abide we ure healent
þe schal acemin ure efter his ahne. *Si compatimur,
conregnabimus* : ȝef we þolieð wið him, we schule blissin
wið him. Nis þis god foreward ? Wat Crist, nis he
nawt god feolahe ne treowe, þe nule scottin i þe lure
35 as eft i þe biȝete. *Glosa : Illis solis prodest sanguis Christi
qui uoluptates deserunt & corpus affligunt.* Godd schedde
his blod for alle, ah heom ane hit is wurð þe fleoð
flesches licunge & pinið ham seoluen. Ant is þet eani

wunder? Nis Godd ure heaued & we his limen alle?
Ah nis euch lim sar wið sorhe of þe heaued? His lim
þenne nis he nawt þe naueð eche under se sar akinde
heaued. Hwen þe heaued sweat wel, þet lim þe ne swet
nawt, nis hit uuel tacne? He þe is ure heaued sweatte 5
blodes swat for ure secnesse to turnen us of þet londuuel
þet alle londes leien on & liggeð ȝette monie. Þe lim þe
ne sweat nawt i swincful pine for his luue, deuleset, hit
leaueð in his secnesse & nis þer bute forkeoruen hit, þah
hit þunche sar Godd; for betere is finger offe þen he 10
ake eauer. Cwemeð he nu wel Godd þe þus bilimeð him
of him seolf þurh þet he nule sweaten? *Oportebat
Christum pati & sic intrare in gloriam suam.* Seinte Marie
mearci, hit moste swa beon, hit seið, Crist þolie pi/ne *f. 98ʳ*
& passiun ant swa habben inȝong in to his riche. Lo 15
deale hwet he seið: swa habben inȝong in to his riche,
swa, & nan oðerweis; ant we wrecches sunfule wulleð
wið eise stihen to heouene þet is se hehe buuen us & se
swiðe muchel wurð; ant me ne mei nawt wið uten swinc
a lutel cote arearen, ne twa þwongede scheos habbe wið 20
ute bune. Oðer þeo beoð canges þe weneð wið lihtleapes
buggen eche blisse, oðer þe hali halhen, þe bohten hit
se deore. Nes seinte Peter & seinte Andrew þeruore
istraht o rode? Sein Lorenz o þe gridil & laðlese meidnes
þe tittes itoren of, tohwiðeret o hweoles, heafdes bicoruen? 25
Ah ure sotschipe is sutel ant heo weren ilich þeose ȝape
children þe habbeð *riche* feaderes, þe willes & waldes
toteoreð hare claðes, forte habbe neowe. Vre alde curtel
is þe flesch þet we of Adam ure alde feader habbeð. Þe
neowe we schulen underuon of Godd ure riche feader 30
i þe ariste of domes dei, hwen ure flesch schal blikien
schenre þen þe sunne, ȝef hit is totoren her wið wontreaðe
& wið weane. Of þeo þe hare curtles toteoreð o þisse
wise, seið Ysaie, *Deferetur munus domino exercituum a
populo diuulso & dilacerato, a populo terribili*: a folc 35
tolaimet & totoren, a folc, he seið, fearlich, schal makien
to ure lauerd present of him seoluen. Folc tolaimet &
totoren wið strong liflade & wið heard, he cleopeð folc

27 riche] ȝape

fearlac, for þe feond is of swucche offruht & offearet.
For þi þet Job wes þullich, he meande him ant seide,
Pellem pro pelle & uniuersa, & cetera: þet is, he wule
ȝeouen fel for fel, þe alde for þe neowe, as þah he seide,
5 ne geineð me nawt to asailin him, he is of þet totore folc
f. 98v —he tereð his / alde curtel & torendeð þe alde pilche of
his deadliche fel; for þe fel is undeadlich þet i þe neowe
ariste schal schine seoueuald brihtre þen þe sunne.
Eise & flesches este beoð þes deofles mearken. Hwen
10 he sið þeos mearken i mon oðer i wummon, he wat þe
castel is his & geað baldeliche in þer he sið iriht up
swucche baneres as me deð i castel. I þet totore folc
he misseð his mearken & sið in ham iriht up Godes
banere, þet is, heardschipe of lif, & haueð muche dred
15 þrof as Ysaie witneð.

M E, leoue sire, seið sum, & is hit nu wisdom to don
se wa him seoluen? Ant tu ȝeld me ondswere—of
tweie men hweðer is wisre? Ha beoð ba seke—þe an
forgeað al þet he luueð of metes & of drunches & drinkeð
20 bitter sabraz forte acourin heale, þe oþer folheð al his
wil & fordeð his lustes aȝein his secnesse & leoseð his
lif sone. Hweðer is wisre of þes twa? Hweðer is betere
his ahne freond? Hweðer luueð him seolf mare? Ant
hwa nis sec of sunne? Godd for ure secnesse dronc
25 attri drunch o rode, ant we nulleð nawt bittres biten for
us seoluen. Nis þer nawiht þrof. Sikerliche his folhere
mot wið pine of his flesch folhin his pine. Ne wene nan
wið este stihen to heouene.

M E, sire, seið sum eft, wule Godd se wracfulliche
30 wreoken up o sunne? Ȝe, mon, for loke nu hu he
hit heateð swiðe. Hu walde nu þe mon beate þet þing
seolf hwer se he hit ifunde, þe for muchel heatunge beote
þrof þe schadewe & al þet hefde þerto eani licnesse?
Godd feader almihti hu beot he bitterliche his deorewurðe
35 sune, Iesu ure lauerd, þet neauer nefde sunne, bute ane
þet he ber flesch ilich ure, þet is ful of sunne! Ant we /
99r schulden beon ispearet þe beoreð on us his sune deað—

þe wepne þet sloh him þet wes ure sunne. Ant he þe
nefde nawt of sunne bute schadewe ane, wes i þe ilke
schadewe se scheomeliche ituket, se sorhfulliche ipinet,
þet ear hit come þerto—for þe þreatunge ane þrof—
swa him agras þer aȝein þet he bed his feader are : *Tristis* 5
est anima mea usque ad mortem. Pater mi, si possibile est,
transeat a me calix iste : sare, quoð he, me grulleð aȝein
mi muchele pine. Mi feader, ȝef hit mei beon, speare
me ed tis time ; þi wil þah & nawt min eauer beo iuorðet.
His deorewurðe feader for þi ne forber him nawt, ah 10
leide on him se luðerliche þet he bigon to greden wið
reowðfule steuene, *Heloy, Heloy, lamazabatani*—mi Godd,
mi Godd, mi deorewurðe feader, hauest tu al forwarpe
me, þin anlepi sune, þe beatest me se hearde ? For al
þis ne lette he nawt, ah beot se swiðe longe & se swiðe 15
grimliche þet he stearf o rode. *Disciplina pacis nostre*
super eum, seið Ysaie. Þus ure beatunge feol on him for
he dude him seoluen bitweonen us & his feader þe þreatte
us forte smiten, ase moder þet is reowðful deð hire
bitweonen hire child ant te wraðe sturne feader hwen 20
he hit wule beaten. Þus dude ure lauerd Iesu Crist,
ikepte on him deaðes dunt forte schilden us þerwið—
igracet beo his milce ! Hwer se muchel dunt is, hit
bulteð aȝein up o þeo þe þer neh stondeð. Soðliche
hwa se is neh him þe ikepte se heui dunt, hit wule bulten 25
on him, ne nule he him neauer meanen, for þet is þe
preoue þet he stont neh him ; & liht is þe bultunge to
þolien for his luue þe underueng se heui dunt us forte
burhen from þe deofles botte i þe pine of helle.

ȜET, seið moni mon, hweat / is Godd þe betere þah *f. 99ᵛ*
ich pini me for his luue ? Leoue mon & wummon, 31
Godd þuncheð god of ure god : vre god is ȝef we doð
þet tet we ahen. Nim ȝeme of þis essample. A mon
þe were feor ifearen & me come & talde him þet his deore
spuse se swiðe murnede efter him þet heo wið uten him 35
delit nefde i na þing, ah were for þoht of his luue, leane
& elheowet, nalde him betere likin þen þet me seide him
þet ha gleowde & gomnede & wedde wið oþre men &

liuede i delices ? Alswa ure lauerd, þet is þe sawle spus, þet
sið al þet ha deð þah he hehe sitte, he is ful wel ipaiet
þet ha murneð efter him & wule hihin toward hire
mucheles þe swiðere wið ȝeoue of his grace, oðer fecchen
5 hire allunge to him to gloire & to blisse þurhwuniende.

NE grapi hire nan to softeliche hire seoluen to
bichearren. Ne schal ha for hire lif witen hire
al cleane, ne halden riht hire chastete wið uten twa
þinges, as seint Ailred þe abbat wrat to his suster. Þet
10 an is pinsunge i flesch wið feasten, wið wecchen, wið
disceplines, wið heard werunge, heard leohe, wið uuel,
wið muchele swinkes : þe oþer is heorte þeawes—
deuociun, reowfulnesse, riht luue, eadmodnesse & uertuz
oþre swucche. Me, sire, þu ondswerest me, suleð Godd
15 his grace ? Nis grace wil ȝeoue ? Mine leoue sustren,
þah cleannesse of chastete ne beo nawt bune ed Godd,
ah beo ȝeoue of grace, vngraciuse stondeð þer toȝeines
& makieð ham unwurðe to halden se heh þing, þe nulleð
swinc þeruore bliðeliche þolien. Bitweonen delices &
20 eise & flesches este, hwa was eauer chaste ? Hwa bredde
eauer inwið hire fur þet ha ne bearnde ? Pot þe walleð
swiðe nule he beon ouerleden, oðer cald weater iwarpe
f. 100r þrin & brondes / wiðdrahene ? Þe wombe, pot þe walleð
of metes & of drunches, is se neh nehbur to þet fulitohe
25 lim þet ha dealeð þerwið þe brune of hire heate. Ah
monie, mare hearm is, beoð se fleschwise & swa ouerswiðe
ofdred leste hare heaued ake, leste hare licome febli to
swiðe, & witeð swa hare heale, þet te gast unstrengeð &
secleð i sunne ; ant þeo þe schulden ane lechnin hare
30 sawle wið heorte bireowsunge & flesches pinsunge,
forwurðeð fisiciens & licomes leche. Dude swa seinte
Agace þe ondswerede & seide to ure lauerdes sonde þe
brohte salue o Godes half to healen hire tittes. *Medicinam
carnalem corpori meo nunquam adhibui* ? : þet is, fleschlich
35 medecine ne dude ich me neaure. Nabbe ȝe iherd tellen
of þe þreo hali men ? Bute þe an wes iwunet for his
calde mahe to nutten hate speces & wes ornre of mete
& of drunch þen þe tweien oþre ; þah ha weren seke,

ne nomen neauer ʒeme hweat wes hal, hwet unhal to
eoten ne to drinken, ah nomen eauer forðriht hwet se
Godd ham sende, ne makeden neauer strengðe of gingiure
ne of zedual, ne of clowes de gilofre. A dei, as ha þreo
weren ifolen o slepe, & lei, bitweone þes twa, þe þridde 5
þet ich seide, com þe cwen of heouene & twa meidnes
wið hire : þe an, as þah hit were, ber a letuaire, þe oþer
of gold a sticcke. Vre leafdi wið þe sticke nom & dude
i þe anes muð of þe letuaire & te meidnes eoden forðre
to þe midleste. Nai, quoð ure leafdi, he is his ahne 10
leche, ga ouer to þe þridde. Stod an hali mon of feor,
biheold al þis ilke. Hwen sec mon haueð ed hond þing
þet wule don him god, he hit mei wel notien, ah beon
þrefter se ancreful, nomeliche religius, nis nawt Godd
icweme. Godd & his desciples speken of sawle lechecreft, / 15
Ypocras & Galien of licomes heale. Þe an þe wes best *f* 100ᵛ
ilearet of Iesu Cristes lechecreft, seið flesches wisdom is
deað to þe sawle. *Prudencia carnis mors. Procul odoramus
bellum*, as Job seið. Swa we dredeð flesches uuel ofte
ear þen hit cume, þet sawle uuel kimeð up & we þolieð 20
sawle uuel forte edstearten flesches uuel, as þah hit were
betere to þolien galnesses brune þen heaued eche oðer
grucchunge of a mistohe wombe; ant hweðer is betere,
i secnesse to beo Godes freo child, þen i flesches heale
to beo þreal under sunne ? Ant þis ne segge ich nawt 25
swa þet wisdom & meosure ne beon ouer al iloket, þe
moder is & nurrice of alle gode þeawes. Ah we cleopieð
ofte wisdom þet nis nan ; for soð wisdom is don eauer
sawle heale biuore flesches heale, & hwen he ne mei nawt
ba somet halden, cheose ear licomes hurt, þen þurh to 30
strong fondunge, sawle þrowunge. Nichodemus brohte
to smirien ure lauerd an hundret weies, hit seið, of mirre
& of aloes, þet beoð bittre speces & bitacnið bittre swinkes
& flesches pinsunges. Hundret is ful tale & noteð perfectiun, þet is ful dede, forte schawin þet me schal ful 35
do flesches pine ase forð as eauer euene mei þolien. I þe
weie is bitacnet meosure & wisdom þet euch mon wið
wisdom weie hwet he mahe don, ne beo nawt se ouer
swiðe i gast þet he forʒeme þe bodi, ne eft se tendre

of his flesch þet hit iwurðe untohen & makie þe gast
þeowe. Nu is al þis meast iseid of bitternesse utewið.
Of bitternesse inwið segge we nu sumhweat, for of þes
twa bitternesses awakeneð swetnesse her ȝet i þis world,
5 nawt ane in heouene.

f. 101r AS ich seide riht nu þet Nichodemus / brohte smirles
to ure lauerd, alswa þe þreo Maries bohten deorewurðe aromaz his bodi forte smirien. Neomeð nu gode
ȝeme, mine leoue sustren. Þeos þreo Maries bitacnið
10 þreo bitternesses; for þis nome Marie as *meraht &*
merariht, þet ich spec þruppe of, spealeð bitternesse.
Þe earste bitternesse is i sunne bireowsunge & i dead
bote, hwen þe sunfule is iturnd earst to ure lauerd. Ant
þeos is understonden bi þe earste Marie, Marie Magda-
15 leine & bi god rihte, for ha, wið muche bireowsunge &
bitternesse of heorte, leafde hire sunnen & turnde to ure
lauerd. Ah for þi þet sum mahte, þurh to muche bitternesse, fallen in to unhope, Magdaleine, þe spealeð tures
hehnesse, is to Marie ifeiet, þurh hwet is bitacnet hope
20 of heh mearci & of heouene blisse. Þe oðer bitternesse
is i wreastlunge & i wragelunge aȝeines fondunges; ant
þeos is bitacnet bi þe oðer Marie, Marie Jacobi; for
Jacob spealeð wreastlere. Þis wreastlunge is ful bitter
to monie þe beoð ful forð i þe wei toward heouene, for
25 þe ȝet i fondunges, þet beoð þe deofles swenges, waggið
oðerhwiles & moten wreastlin aȝein wið strong wrag-
lunge; for as seint Austin seið, *Pharao contemptus surgit*
in scandalum. Hwil eauer Israles folc wes in Egypte
under Pharaones hond, ne leadde he neauer ferd þron,
30 ah þa hit fleah from him, þa wið al his strengðe wende
he þrefter; for þi is eauer bitter feht neod aȝein Pharaon,
þet is, aȝein þe deouel; for ase seið Ezechiel, *Sanguinem*
fugies & sanguis persequetur te : flih sunne & sunne
wule folhin eauer efter. Inoh is iseid þruppe hwi þe
35 gode nis neauer sker of alle fondunges. Sone se he haueð
þe an ouercumen, ikepe anan an oþer. Þe þridde bitter-
f. 101v nesse is i lon/gunge toward heouene & i þe ennu of þis

29 Pharaones] hParaones

world hwen ei is se hehe þet he haueð heorte reste onont
unþeawes weorre, & is as in heouene ȝeten, & þuncheð
bitter alle worltliche þinges ; ant tis þridde bitternesse is
understonden bi Marie Salomee, þe þridde Marie, for
Salome spealeð þes ; & þeo ȝet, þe habbeð þes & reste 5
of cleane inwit, habbeð in hare heorte bitternesse of þis
lif þet edhalt ham from blisse þet ham longeð to, from
Godd þet ha luuieð. Þus lo, in euch stat rixleð bitternesse, earst i þe biginnunge hwen me sahtneð wið Godd,
i þe forðȝong of god lif, & i þe leaste ende. Hwa is 10
þenne o Godes half þe wilneð i þis world eise oðer este ?

AH neomeð nu ȝeme, mine leoue sustren, hu efter
bitternesse kimeð swetnesse. Bitternesse buð hit,
for as þet godspel teleð, þeose þreo Maries bohten swote
smeallinde aromaz to smirien ure lauerd. Þurh aromaz 15
þe beoð swote, is understonden swotnesse of deuot heorte :
þeos Maries hit buggeð, þet is, þurh bitternesse me kimeð
to swotnesse. Bi þis nome Marie, nim eauer bitternesse.
Þurh Maries bone wes, ed te neoces, weater iwent to
wine, þet is to understonden, þurh bone of bitternesse 20
þet me dreheð for Godd, þe heorte þe wes weattri, smechles,
ne ne felde na sauur of Godd namare þen i weater, schal
beon iwent to wine, þet is, ifinden smech in him swete
ouer alle wines. For þi seið þe wise, *Vsque in tempus
sustinebit patiens, & postea redditio iocunditatis* : þe þole- 25
mode þolie bitter ane hwile, he schal sone þrefter habben
ȝeld of blisse. Ant Anna i Tobie seið bi ure lauerd,
Qui, post tempesta/tem, tranquillum facit : & post lacri- f. 102r
mationem & fletum, exultationem infundit : þet is, iblescet
ibeo þu lauerd, þe makest stille efter storm & efter 30
wopi weattres ȝeldest bliðe murhðes. Salomon : *Esuriens*
etiam amarum pro dulci sumet : ȝef þu art ofhungret efter
þet swete, þu most earst witerliche biten o þe bittre.
In Canticis : Ibo michi ad montem myrre, & ad colles
turis. Ich chulle, ha seið, Godes deore spuse, gan to 35
rechleses hul bi þe dun of myrre. Lo, hwuch is þe wei
to rechleses swotnesse bi myrre of bitternesse ; ant eft
i þet ilke luue boc, *Que est ista, que ascendit per desertum*

sicut uirgula fumi ex aromatibus myrre & thuris? **Aromaz**
me makeð of myrre & of rechles ; ah myrre he set biuoren
& rechles kimeð efter—*ex aromatibus myrre & thuris*. Nu
meaneð hire sum þet ha ne mei habben na swotnesse
5 of Godd, ne swetnesse wið innen. Ne wundri ha hire
nawiht ȝef ha nis Marie, for ha hit mot buggen wið
bitternesse wiðuten—nawt wið euch bitternesse, for sum
geað frommard Godd, as euch worltlich sar þet nis for
sawle heale. For þi i þe godspel of þe þreo Maries is
10 iwriten þisses weis, *Vt uenientes ungerent Iesum, non autem
recedentes*: þeos Maries, hit seið, þeose bitternesses,
weren cuminde to smirien ure lauerd—þeo beoð cuminde
to smirien ure lauerd þe me þoleð for his luue—þe
strecheð him toward us as þing þet ismired is, & makeð
15 him nesche & softe to hondlin. Ant nes he him seolf
reclus i Maries wombe? Þeos twa þing limpeð to ancre :
nearowðe & bitternesse ; for wombe is nearow wununge,
þer ure lauerd wes reclus ; ant tis word Marie, as ich
ofte habbe iseid, spealeð bitternesse. Ȝef ȝe þenne i
f. 102v nearow stude / þolieð bitternesse, ȝe beoð his feolahes,
21 reclus as he wes i Marie wombe. Beo ȝe ibunden inwið
fowr large wahes ?—& he in a nearow cader, ineilet o rode,
i stanene þruh bicluset hetefeste. Marie wombe & þis
þruh weren his ancre huses. I nowðer nes he worltlich
25 mon, ah as ut of þe world forte schawin ancren þet ha
ne schulen wið þe world na þing habben imeane. Ȝe,
þu ondswerest me, ah he wende ut of ba. Ȝe, went tu
alswa of ba þine ancre huses as he dude, wið ute bruche
& leaf ham ba ihale : þet schal beon hwen þe gast went
30 ut on ende wið uten bruche & wem of his twa huses : þet
an is þe licome, þet oþer is þe uttre hus þet is as þe uttre
wah abute þe castel.

AL þet ich habbe iseid of flesches pinsunge nis nawt
for ow, mine leoue sustren, þe oðerhwile þolieð mare
35 þen ich walde, ah is for sum þet schal rede þis inohreaðe,
þe grapeð hire to softe. Noðeles, ȝunge impen me
bigurd wið þornes leste beastes freoten ham hwil ha
beoð mearewe. Ȝe beoð ȝunge impen iset i Godes

orchard. Þornes beoð þe heardschipes þet ich habbe
ispeken of, & ow is neoð þet ȝe beon biset wið ham abuten,
þet te beast of helle, hwen he snakereð toward ow forte
biten on ow, hurte him o þe scharpschipe & schunche
aȝeinwardes. Wið alle þeose heardschipes beoð gleade & 5
wel ipaiet ȝef lutel word is of ow, ȝef ȝe beoð unwurðe,
for þorn is scharp & unwurð. Wið þeose twa beoð
bigurde. Ȝe ne ahen nawt to unnen þet uuel word beo
of ow. Scandle is heaued sunne, þet is, þing swa iseid
oðer idon þet me mei rihtliche turnen hit to uuele & 10
sunegin þrefter þer þurh wið misþoht, wið uuel / word *f. 103r*
on hire, on oþre, & sungin ec wið dede. Ah ȝe ahen
unnen þet na word ne beo of ow ne mare þen of deade,
& beon bliðe iheortet ȝef ȝe þolieð danger of Sluri, þe
cokes cneaue, þe wescheð & wipeð disches i cuchene. 15
Þenne beo ȝe dunes ihehet toward heouene. For lo, hu
spekeð þe leafdi i þet swete luue boc: *Venit dilectus
meus saliens in montibus, transiliens colles*: mi leof kimeð
leapinde, ha seið, o þe dunes, þet is, totret ham, tofuleð
ham, þoleð þet me totreode ham, tuki ham al to wundre, 20
schaweð in ham his ahne troden, þet me trudde him in
ham ifinden hu he wes totreden, as his trode schaweð.
Þis beoð þe hehe dunes, as munt of Muntgiw, dunes of
Armenie. Þe hulles, þe beoð lahre, þeo as þe leafdi seið
hire seolf, he ouerleapeð, ne trust nawt se wel on ham for 25
hare feblesce; ne ne mahte nawt þolien swuch totreodunge,
ant he leapeð ouer ham, forbereð ham & forbuheð aþet
ha waxen herre from hulles to dunes. His schadewe
lanhure ouergeað & wrið ham hwil he leapeð ouer ham,
þet is, sum ilicnesse he leið on ham of his lif on eorðe, as 30
þah hit were his schadewe; ah þe dunes underuoð þe
troden of him seoluen & schaweð in hare lif hwuch his
liflade wes, hu & hwer he eode, i hwuch vilte, i hwuch
wa he leadde his lif on eorðe. Þulliche dunes þe gode
Pawel spek of & eadmodliche seide, *Deicimur, set non* 35
*perimus: mortificationem Iesu in corpore nostro circum-
ferentes, ut & uita Iesu in corporibus nostris manifestetur.*
Alle wa, quoð he, & alle scheome we þolieð, ah þet is
ure selhðe, þet we beoren on ure bodi Iesu Cristes

deadlicnesse, þet hit suteli in us hwuch wes his lif on
eorðe. Godd hit wat, þe þus doð, ha pruuieð us hare luue
f. 103v toward ure lauerd. / Luuest tu me? Cuð hit. For luue
wule schawin him wið uttre werkes. *Gregorius: Probatio*
5 *dilectionis exhibitio est operis.* Ne beo neauer þing se
heard, soð luue lihteð hit & softeð & sweteð. *Amor*
omnia facilia reddit. Hweat þolieð men & wummen for
fals luue & for ful luue, & mare walden þolien? Ant
hweat is mare wunder þet siker luue & treowe & ouer
10 alle oþre swete, ne mei meistrin us se forð as deð þe
luue of sunne? Nawt for þi ich wat swuch þet bereð
ba to gederes, heui brunie & here, ibunden hearde wið
irn, middel, þeh, & earmes, mid brade þicke bondes, swa
þet tet swat þrof is passiun to þolien; feasteð, wakeð,
15 swinkeð &, Crist hit wat, meaneð him þet hit ne greueð
him nawt, & bit me ofte teachen him sumhwet wið hwet
he mahte his licome deruen. Al þet is bitter, for ure
lauerdes luue, al him þuncheð swete. Deuleset, ȝet he
wepeð to me wi[ð e]uene sarest, & seið Godd forȝet him for
20 þi þet he ne sent him na muchel secnesse. Godd hit wat,
þet makeð luue, for as he seið me ofte, for na þing þet
Godd mahte don uuele bi him, þah he wið þe forlorene
wurpe him in to helle, ne mahte he neauer, him þuncheð,
luuien him þe leasse. Ȝef ei mon eani swuch þing ortrowi
25 bi him, he is mare mat þen þeof inume wið þeofðe. Ich
wat ec swuch wummon þet þoleð lutel leasse; ah nis
þer bute þoncki Godd i strengðe þet he ȝeueð ham &
icnawen eadmodliche ure wacnesse. Luuie we hare god
& swa hit is ure ahne, for as sein Gregoire seið, of swa
30 muchel strengðe is luue, þet hit makeð oþres god wið
ute swinc ure ahne, as is iseid þruppe. Nu me þuncheð
we beoð icumen in to þe seoueðe dale þet is al of luue
þe makeð schir heorte. /

19 wi[ð e]uene] wiuene

[ON LOVE]

SEINTE Pawel witneð þet alle uttre heardschipes, *f. 104r*
alle flesches pinsunges ant licomliche swinkes, al
is ase nawt aȝeines luue þe schireð & brihteð þe
heorte. *Exercitio corporis ad modicum ualet: pietas
autem ualet ad omnia:* þet is, licomlich bisischipe is to 5
lutel wurð, ah swote & schir heorte is god to alle þinges.
*Si linguis hominum loquar, & angelorum, & cetera: si
tradidero corpus meum ita ut ardeam, & cetera: si distri-
buero omnes facultates meas in cibos pauperum, caritatem
autem non habeam, nichil michi prodest.* Þah ich cuðe, 10
he seið, monne ledene & englene, þah ich dude o mi
bodi alle pine & passiun þet bodi mahte þolien, þah ich
ȝeue poure al þet ich hefde ; ȝef ich nefde luue þerwið
to Godd & to alle men, in him & for him, al were ispillet ;
for as þe hali abbat Moyses seide, al þet wa & al þet 15
heard þet we þolieð o flesch, & al þet god þet we eauer
doð, alle swucche þinges ne beoð nawt bute as lomen
to tilie wið þe heorte. Ȝef þe axe ne kurue, ne spitelsteaf
ne dulue, ne þe sulh ne erede, hwa kepte ham to halden ?
Alswa as na mon ne luueð lomen for ham seolf, ah deð 20
for þe þinges þet me wurcheð wið ham, alswa na flesches
derf nis to luuien bute for þi þet Godd te reaðere þiderward loki mid his grace, & makeð þe heorte schir & of
briht sihðe, þet nan ne mei habben wið monglunge of
unþeawes, ne wið eorðlich luue of worltliche þinges ; for 25
þis mong woreð swa þe ehnen of þe heorte þet ha ne
mei cnawen Godd, ne gleadien of his sihðe. Schir heorte,
as seint Bernard seið, makieð twa þinges : þet tu al þet
tu dest, do hit oðer for luue ane of Godd, oðer for oþres
god & for his biheue. / Haue in al þet tu dest, an of þes *f. 104v*
twa ententes, oðer ba to gederes, for þe leatere falleð in 31
to þe earre. Haue eauer schir heorte þus, & do al þet
tu wult ; haue wori heorte, al þe sit uuele. *Omnia munda
mundis: coinquinatis uero nichil est mundum: Apostolus.
Item. Augustinus: Habe caritatem & fac quicquid uis—* 35
uoluntate, uidelicet, rationis. For þi, mine leoue sustren,

ouer alle þing beoð bisie to habben schir heorte. Hwet
is schir heorte? Ich hit habbe iseid ear: þet is, þet
ȝe na þing ne wilnin, ne ne luuien bute Godd ane, &
te ilke þinges for Godd þe helpeð ow toward him—for
5 Godd, ich segge, luuien ham, & nawt for ham seoluen—
as is mete oðer clað, mon oðer wummon þe ȝe beoð
of igodet; for ase seið seint Austin & spekeð þus to ure
lauerd, *Minus te amat, qui, preter te, aliquid amat quod non
propter te amat*: þet is, lauerd, leasse ha luuieð þe, þe luuieð
10 eawt bute þe, bute ha luuien hit for þe. Schirnesse of heorte
is Godes luue ane. I þis is al þe strengðe of alle religiuns,
þe ende of alle ordres. *Plenitudo legis est dilectio.* Luue
fulleð þe lahe, seið seinte Pawel. *Quicquid precipitur, in
sola caritate solidatur.* Alle Godes heastes, as sein Gregoire
15 seið, beoð i luue irotet. Luue ane schal beon ileid i
seinte Mihales weie. Þeo þe meast luuieð schulen beo
meast iblisset, nawt þeo þe leadeð heardest lif; for luue
hit ouerweieð. Luue is heouene stiward for hire muchele
freolec, for heo ne edhalt na þing, ah ȝeueð al þet ha
20 haueð, & ec hire seoluen—elles ne kepte Godd nawt of
þet hiren were.

GODD haueð ofgan ure luue on alle cunne wise. He
haueð muchel idon us, & mare bihaten. Muchel
24 ȝeoue ofdraheð luue. Me al þe world he ȝef us in Adam /
f. 105r ure alde feader, & al þet is i þe world he weorp under
ure fet—beastes & fuheles—ear we weren forgulte.
*Omnia subiecisti sub pedibus eius, oues & boues universas:
insuper & pecora campi, volucres celi, & pisces maris, qui
perambulant semitas maris.* Ant ȝet al þet is, as is þruppe
30 iseid, serueð þe gode to sawle biheue; ȝet te uuele
seruið eorðe, sea & sunne. He dude ȝet mare—ȝef us
nawt ane of his, ah dude al him seoluen. Se heh ȝeoue
nes neauer iȝeuen to se lahe wrecches. *Apostolus: Christus
dilexit ecclesiam, & dedit semet ipsum pro ea*: Crist, seið
35 seinte Pawel, luuede swa his leofmon þet he ȝef for hire
þe pris of him seoluen. Neomeð nu gode ȝeme, mine
leoue sustren, for hwi me ah him to luuien. Earst, as
33 wrecches] wrecch-ces

a mon þe woheð—as a king þet luuede a gentil poure
leafdi of feorrene londe, he sende his sonden biuoren,
þet weren þe patriarches & te prophes of þe alde testament, wið leattres isealet. On ende he com him seoluen
& brohte þe godspel as leattres iopenet & wrat wið his 5
ahne blod saluz to his leofmon—luue gretunge, forte
wohin hire wið & hire luue wealden. Herto falleð a tale,
a wrihe forbisne.

A LEAFDI wes mid hire fan biset al abuten, hire lond
al destruet, & heo al poure, inwið an eorðene castel. 10
A mihti kinges luue wes þah biturnd up on hire swa
unimete swiðe þet he for wohlech sende hire his sonden,
an efter oðer, ofte somet monie ; sende hire beawbelez
baðe feole & feire, sucurs of liueneð, help of his hehe
hird to halden hire castel. Heo underfeng al as on 15
unrecheles, & swa wes heard iheortet þet hire luue ne
mahte he neauer beo þe neorre. Hwet wult tu mare ?
He com him seolf on ende, schawde hire his feire neb,
as þe þe wes of alle men feherest to bihalden, spec se
swiðe swoteliche & wordes se murie / þet ha mahten deade *f. 105v*
arearen to liue, wrahte feole wundres & dude muchele 21
meistries biuoren hire ehsihðe, schawde hire his mihte,
talde hire of his kinedom, bead to makien hire cwen of
al þet he ahte. Al þis ne heold nawt. Nes þis hoker
wunder ? For heo nes neauer wurðe forte beon his þuften. 25
Ah swa, þurh his deboneirte, luue hefde ouercumen him
þet he seide on ende : Dame, þu art iweorret & þine
van beoð se stronge þet tu ne maht nanesweis wiðute
mi sucurs edfleon hare honden, þet ha ne don þe to
scheome deað efter al þi weane. Ich chulle, for þe luue 30
of þe, neome þet feht up o me & arudde þe of ham þe þi
deað secheð. Ich wat þah to soðe þet ich schal bituhen
ham neomen deaðes wunde ; & ich hit wulle heorteliche
forte ofgan þin heorte. Nu þenne biseche ich þe, for
þe luue þet ich cuðe þe, þet tu luuie me lanhure efter 35
þe ilke dede, dead, hwen þu naldest, liues. Þes king
dude al þus : arudde hire of alle hire van & wes him
seolf to wundre ituket & islein on ende ; þurh miracle

aras þah from deaðe to liue. Nere þeos ilke leafdi of
uueles cunnes cunde, ȝef ha ouer alle þing ne luuede
him her efter ?

PES king is Iesu, Godes sune, þet al o þisse wise
5 wohede ure sawle þe deoflen hefden biset ; ant he
as noble wohere efter monie messagers & feole goddeden,
com to pruuien his luue & schawde þurh cnihtschipe þet
he wes luuewurðe, as weren sumhwile cnihtes iwunet to
donne ; dude him i turneiment & hefde for his leoues
10 luue, his scheld i feht as kene cniht on euche half iþurlet.
His scheld, þe wreah his Goddhead, wes his leoue
f. 106r licome þet / wes ispread o rode, brad as scheld buuen in
his istrahte earmes, nearow bineoðen, as þe an fot, efter
monies wene, set up o þe oðer. Þet þis scheld naueð
15 siden is for bitacnunge þet his deciples þe schulden
stonden bi him & habben ibeon his siden, fluhen alle
from him & leafden him as fremede, as þe godspel seið,
Relicto eo, omnes fugerunt. Þis scheld is iȝeuen us aȝein
alle temptatiuns, as Ieremie witneð : *Dabis scutum cordis*
20 *laborem tuum.* Nawt ane þis scheld ne schilt us from alle
uueles, ah deð ȝet mare, cruneð us in heouene *scuto bone*
uoluntatis. Lauerd, he seið, Dauið, wið þe scheld of þi
gode wil þu hauest us icrunet—scheld, he seið, of god
wil, for willes he þolede al þet he þolede. *Ysaias :*
25 *Oblatus est quia uoluit.*

ME, lauerd, þu seist, hwerto ? Ne mahte he wið
leasse gref habben arud us ? Ȝeoi, iwiss, ful
lihtliche, ah he nalde. For hwi ? Forte bineomen us
euch bitellunge aȝein him of ure luue þet he se deore
30 bohte. Me buð lihtliche þing þet me luueð lutel. He
bohte us wið his heorte blod—deorre pris nes neauer—
forte ofdrahen of us ure luue toward him þet costnede
him se sare. I scheld beoð þreo þinges, þe treo, & te
leðer, & te litunge. Alswa wes i þis scheld—þe treo of
35 þe rode, þet leðer of Godes licome, þe litunge of þe
reade blod þet heowede hire se feire. Eft þe þridde
reisun. Efter kene cnihtes deað, me hongeð hehe i

chirche his scheld on his mungunge. Alswa is þis scheld,
þet is, þe crucifix, i chirche iset i swuch stude þer me
hit sonest seo forte þenchen þerbi o Iesu Cristes cnihtschipe þet he dude o rode. His leofmon bihalde þron
hu he bohte hire luue, lette þurlin his scheld, openin his 5
side to schawin hire his heorte, to schawin hire / open- *f. 106v*
liche hu inwardliche he luuede hire, & to ofdrahen hire
heorte.

FOWR heaued luuen me ifind i þis world : bitweone
gode iferen; bitweone mon & wummon; bi wif & hire 10
child ; bitweone licome & sawle. Þe luue þet Iesu Crist
haueð to his deore leofmon ouergeað þeos fowre, passeð
ham alle. Ne teleð me him god fere þe leið his wed i
Giwerie to acwitin ut his fere ? Godd almihti leide him
seolf for us i Giwerie & dude his deorewurðe bodi to 15
acwitin ut his leofmon of Giwene honden. Neauer fere
ne dude swuch fordede for his fere.

MUCHE luue is ofte bitweone mon & wummon; ah
þah ha were iweddet him, ha mahte iwurðen se unwreast, & swa longe ha mahte forhorin hire wið oþre men 20
þet, þah ha walde aȝein cumen, he ne kepte hire nawt. For
þi Crist luueð mare ; for þah þe sawle, his spuse, forhori
hire wið þe feond under heaued sunne feole ȝeres &
dahes, his mearci is hire eauer ȝarow, hwen ha wule
cumen ham & leten þen deouel. Al þis he seið him seolf 25
þurh Jeremie : *Si dimiserit uir uxorem suam, & cetera.*
Tu autem fornicata es cum multis amatoribus: tamen reuertere
ad me, dicit dominus : ȝet, he ȝeiȝeð al dei, þu þet hauest
se unwreaste idon, biturn þe & cum aȝein, welcume
schalt tu beo me. *Immo & occurrit prodigo uenienti* : ȝet 30
he eorneð, hit seið, aȝein hire ȝeincume & warpeð earmes
anan abuten hire swire. Hweat is mare milce ? Ȝet her
gleadfulre wunder. Ne beo neauer his leof forhoret mid
se monie deadliche sunnen, sone se ha kimeð to him
aȝein, he makeð hire neowe meiden ; for as seint Austin 35
seið, swa muchel is bitweonen Godes neoleachunge &

36 bitweonen] bitweonen bituhhen

monnes to wummon, þet monnes neoleachunge makeð
of meiden, wif, & Godd makeð of wif, meiden. *Restituit,* /
f. 107r *inquit Job, in integrum.*   Gode werkes & treowe bileaue,
þeose twa þinges beoð meiðhad i sawle.

5 NU of þe þridde luue.   Child þet hefde swuch uuel þet
him bihofde beað of blod ear hit were ihealet, muchel
þe moder luuede hit þe walde þis beað him makien. Þis
dude ure lauerd us þe weren se seke of sunne & swa
isulet þerwið þet na þing ne mahte healen us ne cleansin
10 us bute his blod ane ; for swa he hit walde : his luue
makeð us beað þrof—iblescet beo he eaure! Þreo beaðes
he greiðede to his deore leofmon forte weschen hire in
ham se hwit & se feier þet ha were wurðe to his cleane
cluppunges. Þe earste beað is fulluht, þe oðer beoð
15 teares, inre oðer uttre, efter þe forme beað ʒef ha hire
suleð ; þe þridde is Iesu Cristes blod þet halheð ba þe
oþre, as sein Iuhan seið i þe Apocalipse : *Qui dilexit
nos, & lauit nos in sanguine suo.* Þet he luueð us mare
þen eani moder hire child, he hit seið him seoluen þurh
20 Ysaie : *Nunquid potest mater obliuisci filii uteri sui ? Et
si illa obliviscatur, ego non obliuiscar tui* : mei moder, he
seið, forʒeoten hire child ? Ant þah heo do, ich ne mei
þe forʒeoten neauer—ant seið þe resun efter : *In manibus
meis descripsi te.* Ich habbe, he seið, depeint te i mine
25 honden. Swa he dude mid read blod up o þe rode. Me
cnut his gurdel to habben þoht of a þing ; ah ure lauerd,
for he nalde neauer forʒeoten us, dude mearke of þurlunge
in ure munegunge i ba twa his honden.

NU þe feorðe luue. Þe sawle luueð þe licome swiðe mid
30 alle ; ant þet is etscene i þe twinnunge ; for leoue
freond beoð sari hwen ha schulen twinnin.   Ah ure
lauerd willeliche totweamde his sawle from his bodi forte
veien ure baðe togederes, world buten ende i þe blisse of
f. 107v heo/uene. Þus lo, Iesu Cristes luue toward his deore
35 spuse, þet is hali chirche oðer cleane sawle, passeð alle
& ouerkimeð þe fowr measte luuen þet me ifind on
eorðe. Wið al þis luue ʒetten he woheð hire o þis wise.

ÞI luue, he seið, oðer hit is forte ȝeouen allunge, oðer
hit is to sullen, oðer hit is to reauin & to neomen
wið strengðe. Ȝef hit is forte ȝeouen, hwer maht tu
biteon hit betere þen up o me ? Nam ich þinge feherest,
nam ich kinge richest, nam ich hest icunnet, nam ich 5
weolie wisest, nam ich monne hendest, nam ich þinge
freoest ? For swa me seið bi large mon þe ne con nawt
edhalden, þet he haueð þe honden, as mine beoð, iþurlet.
Nam ich alre þinge swotest & swetest ? Þus alle þe
reisuns hwi me ah to ȝeoue luue þu maht ifinden in me ; 10
nomeliche, ȝef þu luuest chaste cleannesse ; for nan ne
mei luuie me bute ha hire halde ; ah ha is þreouald,
i widewehad, i spushad, i meidenhad—þe heste. Ȝef þi
luue nis nawt to ȝeouene, ah wult þet me bugge hire—
buggen hire ? Oðer wið oðer luue, oðer wið sumhweat 15
elles, me suleð wel luue—& swa me ah to sulle luue &
for na þing elles. Ȝef þin is swa to sullen, ich habbe
iboht hire wið luue ouer alle oþre ; for of þe fowr measte
luuen ich habbe icud toward te þe measte of ham alle.
Ȝef þu seist þu nult nawt leote þron se liht chap, ah 20
wult ȝette mare, nempne hweat hit schule beon, sete
feor o þi luue. Þu ne schalt seggen se muchel þet ich
nule ȝeoue mare. Wult tu castles, kinedomes, wult tu
wealden al þe world ? Ich chulle do þe betere—makie
þe wið al þis cwen of heoueriche. Þu schalt te seolf 25
beo seoueuald brihtre þen þe sunne, nan uuel ne schal /
nahhi þe, na wunne ne schal wonti þe ; al þi wil schal *f. 108r*
beon iwraht in heouene & ec in eorðe, ȝe & ȝet in helle ;
ne schal neauer heorte þenchen hwuch selhðe þet ich
nule ȝeouen for þi luue, unmeteliche, vneuenliche, 30
unendeliche mare : al Creasuse weole, þe wes kinge
richest ; Absalones schene wlite, þe as ofte as me euesede
him, salde his euesunge—þe her þet he kearf of—for
twa hundret sicles of seoluer iweiet ; Asaeles swiftschipe,
þe straf wið heortes of urn ; Samsones strengðe, þe sloh 35
a þusent of his fan al ed a time & ane bute fere ; Cesares
freolec ; Alixandres hereword ; Moysese heale. Nalde
a mon for an of þeos ȝeouen al þet he ahte ? Ant alle
somet aȝein mi bodi ne beoð nawt wurð a nelde. Ȝef

þu art se swiðe anewil & swa ut of þi wit þet tu þurh
nawt to leosen, forsakest swuch biȝete wið alles cunnes
selhðe, lo, ich halde her heatel sweord up o þin heaued
to dealen lif & sawle & bisenchen ham ba in to þe fur of
5 helle, to beon deofles hore schentfulliche & sorhfulliche,
world abuten ende. Ondswere nu & were þe ȝef þu const
aȝein me, oðer ȝette me þi luue þe ich ȝirne se swiðe,
nawt for min, ah for þin ahne muchele biheue.

L O þus ure lauerd woheð. Nis ha to heard iheortet
10   þet a þulli wohere ne mei to his luue turnen?—ȝef
ha wel þencheð þeose þreo þinges, hwet he is, & hwet heo
is, & hu muchel is þe luue of se heh as he is toward se
lah as heo is. For þi seið þe salmwruhte, *Non est qui se*
abscondat a calore eius: nis nan þet mahe edlutien þet ha
15 ne mot him luuien. Þe soðe sunne i þe undertid wes for
þi istihen on heh o þe hehe rode forte spreaden ouer al
hate luue gleames ; þus neodful he wes & is aþet tes dei
to ontenden his luue *i* his leoues heorte, & seið i þe
f. 108v godspel, *Ignem / ueni mittere in terram, & quid uolo nisi*
20 *ut ardeat*. Ich com to bringen, he seið, fur in to eorðe,
þet is, bearninde luue in to eorðlich heorte, ant hwet
ȝirne ich elles bute þet hit bleasie ? Wlech luue is him
lað, as he seið þurh sein Iuhan i þe Apocalipse : *Utinam*
frigidus esses, aut calidus; set quia tepidus es, incipiam te
25 *euomere de ore meo*. Ich walde, he seið to his leofmon,
þet tu were i mi luue oðer allunge cald, oðer hat mid alle ;
ah for þi þet tu art ase wlech bitweone twa, nowðer hat
ne cald, þu makest me to wleatien & ich wulle speowe
þe ut, bute þu wurðe hattre.

30 N U ȝe habbeð iherd, mine leoue sustren, hu & for hwi
Godd is swiðe to luuien. Forte ontenden ow wel,
gederið wude þerto wið þe poure wummon of Sarepte,
þe burh þe spealeð ontendunge. *En, inquit, colligo duo*
ligna. Regum iii°. Lauerd, quoð ha, to Helye, þe hali
35 prophete, lo, ich gederi twa treon. Þeos twa treon
bitacnið þet a treo þet stod upriht & þet oþer þe eode

18 luue *i*] luue &

þwertouer o þe deore rode. Of þeos twa treon ʒe schulen
ontende fur of luue inwið ower heorte. Biseoð ofte
towart ham. Þencheð ʒef ʒe ne ahen eaðe to luuien þe
king of blisse þe tospreat swa his earmes toward ow &
buheð, as to beoden cos, duneward his heaued. Sikerliche 5
ich segge hit, ʒef þe soðe Helye, þet is, Godd almihti,
ifint ow þeose twa treon bisiliche gederin, he wule
gestnin wið ow & monifalden in ow his deorewurðe grace,
as Helie dude hire liueneð, & gestnede wið hire þet he
ifond þe twa treon gederin i Sarepte.   10

GRICKISCH fur is imaket of reades monnes blod &
þet ne mei na þing bute migge, ant sond, & eisil,
as me seið, acwenchen. Þis grickisch fur is þe luue of
Iesu ure lauerd, & ʒe hit schule makien of reade / monnes *f. 109*
blod, þet is, Iesu Crist ireadet wið his ahne blod o þe   15
deore rode, ant wes inread cundeliche, alswa as me
weneð. Þis blod for ow isched up o þe earre twa treon,
schal makien ow Sareptiens, þet is, ontende mid tis
grickisch fur, þet, as Salomon seið, nane weattres, þet
beoð worldliche tribulatiuns, nane temptatiuns, nowðer 20
inre ne uttre, ne mahen þis luue acwenchen. Nu nis
þenne on ende bute witen ow warliche wið al þet hit
acwencheð, þet beoð migge & sond & eisil, as ich ear
seide. Migge is stench of sunne. O sond ne groweð na
god & bitacneð idel. Idel akeldeð & acwencheð þis fur.   25
Sturieð ow cwicliche aa i gode werkes & þet schal heaten
ow & ontenden þis fur aʒein þe brune of sunne. For
alswa as þe an neil driueð ut þen oþer, alswa þe brune of
Godes luue driueð brune of ful luue ut of þe heorte. Þe
þridde þing is eisil, þet is, sur heorte of nið oðer of onde. 30
Vnderstondeð þis word. Þa þe niðfule Giws offreden
ure lauerd þis sure present up o þe rode, þa seide he
þet reowðfule word, *Consumatum est.* Neauer, quoð he,
ear nu nes ich ful pinet—nawt þurh þet eisil, ah þurh
hare ondfule nið, þet tet eisil bitacnede, þet heo him   35
(du)den drinken; ant is ilich as þah a mon þet hefde
longe iswunken & failede efter long swinc on ende of

36 (du)den] du *scarcely legible*

his hure. Alswa ure lauerd mare þen twa & þritti зer
tilede efter hare luue, & for al his sare swinc ne wilnede
na þing bute luue to hure; ah i þe ende of his lif, þet
wes as i þe euentid hwen me зelt wercmen hare deies
5 hure, loke hu ha зulden him, for piment of huni luue,
eisil of sur nið & galle of bitter onde. O, quoð ure lauerd
þa, *Consumatum est*; al mi swinc on eorðe, al mi pine
f. 109v o rode, / ne sweameð ne ne derueð me nawiht aзein þis,
þet ich þus biteo al þet ich idon habbe. Þis eisil þet зe
10 beodeð me, þis sure hure, þurhfulleð mi pine. Þis eisil
of sur heorte & of bitter þonc, ouer alle oðre þing, acwencheð grickisch fur, þet is þe luue of ure lauerd. Ant
hwa se hit bereð i breoste toward wummon oðer mon, ha
is Giwes make, ha offreð Godd þis eisil & þurhfulleð
15 onont hire Iesues pine o rode. Me warpeð grickisch fur
up on his famen & swa me ouerkimeð ham. Зe schule don
alswa hwen Godd areareð ow of ei va eani weorre. Hu
зe hit schule warpen, Salomon teacheð : *Si esurierit
inimicus tuus, ciba illum: si sitierit, potum da illi. Sic
20 enim carbones ardentes congeres super caput eius* : þet is,
зef þi fa hungreð, fed him ; to his þurst зef him drunch—
þet is to understonden, зef he efter þin hearm haueð
hunger oðer þurst, зef him fode of þine beoden þet Godd
do him are, зef him drunch of teares. Wep for his sunnen.
25 Þus þu schalt, seið Salomon, rukelin on his heaued
bearninde gleden, þet is to seggen, þus þu schalt ontenden
his heorte forte luuie þe ; for heorte is in hali writ bi
heaued understonden. O þulli wise wule Godd seggen
ed te dome, Hwi luuedest tu þe mon oðer þe wummon ?
30 Sire, ha luueden me. Зe, he wule seggen, þu зulde þet
tu ahtest. Her nabbe ich þe nawt muches to зelden. Зef
þu maht ondswerien, Alle wa ha duden me, ne na luue
ne ahte ich ham, ah, sire, ich luuede ham for þi luue ;
þet luue he ah þe, for hit wes iзeuen him & he hit wule
35 þe зelden.

MIGGE, as ich seide, þet acwencheð grickisch fur,
is stinkinde flesches luue þe acwencheð gastelich
luue þet grickisch fur bitacneð. Hweat flesch wes on

eorðe se swete & se hali as wes Iesu Cristes flesch ? Ant
þah he seide him seolf / to his deore deciples, *Nisi ego* ƒ. 110ʳ
abiero, paraclitus non veniet ad uos : þet is, bute ich parti
from ow, þe hali gast, þet is min & mines feaderes luue,
ne mei nawt cumen to ow; ah hwen ich beo from ow, ich 5
chulle senden him ow. Hwen Iesu Cristes ahne deciples,
hwil þet ha fleschliche luueden him neh ham, foreoden
þe swetnesse of þe hali gast, ne ne mahte nawt habben
baðe togederes, demeð ow seoluen nis he wod, oðer
heo, þe luueð to swiðe hire ahne flesch, oðer eani mon 10
fleschliche, swa þet ha ʒirne to swiðe his sihðe oðer his
speche ? Ne þunche hire neauer wunder ʒef hire wonti
þe hali gastes froure. Cheose nu euch an of þes twa,
eorðlich elne & heouenlich, to hweðer ha wule halden ;
for þet oðer ha mot leten ; for i þe tweire monglunge ne 15
mei ha habben neauer mare schirnesse of heorte, þet is,
as we seiden ear, þet god & te strengðe of alle religiuns
& in euch ordre. Luue makeð hire schir, griðful & cleane.
Luue haueð a meistrie biuoren alle oþre ; for al þet ha
rineð, al ha turneð to hire & makeð al hire ahne. *Quem-* 20
cunque locum calcauerit pes uester—pes, videlicet, amoris
—uester erit. Deore walde moni mon buggen a swuch
þing þet al þet he rine to, al were his ahne. Ant ne
seide hit þruppe feor, ane þurh þet tu luuest þet god þet
is in an oðer wið þe rinunge of þi luue, þu makest wið 25
uten oþer swinc his god þin ahne god, as sein Gregoire
witneð ? Lokið nu hu muchel god þe ontfule leoseð.
Streche þi luue to Iesu Crist, þu hauest him iwunnen.
Rin him wið ase muche luue as þu hauest sum mon sum
chearre. He is þin to don wið al þet tu wilnest. Ah hwa 30
luueð þing þet leaueð hit for leasse þen hit is wurð ? Nis
Godd betere uneuenlich þen al þet is i þe world ? Chearite
is cherte of leof þing & of deore. Vndeore he makeð
Godd & to un/wurð mid alle, þet for ei worltlich þing ƒ. 110ᵛ
of his luue leaskeð. For na þing ne con luuien riht bute 35
he ane. Swa ouerswiðe he luueð luue þet he makeð hire
his euening. ʒet ich dear segge mare : he makeð hire
his meistre & deð al þet ha hat as þah he moste nede.
Mei ich pruuien þis ? ʒe witerliche, ich, bi his ahne

wordes ; for þus he spekeð to Moyses, þe monne meast
him luuede, *in Numeri : Dimisi iuxta uerbum tuum—non
dicit preces.* Ich hefde, quoð he, imunt to wreoke mine
wreaððe i þis folc ; ah þu seist i ne schal nawt. Þi word
5 beo iforðet. Me seið þet luue bindeð. Witerliche luue
bint swa ure lauerd þet he ne mei na þing don bute þurh
luues leaue. Nu preoue her of, for hit þuncheð wunder.
Ysaias : Domine, non est, qui consurgat & teneat te : lauerd,
þu wult smiten, seið Ysaie : weilawei, þu maht wel, nis
10 nan þet te halde—as þah he seide, ȝef ei luuede þe riht
he mahte halden þe & wearnen þe to smiten. *In Genesy
ad Loth : Festina & cetera. Non potero ibi quicquam facere
donec egressus fueris illinc* : þet is, þa ure lauerd walde
bisenchen Sodome þer Lot his freond wes inne, Hihe þe,
15 quoð he, utward, for hwil þu art bimong ham, ne mei
ich nawt don ham. Nes þes wið luue ibunden ? Hwet
wult tu mare ? Luue is his chamberleng, his conseiler,
his spuse, þet he ne mei nawt heole wið, ah teleð al þet
he þencheð. *In Genesy : Num celare potero Abraham que
20 gesturus sum ?* Mei ich, quoð ure lauerd, heolen Abraham
þing þet ich þenche to donne ? Nai o nane wise. Nu
con þes luuien þe þus spekeð & þus deð to alle þe
him inwardliche leueð & luuieð. Þe blisse þet he ȝarkeð
ham, as ha is uneuenlich to alle worldes blissen, alswa
as ha is untalelich to world/liche tungen. *Ysaias :*
26 *Oculus non uidit, deus, absque te que preparasti diligentibus
te. Apostolus : Oculus non uidit, nec auris audiuit, &
cetera.* Ȝe habbeð of þeos blissen iwriten elleshwer,
mine leoue sustren. Þis luue is þe riwle þe riwleð þe
30 heorte. *Confitebor tibi in directione, id est, in regulatione
cordis. Exprobratio malorum, generatio que non direxit cor
suum.* Þis is þe leafdi riwle. Alle þe oþre seruið hire, &
ane for hire sake me hat ham to luuien. Lutel strengðe
ich do of ham, for hwon þet þeos beo deorewurðliche
35 ihalden. Habbeð ham þah scheortliche i þe eahtuðe dale.

NOTES

1–3. These lines belong to AW Part 5 on Confession. **dead-bote.** The *ea* invariable in first element of this compound (common in KG texts) is probably from association with *dead*, ' dead '. As simplex in AW, *dede*, ' deed ' [OE *dǣd*, first element in OE *dǣd-bōt*] is never written with *ea*. In the 12th c., teaching on confession (see J. A. Spitzig, *Sacramental Penance in the Twelfth and Thirteenth Centuries*, Catholic University of America, Washington (1947)) was first systematically analysed into the three stages, contrition, (verbal) confession, and satisfaction. Satisfaction (*dead-bote*) was conceived of as both punishment for and medicine against sin.

4ff. The repetition of **Al . . . al . . . al . . .** comes as an echo of the priest's absolution at the end of Part 5 (*f. 94r*) : ' All the good that thou ever dost, and all the evil that thou ever sufferest for the love of Jesus Christ within thy anchoress's walls, all I prescribe for thee [as penance], all I lay upon thee in remission [of sins].'

6f. i se derf ordre, in so rigorous a religious life. For the form *derf* cp. ON *djarfr*, ' bold ' ; for the meaning cp. OE *dyrfan* (infin.), ' torment '. *ordre* does not necessarily imply a constituted religious order. On the enclosed life as a martyrdom, see Introduction, pp. xlv–xlvi **up o Godes rode,** with 3,11,21, anticipates the theme of 5,13ff.

9. Cp. 2 Tim. 2:12. The variation from the Vulgate reading (*si sustinebis . . .*) may arise from a reminiscence of Bernard's *compatimini et conregnabitis* in *On the Love of God* (PL 182, col. 981). **as ȝe scottið,** etc. : cp. ' Hwa se euer wule habbe lot wið þe of þi blisse, he mot deale wið þe of þine pine on eorþe ' (OE Hom I, 187) ; see also **8**,33 and note.

11f. Gal. 6:14 ; quoted by Bernard in the sermon from which AW proceeds to draw. See note on 19 below and Appendix.

13f. Nos opportet, etc. Used as introit and anthem for Holy Cross Day (14 September).

16f. ' I will start off from another level and so work down to this point.' Viz. at **5**,13ff.

17f. ' for the substance is, more or less, St Bernard's.' But *sentence*, which commonly means ' opinion ', ' gist ', may have a more specialised meaning here. J. Leclercq, *Études sur S. Bernard, Analecta sac. ord. Cisterciensis*, Rome (1953), pp. 45–83, distinguishes between those sermons of Bernard surviving in elaborated literary form and *sententiae* (summaries of sermons) preserved from note-takers' reports. The author of AW may have known Bernard's sermon in this latter form, i.e. as a *sentence*.

19ff. From here to 5,33 the author of AW closely follows Bernard's Sermon VII for Lent (PL 183, cols. 183–6 : see Appendix), delivered by Bernard before monks, but in AW adapted for recluses. **Preo manere men.** *Manere* [OFr *man(i)ere*] is a substitution into the common ME construction with *cunne* : cp. 7,31.

31

22. **Iesuse.** With names of foreign origin ending in -*s*, a genitive in *e* is not uncommon : so *paraise*, **6,37**, *Creasuse, Moysese*, **25,31,37** ; *Iesues*, **28,**15 shows a variant.

24ff. 1 Pet. 2:11 ; in Bernard's sermon.

27. **el þeodie,** OE *elþeodig*, commonly in OE for ' pilgrim '. The prefix *el-* [OE *æl-, el-*, ' strange ', ' foreign '] is rare in ME, but cp. *elheowet*, **11,**37. On the development in OE literature of the theme of human life conceived as a pilgrimage towards the heavenly home, see G. Ehrismann, *PBB* **35** (1909), 209–39. By the end of the 12th c. pilgrimage within England and oversea had become a popular religious activity of social, commercial, and artistic importance : see D. M. Stenton, *English Society in the Early Middle Ages* (1951), pp. 222–3.

p. 4

5f. Heb. 13:14 : in Bernard's sermon, but there introduced earlier.

7. **beoð bi þe leaste,** they make do with the least. For the idiom cp. *beoð bi warme cappen*, AW *f.* 113*v*, ' make do with warm caps ', and see Hall, EME II, 393, and G. V. Smithers, *Kyng Alisaunder* II, EETS 237 (1957), p. 95. The change of person as here, from *we* (6) to *ha* (7), is common in ME : cp. **13,**29.

11. **[wið].** A scribal omission occasioned perhaps by the shape and ending of preceding *gað*.

12. **ane** is emphatic—' a single saint's bones ' opposed to *Godd seolf & alle his hali halhen* (14). **sontes,** a rare but regular phonological development from OE *sanct*, beside the commoner ME *sein, seint(e)* as title drawn from ecclesiastical French use. **James.** Santiago of Compostela in Galicia, Spain, reputed from the 9th c. to possess the bones of the apostle James (the Great), became during the 12th c. one of the great shrines of Christendom and the national shrine of Spaniards in their struggles against the Moors : see *Butler's Lives of the Saints*, new ed., rev. H. Thurston and D. Attwater (1953), III, 182–3. **Giles.** According to the ' utterly untrustworthy ' legend of 10th c. origin, Giles, a hermit of noble birth, was nourished in his forest retreat by a hind which was hunted by Flavius, a king of the Goths. Giles became spiritual adviser to Flavius, who established the hermit in a monastery to be known as Saint-Gilles, in Provence. This monastery conveniently situated on main pilgrim routes, strenuously fostered the cult of its patron, who became one of the great popular saints of the late Middle Ages : see *Butler's Lives of the Saints*, IV, 457–9.

14. **Godd.** This conventionalised spelling in *dd* (MS godd), common to KG and some other EME texts, was devised apparently to distinguish noun [OE *god*, ' God '] from adj. [OE *gōd*, ' good '].

16. ' **St Julian's house '.** There are a number of tangled legends of various Julians, but this is certainly a reference to St Julian the Hospitaller, who according to the pious romance killed his parents by mistake, and in remorse built, and with his wife kept, a hostel for poor travellers. He became a type of hospitality : cp. *Canterbury Tales*, A.340 ; *Sir Gawain and the Green Knight*, 774. His popularity in England was perhaps boosted by a confusion with an early bishop Julian of Le Mans, celebrated in England in the 12th c., probably because Henry II was born in that town : see *Butler's Lives of the Saints*, I, 314 and 183. No mention of SS James, Giles, or Julian is made in Bernard's sermon.

18ff. ' . . . for invariably, although pilgrims, as I said before, keep going forwards and do not become residents in the city of the world, on occasion, something they see by the road looks attractive to them and they stop awhile—though not permanently—and many things happen to them by means of which they are hindered, with the result —more is the pity—that some get home late, and some never at all.' **allegate** (see *MED s.* al-gate(s), 2. (*a*) and (*c*)) is contrasted with **sum chearre** (21). The suppression of subject pronoun, as in 20 and 22, is frequent in AW (cp. 7, 10, 15, above) : see W. F. J. Roberts, *LMS* 1 (1937), 107–15.

22. **edstuteð.** An infin. *etstutten* exists beside *etstunten* in KG texts ; both acquire the senses of ME *etstonden.* *etstutten* is assumed to derive from ON *-stytta*, earlier *stynta*, but words with this late Scandinavian assimilation to *tt* are rare in ME : see d'Ardenne, SJ, p. 166.

29. **Godd wat.** Cp. **5**,14, **8**,33, **18**.2 etc. ; in French, *deu-le-set*, **9**,8, **18**,18. On this type of expression which is asseverative rather than expletive, see C. T. Onions, *RES* 4 (1928), 334–7. H. E. Allen, *PMLA* **44** (1929), 673–5, considered such uses an identifiable feature of the style of the author of the Rule.

31ff. Coloss. 3:3–4. The idea of eternal life in glory recalls to the author the standard text in accounts of beatitude (Matt. 13:43), ' Then shall the righteous shine forth as the sun ' (cp. **9**,31, **10**,8, **25**,25f), and the common metaphor of Christ as sun (cp. **26**,15 ; AW *f.* 12*v*, ' the true sun which is Christ '). The development of the theme is treated at length by F.-J. Dölger, *Sol Salutis*, Munster (1920).

36. **ant** renders Lat. *&* (33) : see *MED, s.* and 7.

38. **monihwet** subject to eileð. **Þe deade**, etc., lit. ' To the dead it is of no account though, etc. ' : cp. **5**,29. On the anchorite life regarded as a death, see Introduction, pp. xxxiv-xxxv.

p. 5

6f. Gal. 2:20.

8ff. simplifies Bernard's explanation.

14ff. Gal. 6:14 : cp. **3**,11. Here AW does not take up Bernard's reference to St Paul's flight to the third heaven : see Intro., p. lvii.

17. **þruppe.** At **3**,14ff.

18. **mi lauerd** in logical (but not grammatical) apposition with the genitive Iesu Cristes.

21. **ancre.** Lat. *anáchoreta* giving (probably through use in Celtic church (see M. Förster, *ESt* 56 (1922), 204–9)), OE *ancre* (*masc.*). Probably the same OE form could be used as *fem.* The ME form is commonly *ancre*, but the vowel length is often uncertain. In AW a form with *o* + nasal is not found (see A. Pogatscher, *ESt* 27 (1900), 220–1). The form in OE and ME seems to have been controlled not only by Lat. but also by popular etymologies. In OE, *āncre* appears, by association with *ān*, ' alone ', and a further connection was made with OE *ancor*, ' anchor '. This etymology was exploited in AW *f.* 39*r* (Salu 63), ' For this reason is ancre called *ancre*, and under the church is anchored, as an anchor (*ancre*) under the ship's board in order to hold the ship.' See also H. Käsmann, *Studien zum kirklichen Wortschatz des Mittelenglischen 1100–1350*, Tübingen (1961), pp. 336–7.

24ff. A summary, with an emphasis on penitence, not found in Bernard's sermon.

27. unnet is to be construed also with spekeð : ' indeed talks foolishly at times. . . .'

33. hure ouer hure. An idiom for a superlative : cp. reowðe ouer reowðe, AW f. 60v, f. 79v ; mihte ouer alle mihtes, HM 13.

p. 6

3. See 3,13.

4. oþre, MS ordre. A censure of other religious ways of life, which would be suggested by reading ordre, is unlikely. The other early MSS (N, C, G, T) support oþre. ' Whatever may be the case with others who . . .' : for this construction, cp. SW 186 and Wilson's note thereon.

7ff. ' Many a man is willing to suffer physical pain in some ways but is unable to bear the humiliation of being considered of no account.' Syntactically, however, beon . . . scheome (8–9) is probably best taken as a conjuncture (by means of (first) ne) of the objects extracted from the two clauses, beon itald unwurð ne mahte he þolien and scheome ne mahte he þolien—an inelegant syllepsis. For the sentiment, cp. Wooing of our Lord (OE Hom I, 279).

12ff to 8,13 draws upon the Declamations from St Bernard's Sermons (also known as the Colloquy of Jesus with Peter), chaps. xxxvi ff : see R. W. Chambers, RES 1 (1925), 19. The Declamations, usually ascribed to Geoffrey of Auxerre, Bernard's disciple and biographer, may well have been put together from authentic Bernardine material ; see the rather inconclusive survey, J. Leclercq, Études sur Saint Bernard, especially p. 127. The Declamations are handled freely in AW : here cp. ' And everything which deters the children of this world from the way of life and discipline, everything which for the time being harasses the servants of God, consists in these two things which the prophet recommends in one verse, " See my humility and my toil " (Ps. 35:18). These therefore are the sides of the ladder, contempt and adversity [vilitas et asperitas], into which the steps of virtue and inward grace are inserted ' (PL 184, col. 460). The idea of a ladder of perfection was certainly best known through Benedict's Rule, chap. vii, On Humility, ' The ladder is our life in the world, which if the heart is humbled, is lifted up to the Lord in heaven. The sides . . . are our body and soul', between which are fixed the different grades of humility. This is one of the very few reminiscences of Benedict's Rule in AW, and seems to be accounted for entirely by the Bernardine source. Vilitas et asperitas are also linked by Adam the Scot, first a Praemonstratensian canon of Dryburgh, then, coming under the influence of Hugh of Lincoln, a Carthusian at Witham, Somerset, one of the original English Charterhouses. On Adam, who died c.1210, see J. Bullough, Adam of Dryburgh (1958). Cp. his Quadripartite Exercise of the Cell, ' So here is vilitas and asperitas in your way of life . . . . I refer vilitas to humiliation, and asperitas to mortification (PL 153, col. 808 : cp. also PL 198, col. 591, and see notes on 7,10ff and 16,22).

17. Dauið, a common spelling to indicate the medieval Lat. pronunciation : see A. Pogatscher, QF 64 (1888), 175f. A usual interpretation of the name David is ' desirable ', ' beloved son ' ; so PL 23, col. 1275. This interpretation accounts for Godes deorling (26).

18ff. **Ps. 25:18** as quoted in *Declamations* : see note on 12ff.

23. **í sar & í sorhe.** For examples of this phrase, common in OE homilies and in KG texts, see D. Bethurum, *JEGP* 34 (1935), 562.

31. **See 2 Kings 2:11.** Elijah's ascent to heaven without knowing death is not treated in *Declamations*. It often received pictorial treatment in 12th c. illumination : see T. S. R. Boase, *English Art 1100–1216* (1953), p. 65, etc. Allegories of chariots and drivers are common in medieval literature : see E. R. Curtius, *European Literature and the Latin Middle Ages*, Eng. trans. (1953), p. 120, n. 34: In the *Book of Sentences*, Bernard explained Elijah's chariot as drawn by 'love' and 'desire' (*PL* 184, cols. 1146, 1151).. In the Bernardine *Short Commentary on the Song of Solomon*, a chariot (one of several) has wheels of prayer and bodily discipline (*PL* 184, col. 426).

34. **ah wel mei duhen.** Apparently an elliptical colloquialism (occurring elsewhere AW *f.* 15*r*, *f.* 113*r* and *v*, and in Layamon's *Brut*, 12754) : see Hall, EME II. 390–1. *duhen* must represent OE *dugan* 'be worth', 'avail'. The meaning of the phrase to suit all contexts is, 'This (instead of something else which may come to mind) will serve the present purpose.' *ah*, 'but', excludes the possible alternatives of interpretation, that is, of the heat and redness of the wheels (*Ha*, 35), which are not here entertained.

35. A play on **hweolinde**, 'wheeling' [OE *hwēol*, 'wheel' + *pres. part.* ending], which would approximate in pronunciation to *hwilinde* (cp. *a hwilinde wa*, *f.* 49*r*) [OE *hwīlwende* (from *hwīl*, 'time' + stem of *wendan*, 'turn') > *hwilende*, 'transitory']. Cf. Ælfric, *Sigewulfi Interrogationes*, *Anglia* 7 (1884) lines 289–93.

36ff. **See Gen. 3:24.** This passage in AW seems to have been suggested by the gloss on this verse in Genesis in which Elijah is usually mentioned. The flaming sword is explained as the tribulations and labours of this life : see the *Ordinary Gloss* (*PL* 113, cols. 97–8).

p. 7

6f. **wið scheome beon iheowet.** The suffusion of blood in a blush of shame is associated with the shedding of blood on the Cross.

7. **bi**, about (as usual). The quotation is from Phil. 2:8. The addition of *est* (not in Vulgate text) suggests that the author recollected the text in the liturgy where (with *est*) the verse served as an antiphon in Holy Week.

10ff. Cp. Adam the Scot, *On the Way of Life of the Praemonstratensian Canons*, 'For He was made obedient even unto death ; and what does the Apostle want us to understand by adding " the death of the Cross " ? . . . that He showed himself obedient to a death not only cruel, but also shameful ; not only bitter but also ignominious ; there was pain (*asperitas*) in death ; and contempt (*vilitas*) on the Cross' (*PL* 198, col. 591).

13. Cp. *Declamations*, chap. xxxix, ' But what is it to take up the Cross but to embrace toil and humility ? ' (*PL* 184, col. 463).

16. **beggin as an hearlot.** The identity of the verb 'beg' is quite clear, but it is the earliest occurrence of the word in ME, and somewhat isolated : see *MED s.* beggen. The word (and related forms) is usually derived from OFr *béguine*, a female member (*masc. beghard*) of a lay mendicant order, flourishing from the early 13th c. particularly in the Low Countries, who made apostolic poverty an essential part

of their way of life : see *NED s.* beg. But the order itself could not have given rise to the word. The earliest *béguinage* provided with a Rule was established as late as 1246 : and the word *béguine* scarcely appears before 1200. Probably *beg* and *béguine* are ultimately related, but the etymology is altogether obscure : see on *béguine* J. Van Mierlo, *Verslagen en Mededeelingen der Koninklijke Vlaamse Academie voor Taal en Letterkunde*, Ghent (1945), pp. 31–51. In AW *hearlot* offers no help in defining the meaning of *beggin*, for the early sense and etymology of *hearlot* are also obscure : see *NED s.* harlot. Lay mendicant religious on the Continent acquired a variety of names, chiefly disapproving, such as *bogards*, *lollaerts*, *boni pueri*, *boni valeti*, but there is no evidence to suggest that OFr *herlot* was one of them. However, a recognition and professionalisation of beggary accompanied the religious revolution of the 12th c., and it was to provide the economic basis of the orders of the Friars.

17. beodes mon. One who prayed for, and often, as in this case apparently, was endowed to pray for the welfare and salvation of another. The well-known passage at an earlier point in N, omitted altogether in AW, seems to indicate the provision made for the original recluses. ' Vor mid more eise ne mid more menke not ich none ancre þet habbe al þet hire neod is, þene ȝe þreo habbeð. . . . Vor ȝe ne þencheð nowiht of mete, ne of cloð, ne to ou, ne to ouwer meidenes. Euerich of ou haueð of one ureonde al þet hire is neod ; ne þerf þet meiden sechen nouðer bread ne suuel fur þene et his halle. God hit wot moni oþer wot lutel of þisse eise, auh beoð ful ofte iderued mid wone & mid scheome & mid teone. In hire hond ȝif þis cumeð hit mei beon ham uroure. Ȝe muwen more dreden þe nesche dole þene þe herde . . . vor uein wolde þe hexte cwemen ou, ȝif he muhte mid oluhnunge makien ou fulitowen, ȝif heo nere þe hendure. Muche word is of ou, hu gentile wummen ȝe beoð, vor godleic & for ureoleic iȝirned of monie, & sustren of one ueder & of one moder ine blostme of ower ȝuweðe uorheten alle wordes blissen & bicomen ancren ' (AR N, p. 85/10–27). [' For I know no anchoress who has all she needs with easier access and with more dignity than you three have. . . . For you do not have to think at all about food or clothing for yourselves or for your maid-servants. Each one of you has all that she needs from the same friend, and a maid-servant need go no further than his hall for bread or savoury. God can witness that many others know little of such comfort, but are often afflicted with misery and shame and vexation. If this should come into their hands it may be of comfort to them. You may have to dread the smooth more than the rough. . . . For gladly would the Evil One please you if he could, with flattery make you ill-disciplined if you were not too clever for him. There is much talk about you, how you are women of gentle birth, sisters, of one father and one mother, courted for your goodness and nobility by many, having in the blossom of your youth renounced the delights of the world to become anchoresses.']

18. danger [OFr from Lat. **dominiarium*, ' lordship ']. Originally a feudal term ; here and **17**,14 the meaning (but not the tone) approximates to MnE ' bossing ', and represents an early stage in the semantic development of the word in ME, for which see C. S. Lewis, *The Allegory of Love* (1936), pp. 364–6.

20ff. In developing the theme of the rewards of suffering AW returns to *Declamations*.

24. **Isa. 61:7.** Cp. *Declamations*, chap. xl, ' Therefore in your country you will possess double and everlasting joy shall be unto you. In exile you will everywhere have the double affliction of humility and toil [cp. 6,18ff]. But console yourselves and do not fail, since in your own land, the land in truth of the living, there shall yet remain for you a double reward, of sublimity and delight. For undisturbed rest is intended by the thrones, the height of dignity by the judgment' (*PL* 184, col. 463). This last passage is based on Matt. 19:28, quoted earlier in *Declamations*, but postponed in AW to 8,3.

29f. **super epistolam,** etc. I.e. a gloss on James 1:2, as found in the *Ordinary Gloss* (*PL* 114, col. 671). Around St Jerome's Prologues to his translation of the Bible into Latin—the version established as the Vulgate—was slowly gathered in successive transcriptions over centuries a variety of interpretative material. This material would vary more or less from copy to copy. In the 12th c. Anselm of Laon and others developed these compilations into a more systematic commentary, out of which emerged eventually the accepted *Gloss* : on this development and particularly on the work of the Paris theologians and of Andrew of St Victor (who *c.*1147 became Abbot of Wigmore) on the *Gloss*, see B. Smalley, *The Study of the Bible in the Middle Ages*, 2nd ed. (1952). Dr C. H. Talbot has pointed out privately that ' Gloss ' in AW sometimes refers to the biblical commentaries of Peter Lombard.

31. Historically **cunne** (cp. 20,22) is genitive plural ; but the genitival function was often obscured, and *cunne* is used meaning ' kind ', as a nominative in such phrases as *þe þridde cunne of fikelere* (AW, *f.* 22v).

32f. **as þah he seide,** etc. The rhetorical figure *sermonicatio* (*ad Her.* IV, xliii, 55) used for refining an argument further : cp. 30,10. feorlich [modelled on ON *ferligr,* ' monstrous '] is kept distinct in KG texts from *fearlich,* ' terrible ' [OE *fǽrlic*], as in 9,36 ; see *s.vv.* d'Ardenne, SJ Glossary.

36. **cang** (and related forms) occurs several times in AW and other KG texts. The derivation from OFr *cangoun,* ' changeling ', is supported by AW, *f.* 29r, ' Cang dohter iwurð as mone i wonunge [waning], þriveð as þe cangoun, se lengre se wurse [i.e. as a pining infant].' *Cang dohter* here renders *fatua filia* of Ecclus. 22:3. A changeling was an ill-favoured, often deformed or imbecile child believed to be the offspring of fairies and to have been substituted by them for a normal child stolen in infancy or before baptism. The semantic change to the sense general in KG texts, ' fool ', ' foolish ', is easily understood : see Colborn, HM, p. 117.

37. **place.** Cp. the specialised use of *field* in warfare ; see *NED*, place II.3.c. **Milicia est,** etc. Job 7:1 ; not in *Declamations,* prompted apparently by the knightly turn of the preceding passage in AW.

p. 8

3f. **Matt. 19:28.** See 7,24 note.

5f. **Bernardus.** In *Declamations,* chap. xl (*PL* 184, col. 463), but with *dignitatis* for *honoris* ; but Bernard was fond of the antithesis (which may originate in Gregory, *PL* 76, col. 1217) and uses it elsewhere.

6–9. Cp. SW 277–81, ' Ich iseh þe apostles poure & lah on eorðe, ifullet & bigoten al of unimete blisse, sitte i trones ant al under hare uet þet heh is i þe worlde, ȝarowe forte demen i þe dei of dome kinges & keiseres, & alle cunreadnes of alles cunnes ledenes.' **kinges & keisers**. Also in AW *f.* 38*r*, *f.* 45*v*, an ancient alliterative phrase (but it is usually assumed with *keiser*, from ON *keisari*, replacing a development from native *cāsere*) in common EME use : see D. Bethurum, *JEGP* **34** (1935), 562 ; J. P. Oakden, *Alliterative Poetry in Middle English*, II (1935), 238, 252, 273. **cnihtes & clearkes**. For other instances of use, see Oakden, *loc. cit.*, pp. 238, 252, 275. AW draws on *Declamations* no further after 13, except perhaps at 9,21ff.

15f. Lat. quotation untraced, but probably of liturgical origin.

20ff. Rom. 6:5. In translating, the author follows the Lat. closely. *beon i-impet to þe ilicnesse* is to be understood after **schulen** (24). Rom. 11:15–24 may have suggested a meaning ' engrafted ' for **i-impet**.

25. **libbeð**. In AW the normal pres. pl. form is *liuieð* as 3,19 ; but the normal infinitive is *libben* (but cp. *liuien* in proximity to *lluiende*, 4,15) : on distribution in AW of stems *libb-*, *liui-* (both found in OE), see d'Ardenne, SJ, p. 239.

28f. Phil. 3:20–1. In 29f the context of these scriptural verses is in mind, especially Phil. 3:12 and 18–19, but exactly who ' runs beforehand ', and why, is not clear.

31. See 3,18. The author has now returned to the original proposition of Part 6.

33ff. Cp. *Orison of our Lord*, ' Nis na trewe ifere þe nule naut **s**cottin in þe lure, ase in þe biȝete ' (OE Hom I, 187) : see 3,9 note.

p. 9

1ff. The Church as the Body of which Christ is the head, and all Christians the members, based on 1 Cor. 6:15, 12:12–17, Eph. 1:22–3, 4:15–16, Col. 2:19, etc., is one of the profound Christian commonplaces. Phrases similar to those in AW appear in many OE and ME writings : e.g. Ælfric, *Catholic Homilies*, I, 272 ; *The Homilies of Wulfstan*, ed. D. Bethurum (1957), p. 194 ; *Vices and Virtues*, ed. F. Holthausen, EETS 89 and 159, pp. 27, 131. **Ah nis euch lim**, etc., is exactly parallel with a phrase in a letter of Peter Bernard, fifth Prior of Grandmont, to Henry II, after the death of Becket (1170) (*PL* 204, col. 1172). The notion of sin as a disease which only God could cure is also ancient, implicit in the Old and New Testaments and variously drawn out in the Middle Ages : see R. Arbesmann, *Traditio* 10 (1952), 1–28. At some length, AW *f.* 31*v* (Salu 50) explains how the whole world was in fever and that Christ was the only sound member from which to let blood. This earlier passage is probably recalled here.

6f. **þet londuuel þet**, etc., ' the plague with which all lands were sick, and many still are '. For *liggen* used absolutely in this sense see *NED* *s.* lie, *v.*[1] B.1, c, d and B.3. **on** is semi-adverbial, almost as if it were a separable particle. **londuuel**, ' epidemic plague ', which though frequent in the 12th and 13th cs., would be usually fever (taking the forms of typhus, dysentery, etc.), accompanying the famine conditions associated with economic troubles and the failure of harvest : see C. Creighton, *A History of Epidemics in Britain* (1891), I, 15–17, and on the epidemics of 1189–1203, pp. 35ff.

9. Cp. Matt. 5:30 and Mark 9:43.

10. Godd with function of dative.

11. him, *viz.* God ; he as antecedent to **him seolf** (12). See Glossary *s.* **bilimeð. þe þus bilimeð,** etc. refers to the man who dismembers the Body of Christ by withdrawing from the obligations imposed by membership of that Body.

12f. Oportebat, etc. A conflation of Luke 24:26 and 46, used in this form as versicle in the Mass on Low Sunday.

14. þolie. Infinitive, in imitation of Lat. construction.

16. deale. A word not hitherto satisfactorily explained, but found elsewhere at AW *f. 75r, f. 78r,* as *dele* ; Robert Mannyng, *Chronicle,* ed. T. Hearne (1810), p. 167 ; and somewhat doubtfully, SM, p. 8/27. The sense required in all cases is ' Distinguish the premisses of the argument carefully to understand its force ', ' Let us get this quite clear.' The connection with OE *dælan, gedælan* (so Stratmann-Bradley, *s.v.*) seems inescapable, though not simple. OE *dælan* appears in AW as *dealen,* but its imperatives would be sg. *deal,* pl. *dealeð. deale* as imperative sg. (used perhaps exclamatorily : cp. common use of *loke,* meaning ' lo ') would require in AW an infinitive **dealin,* a Class II weak verb : possibly then a formation on AW form *dale,* ' part ' (3,2 etc.) [=Lat. technical scholastic term *distinctio* : cp. AW *f.* 4r], usually assumed to be a development, not from OE *dæl,* but from OE *gedāl* : see d'Ardenne, SJ, p. 214. AW *deale* as imperative sg. from **dealin* serves as a call of attention to a point of logic or method ; and with this use of **dealin* should be compared the use of Lat. *distinguere* (as well as *dīvisere*) for similar purposes. With this sense of **dealin* can be connected the difficult verb *dayly* (*Pearl* 313) where the stem vowel has apparently been re-formed on basis of ON *deila.* AW *dale* seems to stand in relationship to **dealin* as *tale* [OE *talu,* ' account '] to *tealen* in the collocation *wið talen tealen* (SM, p. 38/21, where Royal MS reads actually *tealin*).

21. wið lihtleapes. A compound *lihtleapes* is unattested out of this context. AR N p. 164/13 reads *mid liht-leapes,* for which the editor suggested emendation to *mid lihtcheapes* (see *NED s.* light, *adj.* III.13.b.), meaning, here, ' on the cheap '. This emendation would draw support from T *f.*88v², *wið lih/te scheapes,* from AR French, p. 261/15, *a legier marchee,* and AR Lat., p. 140/31, *vili precio* ; but a compound *lihtcheapes* seems also unattested elsewhere, the plural is unidiomatic, and the *-ea-* unexpected in AW dialect after *ch* (cp. *se liht chap,* 25,20). The AW reading must be retained (cp. also *wið lichtlepes,* C *f.* 166r) ; but the explanation (though not the contextual meaning) of the phrase is doubtful. (i) *lihtleapes* may be taken as an original adverbial genitive (of the type of *sunderlepes,* ' separately ', *serlepes* (an EME formation), ' individually ') meaning ' in short measures ', ' in driblets ', which has undergone a false analysis into a phrase : cp. *wyth sundyr lepys* ' with separate leaps ', probably from adv. *sundyrlepys* (K. Sisam, *Fourteenth Century Verse and Prose,* p. 11/234 and note, p. 207). (ii) *wið lihtleapes* can be taken (following on 17–18, *wulleð wið eise stihen*), as if the sense were not modified by compounding, to mean ' with easy steps ' ; but the phrase must then be compared with the uncompounded *moni liht lupe* (sg.), AW *f.* 12v, where *lupe* is the normal form in KG texts from OE *hlȳp,* ' leap ', although Ang. *hlēp* is usually assumed to have existed. The conjunction of adj. or adv. *liht*(*lich*) with n. or vb. *lepe*(*n*) is certainly common in ME : see H. Willert, *Die alliterierenden Formeln der Englischen Sprache,* Halle (1911), p. 312. In *Ywain and Gawain* (72) *ful light of lepes* translates the ironic *preu et saillant* of Chrétien of Troyes' *Yvain* (70). For John Capgrave, *Life of St Katharine*, ed. C. Horstmann, EETS 100 (1893), 92/223, *Tyme goth fast, it is full lyght of lope*. Obviously *liht* and *lepe* could be associated idiomatically to convey the sense of flightiness and irresponsibility. Etymologically (i) and (ii) can hardly be distinguished. (iii) A meaning 'with light measure' could be assumed, deriving *-leapes* from OE *lēap*, 'basket', 'measure': note an OE gloss *leoht leap* for Lat. *imbilium* (?), and ME compound *ber(e)lepe*, 'large basket'. Probably (ii) is least unsatisfactory.

22. After **halhen** understand *beoð canges*.

23ff. According to traditions, the apostle Peter was crucified head downwards at Rome during the persecution of Nero, A.D. 64 ; his brother Andrew, crucified on a cross saltire, in Achaia, *c.* A.D. 70 ; the Spaniard Lawrence, archdeacon at Rome in mid-3rd c., was martyred by slow broiling on a gridiron.

24. laðlese meidnes, grammatically could be genitive sg., but in this context probably applies to the host of virgin martyrs in general, with a particular reference to the legend of St Katherine as told in the text which gives the name to KG texts. There, Katherine herself is *to-hwiðeret wið þe hweoles* (SK 1940), and the tyrant's queen, converted by Katherine's example, has her breasts torn off (2098, 2119) ; but St Agatha also endured this last torment : see **12,**32 note. St Katherine of Alexandria, historically a very shadowy figure indeed, suffered, according to legend, under the persecution of Maximin in the 4th c. Her cultus developed in the 11th c. and became exceedingly popular in England : see *Butler's Lives of the Saints*, IV, 420–1. Legends of virgin martyrs run remarkably true to type. SS Juliana, Euphemia, Christina were all torn on wheels ; all these, together with SS Agnes, Margaret, Dorothea, Barbara, etc., etc. were finally beheaded. Appeals to the example of the saints in recommending suffering are common in devotional writing. AW *f.* 33*r* (Salu 55) has cited Andrew, Lawrence, and Stephen. These saints are similarly held up as models in *Declamations*, chap. lviii (*PL* 184, col. 474), and Ailred, *On the Anchorite Life*, chap. xxv (*PL* 32, col. 1460).

25. heafdes bicoruen. *heafdes* is probably genitive sg. used adverbially : see d'Ardenne, SJ, p. 100.

26. Cp. ' al . . . is se sutel sotschipe ', SK 321–2. þeose. An example of an established ME usage by which the demonstrative refers ' to persons or things that have not been previously mentioned, but are prominent in the writer's mind ' (Sisam).

27. riche MS ȝape. The emendation is necessary and obvious ; cp. 30. **willes & waldes.** Adverbial genitives : also AW *f.* 28*v* ; HM 371, 695.

28. The ' tunic of Christ ' was a commonplace in 12th c. theology (cp. Rom. 6:6). The proper analogical interpretation it could bear was much disputed in the bitter controversy over Abelard's orthodoxy ; cp. C. H. Talbot, *Sermones inediti B. Ælredi*, Rome (1952), pp. 20–3.

29. alde feader. See **20,**25, and cp. *Eue ure alde moder*, AW *f.* 13*v* ; *eald-fæder, Beowulf*, 373.

31. See 4,31ff note.

33. weane. Extended form of OE *wēa*, based on gen. pl. *wēana*, was levelled through all cases.

34f. Isa. 18:7.

36. tolaimet, re-formed from OE *lemian*, ' lame ' ; *ai* suggests Scandinavian influence.

p. 10

1. Cp. SK 1244, *offearet & offruht*.

2. he refers to *þe feond*, 1 ; so also in 3 and 4.

3. Job 2:4.

8. Cp. 4,36.

9, 10, 13. The sense of **mearken** changes slightly in each use.

11. On the allegory of the castle of the soul (cp. **16,32**), as familiar to the audience of *Beowulf* as to readers of Bunyan, see R. D. Cornelius, *The Figurative Castle*, Bryn Mawr Monograph (1930) ; this allegory provides the basis of SW.

15. Ysaie. See 9,34.

16ff. First objection against the penitential life. A systematic rejection of proposed objections was a feature of medieval theological argumentation. **me**, used as conjunction in KG texts, to be compared with contemporary AN *mes* [Lat. *magis* > Mn. Fr. *mais*] as conjunction or interjection.

20. sabraz. A medicinal decoction or infusion. *NED* suggests derivation from Provençal *saboratz*, past part. of vb. *saboras* ' season ' ; see *N&Q* **2** (*1st series*) (1850), 204.

21. fordeð from *forðin* [OE *forþian*, ' further ']. The spelling in *d* may be no more than the common careless omission of bar of *ð* ; but see Mack, SM, p. li. With this passage in AW, cp. Peter Damian (1007–72), *Letters*, Book 8, letter vi, ' Moreover physicians of the body permit those of whom they despair to take whatever food they may seek anywhere ; but with threats they forbid all food of poisonous delight to those who, they think, can be cured, and in addition, they make them drink bitter remedies, so that by the swallowing of bitter things, they may recover the sweetness of health. What wonder therefore if the Physician of souls, etc.' (*PL* 144, cols. 474–5) : cp. Peter of Blois, *Twelve Benefits of Tribulation* (*PL* 207, col. 998).

24f. An allusion to the vinegar of Matt. 27:48 as well as to the primitive notion that death itself is a sort of drink : see C. Brown, *Speculum* **15** (1940), 389–99, and G. V. Smithers, *EGS* **4** (1952), 67–75.

27f. Cp. *Orison of our Lord*, ' Ne wene na mon to stihen wið este to þe steorren ' (OE Hom I, 187). AR N, p. 165/27 also reads *steorren* here, with which cp. Geoffrey of Vinsauf, *Poetria Nova* (ed. E. Faral), lines 496–8, ' If you wish to follow Christ, you must add torment to torment. The way to the stars is not with delights (*non itur ad astra deliciis*) ' : see also D. V. Ives, *MLR* **29** (1934), 260.

29ff. Second objection against penance.

34. Cp. Augustine, *Exposition of the Psalms*, Ps. 36:9, ' Since He beats every child He receives, He did not spare His own in whom He found no fault ' (*PL* 36, col. 389) ; and on Ps. 88:2, ' Should the sinful child shun beating, when he sees beaten the Only Son without sin at all ? ' (*PL* 37, col. 1131).

37f. Þe beoreð on us, etc. ; perhaps ' who are ourselves responsible for His son's death (and carry on us) the weapon that slew Him, which was our sin '. Thus wepne (11,1) would be in apposition with deað, which would mean here ' the instrument or cause of death ' ; cp. *NED s.* death, 7. For the double meaning to be given to beoreð on, see *MED s.* beren *v.*(1), 8.(c) and 2.(a).

p. 11

2ff. The flesh of Christ was allegorised as His shadow (a development of Lam. 4:20 ultimately) : see Gregory, *Morals*, Book 33, chap. iii, 5 (*PL* 76, col. 671). On the theme of *umbra Christi*, elaborated by Bernard, see I. Valléry-Radot, *Collectanae ord. Cisterc. ref.* 12 (1950), 331–5. See also 17,28 note.

5ff. Matt. 26:38–9. Peter of Celles (a Cluniac monk, who succeeded his friend John of Salisbury as Bishop of Chartres, died 1183 ; an influential correspondent, and a writer much concerned with the ascetic life : see de Ghellinck, *L'Essor*, pp. 190, 194, etc.), in *On the Discipline of the Cloister* (*PL* 202, col. 1120), has a passage which may have suggested AW 10,34ff, based on and quoting Rom. 8:32 (cp. 10,34), Isa. 53:5 (cp. 16) and Matt. 26:39 (as here). See AW *f.* 30*v* (Salu 49) for earlier expression of Christ's horror at the prospect of death.

12. Matt. 27:46.

14. Cp. Ecclus. 30:1.

16. Isa. 53:5. *disciplina* is taken in this context in the usual monastic sense of scourging. Though used earlier among Celtic religious, penitential scourging was promoted extensively following the example and advice of Peter Damian ; see his *In Praise of Whips* (*PL* 145, cols. 679–86) ; L. Gougaud, *Dévotions et pratiques ascétiques du moyen âge*, Paris (1925), pp. 175–99. In AW the recluses are urged not to wear anything made of iron, or hair, or hedgehog skin, nor to discipline themselves with anything made of these materials, or with a leaded scourge, or with holly or thorns, nor to draw blood without permission ; nor should they sting themselves with nettles, nor scourge the front of their bodies at all : AW *f.* 113*v* (Salu 185–6). But they are advised to scourge themselves as a last defence against temptation, AW *f.*80*r* (Salu 131), and regularly before Holy Communion, AW *f.* 111*v* (Salu 182).

24. bulteð formed on OE *bolt*, ' bolt ', a missile discharged by catapult action.

30ff. Third objection against penance.

33ff. A mon subject to the interrogative *nalde* (37). Cp. the illustration provided by John of Fécamp (1028–78, an initiator of the new piety in northern Europe and a master of devotional prose) in a meditation incorporated in the 12th c. into the Anselmian *Book of Prayers and Meditations*, ' For if a bride were so passionately attached to her husband that she for the degree of love could enjoy no peace of mind and suffered the absence of her beloved with the greatest grief, with what love, then, with what zeal . . . should the soul whom thou hast espoused . . . love thee, true God and fairest Bridegroom.'

Prayer xvii (*PL* 158, col. 896). Also Stephen of Grandmont (the founder *c.*1100 of an eremitical order near Limoges), in his *Book of Sentences*, chap. lxxxiv, ' And this example can be noted : if when a husband is absent from his wife, another man speaks to her of adultery, and she does not consent in any way, will the husband love her any the less when he returns ? ' (*PL* 204, col. 1119).

37. elheowet [OE *el*, ' strange ' + *hiwod*, ' coloured '] (cp. 3,27) occurs elsewhere only in SW 64.

38. wedde. From OE *wēdan*, ' be out of one's senses '.

p. 12

1. Cp. AW *f.* 3r (Salu 4) for the soul as a widow who through her sin has lost her spouse Christ.

6ff begins the transition to the adaptation of material from Ailred, with which the author of AW seeks to show the proper moderation to be observed in mortifying oneself.

9. Ailred, born at Hexham 1109, the son of an hereditary and noble priest, brought up at the court of Scotland as companion to the son of King David ; abandoned the court in 1135 to join the new Cistercian foundation at Rievaulx (Yorks) ; abbot of Revesby (Lincs) 1142, of Rievaulx from 1146 until his death 1167 ; canonised 1191. His connections, learning, intelligence, and sanctity made him the outstanding churchman of the north of England in the 12th c. His writings include historical works, sermons, devotional and ascetical treatises in which the ethics of Cicero blend attractively with the ascetic piety of Bernard. His life was written by his disciple, Walter Daniel, *Life of St Ailred*, ed. Sir F. M. Powicke, new ed. *Nelson's Medieval Classics* (1950). AW uses on several occasions Ailred's *On the Anchorite Life*, see Introduction, pp. xxxvi–xxxvii. Here cp. chap. xxvi, ' Chastity is never won nor kept by the young, without great contrition of heart and affliction of the body ' (*PL* 32, col. 1460). AW continues to draw upon Ailred up to 13,31. H. E. Allen, *PMLA* 44 (1929), 655–7, sets out these correspondences.

11. leohe. OE *hlēow*, ' shelter ', see *NED* lee, *n.*[1], but blended with ON *lega*, ' lair ', ' lying (in bed) '.

15. wil ȝeoue. A virtual compound noun, similarly applied SM, p. 38/15. ' Godes grace . . . wil ȝeoue onoseruet ', ' a free gift undeserved '. *wil* is also compounded in *wilcweme*, ' freely satisfied ' (AW *f.* 85v, SK 1728, SJ 282). AW has already condemned the man who thinks he can draw upon grace when he chooses, *f.* 92r (Salu 150). Here AW follows Ailred, ' For continence is indeed the gift of God and no one can be chaste unless God grant it ; nor must His gift be ascribed to any merit of ours but to His freely-given grace ; yet He judges those unworthy of such a gift who refuse to undergo any labour for it and wish to keep chaste among delights, continent while feasting . . . to seem to bind themselves with flames and not to burn ' (*PL* 32, col. 1460). Ailred himself in later years was much troubled by the thought of his incontinence when young.

17. vngraciuse, either plural adj. as n., or adverbially.

18. þe, dependent on subject of stondeð, 17.

20f. Hwa bredde, etc. Cp. Prov. 6:27, a text commonly alluded to in similar contexts, e.g. by Andrew the Chaplain, *The Art of Courtly Love*, trans. J. J. Parry, New York (1941), p. 123 and note.

21f. **Pot þe walleð**, etc. Probably a reminiscence of Job. 41:11, and of Gregory's commentary on it in *Morals*, Book 33, chap. xxxvii, 66 (*PL* 76, col. 715).

22. **nule he beon ouerleden**, etc. The sense (gluttony ' spills over ' into lust) is established by the following sentence, *þe wombe*, etc. (23ff). Past part. *ouerleden* [OE *-hladan*, ' load, fill ', ' draw (water) '] requires the meaning (not as *NED s.* overlade) ' filled to excess ' with *ouer-* used as *NED s.* over- (in combination) 5. **oðer** expresses a conditional relationship, not a logical alternative (cp. *NED s.* or, *conj.*² B.4.), and is modified by the negative in *nule*. Translate ' unless '.

24. Cp. AW *f.* 76*v* (Salu 125), ' Lechery rules in the loins ' ; *f.* 78*r* (Salu 128), ' Lechery comes of greediness and carnal ease '. Peter the Cantor, *Verbum Abbreviatum*, chap. cxxxiv (*PL* 205, col. 329), provides the phrase, ' The belly and the genitals are neighbours ', often cited in the 12th c.

26ff. Cp. Ailred, *On the Anchorite Life*, ' But some are held back from solitary exercises by fear lest, forsooth, they should fall ill on account of excessive abstinence or immoderate vigils ' (*PL* 32, col. 1461).

31. **forwurðeð . . . leche.** Similar use of the verb [OE *forweorþan*, ' perish '] occurs AW *f.* 114*v*, ' Ancre ne schal nawt forwurðe scolmeistre '. *leche* appears to be a singular, out of agreement with *fisiciens*. In KG texts genuine noun-plurais in *-e* are scarcely recorded : see d'Ardenne, SJ, pp. 210, 214. But there may have been some uncertainty (between *-s* and *-n*) as to the plural of this noun [OE *-ja* stem *lǣce*, pl. *lǣcas*], as with a few other nouns ending in *-e* (*wrecche*, *ancre*) : *ende*, also original masc. *-ja* stem noun, seems to lose a recognisably plural form in EME.

32. **Agace.** The regular ME form of *Agatha* (cp. *Boece* for *Boethius*). Agatha, another virgin martyr, according to legend was a nobly born Sicilian who suffered under the Decian persecution A.D. 253. Cast into prison after torture and mutilation, she was visited and healed by St Peter. She was eventually beheaded : see *Butler's Lives of the Saints*, I, 255–6.

33f. **Medicinam**, etc. Used as anthem on St Agatha's day (5 February). See also H. E. Allen, *PMLA* 44 (1929), 660–1.

35ff. Pretty certainly a story of Cistercian origin. The closest early parallel is on *f.* 81*v* of British Museum MS Addit. 15723, of late 12th c., containing many Cistercian stories. Here a monk of Clairvaux, a doctor, has disdained to eat the coarse food provided and sees the Blessed Virgin give syrup to his less fastidious fellows. A similar story is told in the *Mighty Beginnings of the Cistercians*, Part III, chap. xix (*PL* 185, col. 1077, and cp. also col. 1365). The story of the Fastidious Monk became popular : see also the French poem *Miserere* by the Recluse of Molliens, ed. A.-G. von Hamel, Paris (1885), p. 265 ; Caesarius of Heisterbach, *Miracles*, ed. A. Hilka, III, Bonn (1937), 172.

p. 13

3*f.* **makeden . . . strengðe of.** An idiom (following OFr *faire force de . . .*) used several times in AW : cp. 30,33 ; *f.* 4*r*, etc. **gingiure . . . zedual . . . clowes de gilofre.** All three spices were recommended for (among other ailments) digestive complaints : see G. Frisk, *A ME Translation of Macer Floridus de viribus herbarum*, Uppsala (1947), pp. 179 and 181. The three spices are also named together in the ME lyric ' Annot and John ' (*The Harley Lyrics*, ed. G. L. Brook (1948), p. 32/40).

4. A dei. Formally from OE *on dæg*, ' by day ', but here meaning ' one day ', and providing an earlier example of the analysis into article (or numeral) + noun than those provided in *MED s.* a dai, adai.

5. ifolen o slepe. Past part. of OE *fēolan* (Class III > IV strong verb), ' enter ', but even in LOE in this phrase confused in use with *gefallen*, ' fallen '.

11. of feor, ' from afar ' ; an analytic form of *feorran* : cp. Fr. *de loin*.

13f. ah beon, etc., ' but to be so devoted to it, especially for those called devout to be so devoted. . . .' The author is playing on **ancreful** (and probably on **nomeliche,** ' especially ', but also here ' by name '). *ancreful* is a formation from ME *anger* [ON *angr*, ' distress ', probably influenced by Lat. *angor*], with the pun on *ancre*, ' recluse ' ; the same play on *ancreful* occurs AW *f.* 66r.

15f. Cp. the *Mighty Beginnings of the Cistercians*, Part III, chap. xix, which continues the story referred to on **12,**35 above, with a condemnation of ' those brothers who seem to follow rather the schools of Hippocrates than the schools of Christ ' (*PL* 185, col. 1078). But this taunt was often on Bernard's lips, as in *PL* 183, cols. 938–9, a sermon which may have been recalled here in AW. **desciples.** The *s* is reinserted from Lat. *discipulus* ; *deciples*, as **22,**15, **29,**2,6, is the usual EME form from OFr.

16 Ypocras. The Greek Hippocrates (5th c. B.C.), the ' father of medicine ', reputed author of a collection of clinical works which provided the basis of medical theory and practice throughout the antique and medieval world. **Galien.** Claudius Galen, the Graeco-Roman physician (late 2nd c. A.D.), born in Asia Minor, practised at Alexandria and Rome. In his writings he provided a complete survey of Greek medicine which remained standard for the Christian and Arabic worlds into the 16th c.

18. Prudencia, etc. Rom. 8:6. **Procul,** etc. Job 39:25, also used by Ailred, *On the Anchorite Life*, to which AW now returns, ' " We smell the battle afar off ", and thus we fear the death of the body before it is felt ; so that terrified, we neglect the sickness of the soul which we feel at the present, as if it were more bearable to suffer the fire of lust than a rumbling in the belly ; rather should it be more bearable to shun the wantonness of the flesh in severe and long illness than to be reduced to a healthy and sound servitude to it ' (*PL* 32, col. 1461).

25ff. The doctrine (Aristotelian at far remove) of the Golden Mean, often put to homiletic use : cp. AW *f.* 78r (Salu 127) ; Hall EME, II, 448. AW is still following Ailred, ' I refer to prudence [*discretio*], which is both mother and nurse of all virtues . . . because we often conceal the commerce of pleasure under the false name of prudence. But true prudence is to put the soul before the flesh and where both are in danger, and if salvation for the former cannot be obtained without discomfort for the latter, to neglect the latter for the welfare of the former ' (*PL* 32, col. 1462). Here Ailred may be following

Bernard, Sermon III on the Circumcision (*PL* 183, col. 142) : cp. 1 Tim. 4:8.

30. cheose, infinitive parallel to *don* (28).

31ff. See John 19:39. Nichodemus is introduced apparently through the association of *meosure* and the measure of spices brought to Christ's tomb. With what follows compare an anonymous 12th c. *Meditation on the Passion and Resurrection*, ' These [myrrh and aloes] are indeed bitter things, but they remove corruption ; whereas mortification of the flesh is indeed painful, yet otherwise neither the mind, nor the flesh itself is kept incorrupt. " About a hundred pound " (John 19:39). O good and full measure ! There must be a weighing out between body and soul with most subtle wisdom [*discretione*], that each may rejoice to have full measure to itself and there may be peace and equality between flesh and spirit, so that measure may be maintained and perfection be not lacking ' (*PL* 184, col. 757). The connection between this *Meditation* and AW seems close ; but the spices were often interpreted as bitternesses and as mortifications.

34. Hundret, etc. According to Gregory, *Morals*, Book 30, chap. xxv, 74, hundred is usually to be understood to imply ' the fulness of perfection ' (*PL* 76, col. 565).

p. 14

2, 3. utewið, inwið. Both are characteristic KG forms. The distinction between the control of behaviour and the inner discipline of the spirit runs through AW and is marked in most treatises on asceticism. Ailred in *On the Anchorite Life* deals first (chaps. i–xlvi) with the practice of virtue (*effectus operis*), and in the remainder of the book (chaps. xlvii–lxxvii) with the cultivation of the right disposition of heart (*affectus mentis*), which is nourished by meditation. Part 6 of AW has here reached a turning point, and out of the remaining argument in this part develops the theme of Part 7, but it is characteristic of the development of AW that the break is bridged by continuing with Nichodemus.

7. þe þreo Maries. See Mark 16:1, Luke 24:1, texts often used for Eastertide sermons, and providing the basis for the famous *Quem quaeritis* trope of liturgical drama. In the following passage, AW uses stock material throughout, but no treatment has been found which reproduces exactly the combinations of interpretation and etymology. The German Geoffrey, Abbot of Admont from 1137 to 1165 (an effective and eclectic monastic preacher), using this text (Mark 16:1), etymologises *Magdalena* as *turris*, *Jacobus* as *supplantator*, *Salome* as *pacifica*, and interprets the ointments as salves of contrition, devotion, and love (*PL* 174, cols. 797–8).

8. aromaz through OFr from Lat. *aromata*, which, according to Isidore of Seville in *Etymologies*, Book 17, chap. viii, 1, ' are things of fragrant odour sent from India or Arabia or elsewhere ' (*PL* 82, col. 620).

10. *Amarum mare*, ' bitter sea ' is given by Jerome (*PL* 23, col. 1229) as an etymology of Mary ; there were others.

11. þruppe. At AW *f.* 84r (Salu 137), in treating the bitterness of confession, ' Judith þe spealeð schrift, ase ich ofte habbe iseid, wes Merarihtes dohter, and Iudas þet is ec schrift, wiuede o Thamar.

Merariht & Thamar ba ha spealieð an on ebreische ledene. . . . Bitter sar & schrift, þet an mot cumen of þe oþer, as Judith dude of Merariht, etc.' The author's knowledge of the Hebrew word [Heb. *marah*, ' bitterness '] is likely to have been acquired from one of the collections of etymologies : see Introduction, p. xxvii.

16. See Luke 8:2.

18. The usual interpretation of Magdalene ; so *PL* 23, col. 1214.

19, 21. Hope and the bitterness of wrestling have been associated earlier in AW *f.* 20*r* and *v* (Salu 34–5).

23. The more usual interpretation of Jacob is ' supplanter ' (cp. note on 7 above), but ' wrestler ' is also found, as in Peter Lombard (*PL* 191, col. 1188).

24ff. for þe ȝet . . . wragelunge, ' for those who are still agitated at times by temptations, which are the catches [as in wrestling] of the devil, and have to fight back with a bitter struggle '.

25. þe (first) is the relative particle (with omission of pronoun) parallel with relative *þe* (24), both with antecedent *monie*.

27. No work ascribed to Augustine, genuine or spurious, so far examined has yielded up this quotation. The notion is not uncommonly educed from Exod. 14:5 : cp. AW *f.* 59*r* and *v* (Salu 97–8).

29. Pharaones. MS hParaones. For the occasional uncertainty of KG scribes with *h*, see d'Ardenne, SJ, p. 201.

31. For this construction with neod, see Wilson's note on SW 225.

32f. Based on Ezek. 35:6, which gives however no suggestion of flight. The equivalence of blood and sin, assumed here, is stated at AW *f.* 31*r* (Salu 50) ; also *f.* 32*v* (Salu 53–4).

34. þruppe. Viz. at the beginning of Part 4 on Temptations, AW *f.* 47*v* (Salu 78).

p. 15

1. ei is explained by d'Ardenne, SJ, p. 151, as contraction of OE *ǣnig* in unemphatic use. onont, a characteristic form of KG texts, probably a blend of OE *on-efn* and ON *jamt*, with substitution of *o* before nasal : see Colborn, HM, p. 112.

5. Salome, with the usual interpretation : see 14,7 note.

8ff. A recapitulation of the distinctive bitternesses (i) of penitence at conversion, (ii) during the course of a life of virtue, (iii) in the longing for heaven. Hereafter AW comes to the direct transition to the treatment of Love, by a re-adaptation of the three Maries.

12f. Cp. the 12th c. pseudo-Augustinian *Manual*, chap. xxvii, ' Pour out bitterness and you will be filled with sweetness ' (*PL* 40, col. 936).

13. swetnesse. Cp. swote (14), swotnesse (16). J. H. Fisher, *JEGP* 50 (1951), 326–31, suggests that ME *swote* (Lat. *suavis*), ' agreeable ' (primarily of smell, as here), should be distinguished from ME *swete* (Lat. *dulcis*), ' sweet ' (primarily of taste, as in 23 below).

18ff. See John 2. Cp. Baldwin of Ford (Cistercian Archbishop of Canterbury, 1180–90, died a Crusader in the Holy Land), *Tract on the*

Sermon on the Mount, ' . . . and by the grace of inward sweetness and smoothness coming from above, everything which is bitter is absorbed into joy of the heart, and the waters of tears flow like rivers of honey. So at the suggestion of His mother to Jesus, "They have no wine ", the water of sadness was turned into the wine of joy ' (*PL* 204, col. 508).

24f. Ecclus. 1:29.

27f. Tobit 3:22, with *qui* for Vulgate *quia*.

31f. Prov. 27:7. The so-called Sapiential books of Scripture were ascribed to Solomon—þe wise (24).

34f. Song of Sol. **4:6.**

38f. *Ibid.*, 3:6. The Beloved of the Song was traditionally taken as God's dear spouse, the Church : see Introduction, p. xlix. Nearly a score of expositions of the Song of Solomon remain from the 12th c., several by Englishmen, including Isaac of Stella (*d.* 1165), Gilbert of Hoyland (*d.* 1172)—both were Cistercians—Bishop Gilbert Foliot (*d.* 1188), and Alexander Neckam (*d.* 1217). Usually these commentaries were not intended as exegesis but as expositions of the mystical union of the soul with God, following thus the aim and methods of Bernard in his Sermons on the Song. Courtly material is often incorporated in these works : there are debts to Ovid as well as to Cicero. With the following exposition in AW, cp. Peter of Blois, Sermon IX on the Epiphany, which is indebted to an Epiphany sermon by the Cistercian abbot (*fl.* 1140), Guerricus of Igny (near Rheims) (*PL* 185, cols. 48–9), and provides a train of thought and quotation similar to AW here. The austere life of a certain unnamed holy man is spoken of at some length as exemplifying the bitterness of myrrh, but these austerities become a source of sweetness to him, ' myrrh is for chose at the beginning, incense for those on the way.' Song of Sol. 3:6 and 4:6 are quoted (as in AW). ' In both cases, incense follows and myrrh comes first ' (*PL* 207, col. 588). Cp. **16,2.**

p. 16

4, 5. swotnesse, swetnesse. See note on **15,12.**

10f. Mark 16:1. **non autem recedentes** added by the author.

12f. **þeo beoð cuminde,** etc. The obscurity arises from the identification of *þeos Maries* with *þeose bitternesses* (11), and from too close a following of the Lat. text, ' . . . those bitternesses which men suffer for His love are the approaches (*lit.* the (ones) coming) to anoint our Lord.' For a similar substantival use of *cuminde*, cp. SW 44, ' þe (*relative*) . . . bihalde alle þe cuminde hwuch beo wurðe in ȝong.'

22f. Apparently to be connected with Adam the Scot (see **6,12** note), *On the Way of Life of the Præmonstratensian Canons*, ' Surely from this instance of the tomb, we are expected to enquire in what other places His sacred body was laid. Instantly we recall the virgin's womb, the narrowness of the cradle, the gallows of the cross. These are three places : the tomb is the fourth ' (*PL* 198, col. 471). But cp. also Peter the Cantor, *Verbum Abbreviatum*, chap. lxxxvi (*PL* 205, col. 259), and *Wooing of our Lord*, ' Mi bodi henge wið þi bodi neiled o rode, sperred querfaste wið inne fowr wahes & henge i wile wið þe, & neauer mare of þi rode cume, til þat i deie ' (OE Hom I, 285). An emphasis known to the rhetoricians as *aposiopesis* or *abscisio* (see *ad Her.*, **IV, lix,** 67) is produced in 22, by stopping short and breaking the

sense. cader, Welsh *cadair*, ' frame ', ' cradle ', used also HM 537 and 553.

23. **hetefeste** [OE *hete*, ' hate ' + *fæste*, adv.], a compound peculiar to KG texts.

24. **worltlich,** ' secular', as opposed to ' living in religion '. AW *f.* 6*v* distinguishes the timetable followed *in alle religiuns*, ' in all monastic and regular orders ', from that followed by *preostes of þe worlt*, ' parish and other secular clergy '.

28. **wiðute bruche.** In allusion to the Virgin-birth and to the Resurrection from the sealed tomb.

33ff. Such disclaimers occur several times in AW (*f.* 13*r*, *f.* 17*r*, *f.* 23*r*, *f.* 31*v*, etc.), and in Ailred, *On the Anchorite Life* (*PL* 32, col. 1454, etc.). They may suggest that the author of the Rule had in mind a larger audience than the three sisters, but palliations of over-candid speech (*licentia*) were enjoined in rhetorical training : see *ad Her.*, IV, xxxvii, 49.

35. **inohrea ðe,** ' quickly enough ' [OE *genoh* + form of *hraðe*, ' quick '], common in AW and found in other KG texts.

36. The idea of the soul as a sapling in God's orchard is probably suggested by Isa. 5:1–6 and Jer. 2:21.

p. 17

2. **neoð þet.** A comparable but partial assimilation of *neod* occurs OE Hom I, 9, *neot þet* ; but cp. ON *nauð*.

3. **snakere ð.** A frequentative related to OE *snīcan*, ' creep ' ; cp. AW *f.* 79*r* ; ' tes dogges of helle cume snakerinde ' ; *f.* 89*r* : smit [þe dogge of helle] . . . þet him laði & drede to snecchen eft toward te.'

4. **schunche.** A rare verb, occurring also AW *f.* 65*v* ; SJ 301; *aschunche*, *Harley Lyrics*, ed. Brook, p. 40/45 ; probably a dialectal blend in form and meaning of such words as *schuhten, schunien, schunte, blenchen* : see d'Ardenne, SJ. p. 164.

5f. I.e., be glad if little notice is taken of your austerities. But on the other hand (8f) do not be so careless of what men say of you that you fall into disrepute.

9ff. **þet is . . . wið dede.** Probably an insertion by the reviser of the Rule responsible for AW. It provides an adequate definition of scandal in the ecclesiastical sense : see *Catholic Encyclopedia*, *s.* scandal.

11, 12. **sunegin, sungin.** The latter form is the more normal development from OE *syngian*, ' sin ', but *sunegin* appears more commonly in AW, probably by analogy with *munegin* [OE *mynegian*, ' recall, recount '] : see d'Ardenne, SJ, pp. 166–7. **wið uuel word,** etc. Apparently ' with evil report about her in respect of another ', or ' . . . as it appears to another '. The anchoress should not behave so that even a false report about her behaviour can provide an occasion of sin in another. Throughout the author has insisted on the necessity of maintaining a good reputation : so *f.* 21*v* (Salu 36), *f.* 28*v* (Salu 46) ; and at *f.* 34*r* (Salu 56) advice is given in dealing with *misdede oðer missahe*.

13. Cp. 5,2ff.

14. beon, infinitive after *ahen* (12). **danger.** See **7,**17 note. **Slurl,** scarcely a baptismal name ; its force is indicated by *NED s.* slurry, *vb.* ' dirty, smear ' ; slur, slurry, *n.* ' thin, sloppy mud '—all of obscure origin, but *NED* compares MDu *slore* (Dutch *sloor, sloerie*), ' a sluttish woman '.

16. Mountains are often interpreted as types of the higher spiritual life. AW *f.* 47*v* (Salu 78) speaks of ' the hill of high and holy life '. Cp. *f.* 52*r* (Salu 86) ; and at *f.* 44*r* (Salu 71) is an exhortation to ' climb hills with Christ '. A variety of interpretation for *mons* is provided by Gregory, *Morals,* Book 33, chap. i (*PL* 76, cols. 668–9).

17ff. Song of Sol. 2:8. The sense of the passage is involved because of the attempt to combine two mutually excluding metaphors : (i) that the beloved (Christ) leaps on and tramples the mountains, which signify those who lead the most arduous spiritual life ; (ii) that Christ Himself is the type of the highest life (and thus a mountain) who was shamefully trampled upon and abused by the world. On this use of *inculcatio,* see Introduction, p. lxx. Translate, ' My love comes leaping, she says, upon the mountains, that is, tramples them, disfigures them, permits them to be trodden on, to be grievously ill-treated and shows upon them His own footprints, so that one may follow His track in them to discover how He was trodden on as the footprints on Him show.' Peter of Celles provides an elaborate sermon on this theme of following in the footsteps of Christ (*PL* 202, cols. 725ff).

20. tuki . . . al to wundre. A set phrase in KG texts : cp. **21,**38. For this use of *wunder* developed in LOE, see Hall, EME II, 256.

21. trudde, pres. subjunctive (*truddeð,* 3 sg. pres., *f.* 63*r*) from OE *tryddian,* ' step ', ' follow the track ', cp. *NED s.* trod, *vb.*

22. ifinden, infinitive dependent on *trudde.*

23. Muntgiw. OE *munt-geof, -giu,* Lat. *mons Jovis* ; but the word is used in OE for the Alps in general, usually encountered by Englishmen on the pilgrim route Boulogne–Metz– Gt St Bernard–Aosta–Milan to Rome (see G. B. Parks, *The English Traveller to Italy,* I, Rome (1954), pp. 6, 46–7, 186, etc.), and hence the name *Muntgiw* is sometimes restricted to peaks along this route. But Honorius of Autun (*PL* 172, col. 130) and others (better acquainted than the English with the path to Rome up the Rhine valley) give this name of the Mount of Jove to St Gotthard.

24. Armenie. In AV and Vulgate, Armenia is the name given to the Biblical Hebrew Ararat, the highland region lying between the Black and Caspian Seas, containing the peak upon which Noah's Ark came to rest.

24ff. ' The hills which are lower, those, as the lady says, He leaps over, neither does He rely on them so much because of their weakness ; nor might they endure such trampling, and He leaps over them, avoids them, turns aside from them, until they grow higher.'

28ff. For the metaphor of the shadow, see **11,**2 note. Guerricus of Igny, preaching on Song of Sol. 2:17, provides various interpretations of shadow ' in the manner of our master Bernard ', and includes this idea of the shadow of Christ lying on the mountains of spiritual life (*PL* 185, col. 186).

29. lanhure. Also **21,**35 ; in KG texts replaces—but not invariably (*hure & hure*, AW *f*. 31*r*)—the more usual ME *hure & hure*, ' at least '. *lanhure* is apparently a reduction of exclamatory *lā* (' lo ! ') *ond hure* [OE *huru*, adv. ' however '].

35ff. 2 Cor. 4:9–10.

38ff. A recapitulation of earlier themes : cp. 5,33ff.

p. 18

2ff. Part 6 is to end with proof by *exempla* : see Introduction, p. lxiv.

3. Cp. John 21:16–17.

4f. Gregory, *Homilies on the Gospels*, Book 3, Sermon xxx, 1 (*PL* 76, col. 1220), in constant medieval use, quoted e.g. by Peter the Cantor, *Verbum Abbreviatum* (*PL* 205, cols. 277, 278, 284, 342).

6f. Amor omnia, etc. Adapted from Augustine, Sermon lxx, ' All horrid and savage things, love makes easy and insignificant ' (*PL* 38, col. 444): in varying form a 12th c. commonplace ; so Peter of Blois, *Twelve Benefits of Tribulation* (*PL* 207, col. 993), and Peter Comestor, Sermon xvi, ' Love and do what you like [see 19,35 note] ; all difficulties are made easy for the lover ' (*PL* 198, col. 1767). Cp. also *PL* 184, col. 1164.

11ff. No doubt many hermits and recluses indulged in similar practices, but the austerities of this unknown holy man closely resemble those recorded by Peter Damian of the Italian, Dominic, the so-called *loricatus* (955–1060), who ' wore for about three years an iron corslet next to the skin, but girt about the body with two iron hoops and his arms fastened by another pair ' (*PL* 144, col. 1017). By the 12th c. this type of austerity had spread to England. Much the same sort of equipment was worn by Edmund Rich (*c*.1170–1240), Archbishop of Canterbury from 1234 : see V. McNabb, *MLR* 11 (1916), 6–7, but also H. E. Allen, *PMLA* 33 (1918), 544–5. An earlier *loricatus* in England was a William, knight of Hugh Lacy, who *c*.1100 retired to Llanthony (Monmouthshire) and wore ' an habergeon with which to defend himself against the darts of the Enemy '. Godric of Finchale wore out three shirts of chain-mail during his long seclusion. On *loricati* see R. M. Clay, *Hermits and Anchorites of England* (1914), p. 119, and M. Bell, *John, Abbot of Ford, Life of Wulfric of Haselbury*, *Somerset Record Society*, XLVII (1933), pp. 133–4.

12. here, n. (see *NED* haire), haircloth, especially as made up into hairshirts, worn next to the skin. Hairshirts are recommended at AW *f*. 37*v* (Salu 61) ; but cp. the passage from *f*. 113*v* referred to 11,16 note.

19. wi[ð e]uene. MS wiuene sarest, ' sorest of women ' (so also T), has no relevance in this context. The scribes of N and C attempting apparently a correction of the same reading *wiuene sarest*, wrote *monne sarest*, which improved nothing but the gender. The emendation proposed implies at some earlier stage of transcription the omission of *ðe*, which is readily understandable. *euene* (cp. **13**,36) is in common use in KG texts (see *MED* s. evene), deriving from ON *efnl*, ' material ', ' means ', ' state '. The nuances of meaning in ON are various ; so too in ME, where there were apparently associations added from adj. *even* (see *MED* s. even, adj. 12.(e)), and also from OE *hæfen*, n. ' having ' (cp. *NED* s. having, *n*.3). Within the range of EME usage, a meaning of ' in bitterest fashion ' for *wið euene sarest* here is acceptable.

21. luue as subject to *makeð*. ' Love brings that about . . . that not for anything that God might do hurtfully towards him—though He should cast him into hell with the lost—could he ever, it seems to him, love Him the less.' Several contemplatives of the later medieval centuries affirmed their attachment to God in similar terms : see H. E. Allen, *The Book of Margery Kempe*, EETS 212 (1940), 340.

25. mat, from OFr *mat*, originally ' mated at chess '.

29. Gregory, *Pastoral Care*, Book 3, chap. x (*PL* 77, col. 63), and also in his *Letters* (*PL* 77, col. 900) ; the quotation is made in Lat. AW *f.* 77*r*.

31. þruppe. Viz. at AW *f.* 77*r* (Salu 126) ; cp. **29,**24.

p. 19

2ff. Cp. the iterative construction with *al* which begins Part 6 and 15ff below.

4f. 1 Tim. 4:8. But Vulgate reads *exercitatio*, and *utilis est* for *ualet*. The same quotation has already been applied to the Outer Rule at AW *f.* 1*v* (Salu 2).

7ff. 1 Cor. 13:1 and 3, but rearranged.

11. ledene. Already in OE *læden* [Lat. *latina*] had acquired a general sense of ' tongue ', ' language '.

15ff. A desert father, an abbot Moses (probably a Libyan of the 4th c.) was introduced as speaker in *Collations* 1 and 2 by John Cassian (*c.*360–435), who after visiting the famous monastic communities of the deserts, introduced Eastern habits and thought into the monasteries of southern France, and thence they came into Western Christendom generally. Cassian's writings had been known in Anglo-Saxon England, but the type of spirituality of which he bears record became particularly attractive in the 12th c. (see also Introduction, p. xlvii). In *Collation* 1, Cassian investigated the purpose of the monastic life. Even as the farmer continues his work through bad weather because he knows the end of his labours, so should the monk (chap. ii). The aim is purity of heart (chap. iv). For this end everything else is to be endured (chap. v). 1 Cor. 13:1–3 is quoted (cp. 7ff here). Hardship is of no avail without charity, ' which consists in purity alone ' (cp. **20,**10) (chap. vi). ' Fasts, vigils, solitary life, meditation on the Scriptures, it behoves us to practise these, on account of the principal aim, and that is purity of heart which is charity. . . . So anyone will fashion . . . for himself the tools (*ferramenta*) of an occupation, not so that he may possess them superfluously, nor simply for the advantage of possessing them, but so that he may usefully attain through their use to practical achievement and the end . . . for which they are instrumental' (chap. vii) (*PL.* 49, cols. 481–90 : cp. also *Collation* 21, chap. xv, col. 1191). Chapters i-iv of *Collation* 1 are used in a pseudo-Anselmian ascetic tract (*PL* 158, cols. 1021–3). But much the same teaching based on 1 Cor. 13 can be found in Bernard (*PL* 182, cols. 905–8) ; William of St Thierry (*PL* 184, col. 322) ; Richard of St Victor (*PL* 196, col. 1206), and elsewhere. But AW seems to make a direct if not close verbal contact with Cassian's *Collation.*

23. loki is subjunctive ; **makeð** (unexpectedly) indicative.

24. monglunge. Verbal noun from an infinitive *monglin* (apparently only in AW), a frequentative formation from OE *gemong*, ' mixture ', ' intercourse '.

26. woreð, cp. *wori* (33). Both are to be connected with OE *wērig*, ' weary ' and *wōrian*, ' wander ', ' fall to pieces ' : see J. R. R. Tolkien, *RES* **1** (1925), 212. **þe ehnen of þe heorte.** Also *f. 23v, f. 72r*, etc., *oculus cordis* or *mentis*, ' the mind's eye ', frequently found in spiritual writers (cp. Eph. 1:18). Such transfers of sense to spirit (producing even ' your heart's nose ', AW *f.* 58v), provided the basis of the psychological theory of the exact correspondence between the *homo interior* and the physical man.

28. twa þinges, subject to **makieð.** Bernard, *Tractate on the Office and Duty of Bishops*, chap. iii (*PL* 182, col. 817).

31. ' The love of God and the love of our neighbour are distinct as precepts but in practice fall together ' : so Augustine (*PL* 38, col. 1223), Gregory (*PL* 76, col. 1199), and often repeated in 12th c.

33f. sit. On this use see *NED s.* sit, *vb.* B. 15. **Omnia munda,** etc., Titus 1:15.

35f. Augustine, *On the Epistle of John*, Tract vii (*PL* 35, col. 2033). This famous phrase is often found in 12th c. writers : Ailred (*PL* 195, col. 612), Adam the Scot (*PL* 198, col. 516), Peter of Blois (*PL* 207, col. 774). Cp. **18,** 6f note, and see H. E. Allen, *PMLA* **33** (1918), 519, 530. But the phrase could be easily put to dangerous uses ; witness the protests of Hugh of St Victor (*PL* 176, col. 546) and Richard of St Victor (*PL* 196, col. 323), and probably the author of AW felt it necessary to add his restrictive explanation *uoluntate rationis*—' by the determination of reason '.

p. 20

2. ear. At **19,**27ff. What follows here is a definition in the Augustinian style much favoured by 12th c. devotional writers : as William of St Thierry, ' When indeed I love anything for thy sake, I do not love that thing but rather love thee, for whose sake I love what I love ' (*PL* 184, col. 373). But Bernard's description in *Short Commentary* ' of a pure affection ' is especially notable, ' by which God is loved only on account of God, nor is anything to be loved with God, except in God and on account of God ' (*PL* 184, col. 429). J. Leclercq, *Études sur S. Bernard*, p. 120, note 2, shows that this particular formula was often taken up by Bernard's successors.

6f. mete oðer clað, etc. Apparently a reference to the worldly goods (cp. 1 Tim. 7:8) and servants with which the anchoresses have been provided by their friend : see 7,17 note.

8. Augustine, *Confessions*, Book 10, chap. xxix (*PL* 32, col. 796), quoted in 12th c. devotional works such as *Soliloquies of the Soul with God* (*PL* 40, col. 880).

10. On this equation of purity and love, see Cassian's phrases quoted in note on **19,**15ff and Introduction, p. xlvii.

11f. I þis is al þe strengðe, etc. The same phrases occur **29,**16ff and in the Introduction to the Rule, where the author calls the Inner Rule guarding the heart, the rule of charity, as described in 1 Tim. 1:5, ' out of a pure heart, and of a good conscience, and of faith unfeigned ' (AW *f.* 1v (Salu 1–2)).

12. Rom. 13:10.

13. Gregory, *Homilies on the Gospels*, Book 2, Homily xxvii (*PL* 76, col. 1205), quoted by Adam the Scot (*PL* 198, col. 515).

16. Mihales weie. The archangel Michael considered not so much in his original rôle as angel of death, but chiefly as the conductor of souls after death : see *DAC, s.* Anges psychopompes. In representations of the Doom, Michael is sometimes shown superintending the weighing of the soul against its evil deeds (see E. Mâle, *L'art religieux du XIIIe siècle en France*, 4th ed. Paris (1919), pp. 438–41), but much less commonly in England than in France, according to P. Brieger, *English Art 1216–1307* (1957), p. 181. Þeo þe meast luuieð, etc. reproduces an Augustinian saying : cp. *PL* 40, col. 1055.

18. In Anglo-Norman courts the steward, *dapifer*, one of the great officers of state, had charge of the royal hall and its provisioning : see D. M. Stenton, *English Society in Early Middle Ages*, pp. 22f.

19. freolec. Formations with *-lec* [ON *-leikr*] usually replacing OE *-nes* in abstract nouns from adjectives are found in KG texts, cp. *feierlec*. But OE *-lac* is retained in compounds formed from noun or verb ; so *fearlac, schendlac*.

20f. elles ne kepte, etc., otherwise God would set no store by her offices. *hiren*, disjunctive ' hers ', acquiring *-n* by analogy with *min, þin*.

22ff. Now are advanced reasons why God is to be loved (see Introduction, pp. l–li), primarily in gratitude for gifts received and promised. Alcher of Clairvaux *(fl.* 1160), *On the Love of God*, chap. xvii (*PL* 40, col. 861), provides close verbal parallels here ; but this exceedingly common 12th c. devotional theme is not treated systematically in AW ; it is used as a brief introduction to the theme of the wooing. A similar application can be seen in Baldwin of Ford, *Tractate 10* on Song of Sol. 8, ' " Set me as a seal [*signaculum*, taken by Baldwin as ' heraldic device '] in thy heart "—as if He should say, " Love me, as I love thee. Keep me in thy mind, in thy memory, in thy longing, in thy sighing, in thy groans and sobs. Remember, man, what I have created for thee, how far I set thee over other creatures . . . how I set everything under thy feet [Ps. 8:7 ; cp. 27]. Remember not only how much I did for thee but what hard and shameful things I suffered for thee, and take care lest thou dost evil in return, lest thou lovest not thyself. For who so loves thee as I ? Who made thee but I ? Who as defender of thy life took upon him the peril of combat save I ? [cp. **21,**31]. To make exchange of love with me, extend thy arms, put forth thy strength, set me as an emblem upon thy arms. Fight for me, as I for thee . . ." ' [*PL* 204, col. 514]. Particularly with 24–6, cp. ' Crist us ȝef moni freo ȝeue seoððen he com on þisse midelerd, nawhit for ure ernunge, but for his muchele mildheortnesse, er we were forgult in to helle þurh Adam ure alde feder ' (OE Hom I, 19).

27ff. Ps. 8:7–8.

29. þruppe. Presumably at 4ff above.

30f. ȝet te uuele, etc. An emphatic chiasmus, ' yet earth, sea, and sun serve even the evil '. Cp. Matt. 5:45, Hugh of St Victor, *Soliloquy on the Pledge of the Soul* (*PL* 176, cols. 957–8), and Introduction, p. l.

32f. Se heh . . . to se lahe, etc. This antithesis of ' high ' and ' low ' is a favourite in KG and related texts : cp. **26**,12, HM 342, OE Hom I, 187, 211, etc.

33f. Eph. 5:23 fused with Gal. 2:20.

35. **leofmon** translating *ecclesiam* assumes the traditional interpretation of the lovers in Song of Sol. as Christ and the Church : see Introduction, p. xlix.

37. **Earst**. On the divisions of the argument, ' Why men ought to love God ', see **22**,36 note and Introduction, pp. xlviii–li.

p. 21

1ff. The allegory of God (or Christ) as a king wooing the individual soul as bride is ancient, and indeed a natural enough analogy ; see Introduction, p. xlix. It was elaborated from the 3rd c. by Origen and in Eastern monastic writers, but does not seem to have been used in the West much before the 12th c. An early adaptation is provided by Macarius the Egyptian, Homily 15 (*PG* 34, col. 575), who explains how a rich and mighty king woos and wins a beggar maid. In the 12th c. Hugh of St Victor, *Soliloquy on the Pledge of the Soul*, turns the story of Esther into a similar allegory (*PL* 176, cols. 964–5). See also Stephen of Grandmont, *Book of Sentences*, chap. xix (*PL* 204, col. 1131). Anselm provides similar parables in his *Similitudes* (*PL* 159, cols. 618, 640), also Ailred, *Sermones inediti*, ed. Talbot, p. 40. But in these allegories, variations on the King Cophetua and the Beggar-maid story, the centre of interest is marriage not the wooing. AW shows the modifications effected by the new chivalric and courtly conventions. The king becomes a royal knight, the soul, the highborn lady of romance, who is disposed to receive the polite and passionate advances of the lover with disdain. Sister Marie de Lourdes de May, *The Allegory of the Christ-Knight in English Literature*, Catholic University of America, Washington (1932), sought on rather scanty evidence to show that Bernard was influential in establishing the new conventions in devotional writing. See further 9ff, note.

2ff. Reminiscences of the parable of the Wicked Husbandmen (Matt. 21) are incorporated to illustrate the belief that the prophets and patriarchs of the Old Testament were the forerunners of Christ.

4. **leattres isealet**. Letters from the sovereign to a particular person for a particular purpose were closed and sealed on the outside (*litterae clausae*) and recorded in Close Rolls.

5. **leattres iopenet**. Letters patent were addressed by the sovereign ' to all to whom these presents shall come ', to indicate the grant of some privilege and to proclaim it publicly. The distinction between letters closed and patent is aptly applied to the Scriptures, for the Old Testament was considered ' a wrapping up ' of the New, and the New Testament an unfolding of the Old : see e.g. Augustine, *City of God*, Book 16, chap. xxvi. **wrat wið his ahne blod**, i.e. by the Passion. This conceit (based on 1 Col. 2:13–14), by which the Atonement is spoken of as a written legal instrument, was elaborated later as the Charter of Christ, drawn up in imitation of a deed of gift : see M. C. Spalding, *The ME Charters of Christ*, Bryn Mawr Monograph 15 (1914). In the *Long Charter*, the deed is executed on the parchment of Christ's skin, the pens were the scourges, the letters the wounds, the sealing-wax the blood.

6. saluz. The greeting with which a letter written in Anglo-Norman would commonly begin ; but here there is also the play on the meaning ' salvation '.

9ff. Wilbur Gaffney, *PMLA* 46 (1931), 155–69, collected 13 versions of this *exemplum* of which AW provides the earliest and *Piers Plowman* the most famous. Later, Christ is usually presented as a knight in tourney, but in AW the likeness is worked out chiefly in contemporary terms of siege warfare. At *f.* 29*r* (Salu 49) the anchoress has been compared with a lady of a castle : see **10,11** note.

10. eorðene castel. The figurative castle of man's body. But during the 12th c., particularly during the reign of Stephen (1135–54), local defences in England often consisted of earthworks crowned with wooden stockades. From the end of the 11th c. the great royal castles had been built of stone.

13. beawbelez. According to A. T. Baker, *MÆ* 2 (1933), 137–9, *beaubelet* is not to be given a primary meaning ' plaything ', as if it were a reduplicated form of OFr *bel*, ' pretty ' ; instead it refers to ' some much more costly object suitable for a present from one prince to another '. Roger of Howden, *Chronicle*, ed. W. Stubbs, RS IV (1871), 83, distinguishes Richard I's separate legacies of his castles, his ready monies, and his *baubella*, ' personal valuables '.

15. as on unrecheles. The same idiom as AW *f.* 26*r* : ' Crist spekeð as o wreaððe, & seið as o grim hoker & o scarn to þe ancre . . . seið as o grome & o scarn. . . .' In these examples the prep. *o(n)* is used with nouns, but a similar construction appears with negatived adj. in OE *on ungearwe*, ' at unawares ' (*Sweet's Anglo-Saxon Reader*, 10th ed. (1946), p. 25/69), and in Orm, *Dedication*, 82, *onn unnitt & onn idell*. But perhaps *unrecheles* is to be considered a noun, cp. the use of *ʒemeles*, ' heedlessness ', AW *ff.* 12*r*, 56*v*, 80*r*, etc. ; SW (R) 387. In OE, *receleas* and *ʒemeleas* are frequently associated : see BT & Suppl. *s. vv.* The twice-negatived form *unrecheles* is of a type with *unroles*, ' restless ', HM 526 ; *unwitlese*, ' witless ', SM, p. 20/13 : see *NED s.* un- *prefix*, 5.a.

19. Cp. Ps. 44:2. Often applied to Christ.

24. Al þis ne heold nawt. On the intransitive use of this vb. in negative (or interrogative) sentences, see *NED s.* hold, *vb.* 25.

30. scheome deað (cp. *scheome sunnen f.* 87*v*). The feminine noun [OE *scamu*] retains an indefinite genitive force, although indistinguishable in form from the first element of a compound. Cp. *heorte blod* (**22**,31), *luue boc* (**15**,38, **17**,17), *luue gleames* (**26**,17), etc.

35f. ' . . . that thou love me at least for the sake of that same deed, (when I am) dead, even if thou wouldst not (when I was) alive.'

p. 22

1f. of uueles cunnes cunde is completely analysable, see Glossary, *s. cunnes* ; but the retention of inflexion of *uueles* anticipates the development of late ME fossilised forms such as *anescunnes*, *wolueskynnes*, etc.

6. goddeden, a compound established in OE ; cp. Lat. *benefactum*.

8f. The reference to past times in **as weren sumhwile cnihtes iwunet to donne** is at first sight puzzling, for the earliest record of an historical tournament in England at which ladies were present, i.e. of something which can plausibly be described as a love-tourney, is in 1215 at Staines, where the prize of a bear was presented by a lady : for the early history of the tournament in England see N. Denholm-Young, *Studies in Medieval History presented to Sir F. M. Powicke* (1948), pp. 240–68, and D. M. Stenton, *English Society in the Early Middle Ages*, pp. 78–87. Such tournaments as were held in the late 12th c. were conducted as mass mêlées. Even on the Continent, where development went faster, the presence of ladies is not usually noted before the 13th c. It seems then that AW is looking back to an ideal past, and that the reference is to Geoffrey of Monmouth, *History of the Kings of Britain*, Book 9, chap. xiii ; see H. E. Allen, *MLR* **29** (1934), 173. Arthur's coronation is described. ' The knights . . . were famous for feats of chivalry . . . and the women no less celebrated for their wit . . . and esteemed none worthy of their love but only such as had given proof of valour in three several battles.' In the next chapter comes an account of the coronation festivities, when the knights devised an entertainment in imitation of a fight on horseback : ' and the ladies placed on top of the walls as spectators . . . darted their amorous glances at the courtiers the more to encourage them '. Geoffrey's account may have reflected some aspects of tournaments held in Stephen's reign, but in the main is an idealisation which was to be taken over in turn by Wace and Layamon. See J. S. P. Tatlock, *The Legendary History of Britain*, Berkeley and Los Angeles (1950), pp. 301–2.

11. Cp. Bernard, Sermon v on Ps. 91 (*Qui habitat*), ' Not unfittingly . . . is the grace of the divine protection compared with a shield [using Ps. 5:12 as in 21], which in the upper part is wide and broad to guard the head and shoulders, but lower down is narrower . . . and tapers towards the shins ' (*PL* 183, col. 196). Earlier AW has counselled the recluses to make the Passion their shield, *f.* 80r (Salu 130).

13. In older crucifixes, the feet of Christ are affixed separately to the cross, side by side, and this style persists as the orthodox fashion until at least 1300 : see P. Thoby, *Le Crucifix*, Nantes (1959). But at some time about 1200 it became fashionable to represent the feet, one laid on top of the other, fastened with one nail : see B. White, *MLR* 40 (1945), 207. A. Andersson, *English Influence in Norwegian and Swedish figure sculpture in wood, 1220–70*, Stockholm (1949), pp. 286–8, says, ' Our knowledge of the origin of the new crucifix type is very incomplete ', and suggests that devotional writings should be investigated further. An early reference to the fastening of the feet with one nail is to be found in Meditation 10 in the Anselmian collection (*PL* 158, cols. 761–2). According to A. Wilmart, *Auteurs spirituels et textes dévots du moyen âge latin*, Paris (1932), p. 194, note 4, the earliest version of this Meditation is found in Bibl. Roy. Brussels MS 5246–52, which he dates at the beginning of the 13th or possibly at end of the 12th c. Cp. also T. S. R. Boase, *English Art 1100–1216*, p. 286. After monies wene suggests the novelty of the 3-nail crucifix. It seems likely that the iconographic change was a by-product of the new devotion to the physical Passion of Christ, which flourished outside the monasteries in the last decades of the 12th c., at first particularly in the Low Countries, but also in England, and was exemplified most astonishingly in the stigmatisation of Mary of Oignes, and later of Francis of Assisi (who is credited with a belief in the 3 nails).

16. **habben ibeon his siden.** The phrase is explained by John of Salisbury, *Policraticus*, ed. C. C. Webb (1922), Book 5, chap. ii, 1, 283, ' Those who always attend a prince are likened to his sides ' ; and Peter of Blois, *Twelve Benefits of Tribulation*, ' . . . by " side ", brother is to be understood ' (*PL* 207, col. 999). The flight of the disciples contravened the spirit of feudal loyalty : cp. AW *f.* 28*r* (Salu 46), *f.* 30*r* (Salu 49).

18. Matt. 26:56.

19f. Lam. 3:65.

21f. Ps. 5:12 : see note on 11 above.

25. Isa. 53:7. The conclusion of this verse had been used AW, *f.* 33*r* (Salu 54).

26ff. The necessity of the Passion as the only possible means of our redemption was debated in the schools of Paris in the 12th c. as an issue raised by the teaching of Abelard. Peter of Poitiers, Chancellor of the University (*d.* 1205), in his *Sentences* (*c.*1175), Book 14, chap. xix, asks, ' Could Christ have saved us in any other way ? ' and answers, ' He could not have saved us in any way more fitting, for He could do nothing which should more move us to love Him than that He should die for us ' (*PL* 211, cols. 1209–10).

27. ȝeoi. An emphatic form of *ȝe*, in replying to a negative proposition ; occurs also *f.* 90*v* (twice). On the phonology, see note by Wilson on SW 245.

33f. In the 12th c. shields were occasionally made of iron, sometimes of *cuir bouilli*, most usually of wood covered with leather. Early in the century they were commonly kite-shape, but later were becoming shorter and equilateral. Heraldic devices on shields appeared in the first half of the century, and were elaborated with the development of the tournament.

36f. **hire,** *sc. þe rode* (35). If the heading **Eft þe þridde reisun** is taken to introduce the theme of the *memoria* of Christ (see Introduction, pp. li–lii), **22**,36 to **23**,7, then the first reason why we should love God would be contained in **20**,37 to **22**,3 (on the proper response to a suitor making honourable proposals), and the second, in **22**,4–36 (on the return of love to the champion who has actually performed so much for us). It is less likely that *þe þridde reisun* should be restricted simply to the interpretation of the ' shield ' ; but then the third use of the shield as a memorial, would follow upon its use (i) as defence (10ff), (ii) as a means of exaltation (20ff).

p. 23

2. **þe crucifix,** usually, by the end of the 12th c. set on a rood screen at the entrance to the chancel, flanked by the figures of the Virgin and St John, forming what in AW *f* 8*v* is called *þe muchele rode*. But here and throughout the author has in mind a more intimate use of the crucifix within the cell. Small crucifixes for devotional purposes seem to have come into use during the 12th c. ; see L. Gougaud, *Dévotions et pratiques ascétiques du moyen âge*, pp. 74–8. In AW *f.* 37*r* (Salu 60) the anchoresses are recommended to have a likeness of Christ and often to look upon it and kiss the places of the wounds. Ailred, *On the Anchorite Life*, desires his sister to have no other ornament or image than ' the figure of the Saviour hanging on the Cross . . . ;

with His extended arms He invites you to His embraces in which you delight ' [cp. 27,3ff] (*PL* 32, col. 1463) ; before this crucifix she should prostrate herself in prayer (*ibid.*, cols. 1456, 1460). Similar use of the crucifix was made by the recluses Godric of Finchale, (see *Nova Legenda Anglie*, ed. C. Horstman (1901) I, 481, 487), Bartholomew of Farne (*ibid.*, p. 102), Henry of Coquet (*ibid.*, II, 23). Used thus, the crucifix often became the focus of a sense experience which induced trance or ecstasy.

4ff. Cp. Bernard, Sermon lxi on Song of Sol., a sermon with which the author of AW shows acquaintance, *f.* 79*v* (Salu 129–30), ' Men pierced His hands and His feet and with the lance gashed His side and through these openings I am permitted to suck the honey from the rock . . . that is, to taste and see how sweet is the Lord. . . . The mystery of His heart is revealed through the wounds of His body. . . . What more clearly than thy wounds, O Lord, proclaim that thou art sweet, gentle, and of great mercy ? ' (*PL* 183, col. 1072), also pseudo-Augustinian *Manual* (*PL* 40, col. 960), and *Wooing of our Lord*, with reference to the wound in the side, ' A swete Ihesu, þu oppnes me þin herte for to cnawe witerliche & in to reden trewe luue lettres, for þer i mai openlich seo hu muchel þu me luuedes ' (OE Hom I, 283). See Introduction, p. lxxiii.

9ff. This classification of loves is apparently the author's own, but there are many classifications in 12th c. writings : see E. Gilson, *The Mystical Theology of St Bernard*, Eng. trans. (1940), pp. 245–6, and the list could be greatly extended outside Bernard. In AW the classification is rhetorical ; see Introduction, p. lx. J. H. Fisher, *Tretyse of Loue*, EETS 223 (1951), p. 149, provides a number of parallels to the first three loves and suggests (p. 150) that the addition of the fourth ' is an echo of the debate on the relationship between body and soul ' current at this time. Basically the division of loves is Aristotelian (cp. *Ethics*, Book 8, chaps. vii and xii). For the use of a similar classification, cp. Baldwin of Ford, *Tractate* 8, *On the Wound of Love*, ' The father loves his sons as his sweetest pledge, and the mother cannot be unmindful of the children of her womb. On each side an indissoluble bond . . . joins comrades together. Husband and wife subordinate the individual ties of blood. . . . But than these the love of Christ is more violent, deeper, more intimate, intense, penetrating, compassionate, sweeter, stronger, more ardent ' (*PL* 204, cols. 478–9) ; and Richard of St Victor, *Four Steps of Violent Love* (highly popular in England later) : ' Therefore let us recognise the transcendence of the love of Christ, which exceeds or even excludes the love of parents, the love of offspring, the affection of a wife, and in addition converts even the very soul of man into an object for his own hate ' (*PL* 196, col. 1207).

13f. An allusion to the old motif, found in the classical story of Damon and Pythias, of a friend who pledges his life for his friend (as in the ' bond ' story of *The Merchant of Venice*). **i Giwerie** will carry a number of meanings here : (i) in pawn with the Jews ; (ii) born in Judaea, the scene of the Incarnation ; (iii) delivered into the hands of the Jews who crucified Him. The Jews in Henry II's reign had had a recognised place in the national economy and were much used by the king in the collection of money. From the beginning of Richard I's reign (1189), outrages directed against the financial monopoly of the Jews were numerous. Hatred was intensified by the fall of Jerusalem and during the preparations for the Third Crusade (1189–92). On the sharp growth of intellectual hostility to the Jews during the late 12th c. see R. W. Hunt, *Studies presented to Sir F. M. Powicke*, pp. 146–9.

17. **fordede.** Probably formed on model of Lat. *profectio* ; see *MED* s. for(e)-dede.

22f. Cp. HM 608 ; ' þu forhorest te wið þe unwiht of helle.' Similarly, Anselm, Meditation 3, ' Espoused of old to the king of heaven, thou hast become the whore of the fiends of hell ' (*PL* 158, col. 726) ; Hugh of St Victor, *Soliloquy of the Pledge of the Soul* (*PL* 176), col. 961.

23f. **feole ȝeres & dahes,** 'for many a full year'. 'A year and a day', a legal phrase still current, usually indicating the time of expiry of a permissible term, here presumably the term during which forgiveness for the adultery might have been reasonably looked for.

26ff. Jer. 3:1.

30f. A loose reference to the parable of the Prodigal Son, Luke 15:20.

35. Apparently a summary reference to Augustine, *City of God*, Book 1, chaps. xvi–xvii, to which will also refer a similar ascription to Augustine in *Vices and Virtues*, ed. Holthausen. p. 131. On the disputed scholastic question of God's power to restore lost virginity, see Peter of Poitiers, *Sentences*, Book 3, chap. xxvii (*PL* 211, cols. 1127–30).

36. **bitweonen** MS bitweonen bituhhen. *bitweone(n)* is the usual form in AW ; *bituhhen* occurs occasionally. The double writing is probably a scribal slip ; the collocation *betwixt and between* (adv.) is not noted in *NED* s. betwixt, B.3. before the 19th c.

p. 24

2. Job 12:23.

5ff. Cp. Anselm of Bury (nephew of the Archbishop, Anselm of Canterbury ; abbot of Bury St Edmunds 1121–48), Meditation 4, in the Anselmian *Book of Prayers and Meditations*, ' A human father and mother are wont to have great affection for those whom they beget ; and if they perceive that the children are troubled by some disease or bodily sickness they will willingly spend money to restore them to health ' ; but Christ does more to cure us (*PL* 158, col. 732). H. E. Allen, *Select English Writings of Richard Rolle* (1931), p. 134, notes in this same figure of the bath of blood, a recurrence of an ancient motif in folklore (as in ME romance *Amis and Amiloun*). Bathing in blood is spoken of as a cure for leprosy in stories of Constantine the Great and of Richard the Lionheart. Deadly sin is often referred to metaphorically as a leprosy ; cp. Hall EME I, 218/141ff. So here the blood of Christ provides the bath to cure the leprosy of sin. In this paragraph there are several phrases which recall 12th c. discussions on confession.

11. **þreo beaðes.** Viz. of baptism, of penitence (as explained in AW Part 6), of redemption (by the blood of Christ). The division is based on 1 John 5:8 ; cp. Alan of Lille, *PL* 210, col. 717. Gregory very commonly speaks of tears as washing away the stains of sin ; see J. Turmel, *Histoire des dogmes*, VI, Paris (1936), pp. 282ff.

17f. Rev. 1:5.

20f. Isa. 49:15. This passage bears a close resemblance to Peter of Blois, *Twelve Benefits of Tribulation*, ' Consider then that Jesus kept in mind the scars of His wounds which He suffered for you, as if a knot were made on a girdle to keep something in mind. As He himself said, " I will not forget thee ; in my hands I have written thee " ' [Isa. 49:16 ; (cp. 23 below)] (*PL* 207, col. 996). Further investigation is necessary into the relationship between AW and the writings of Peter of Blois (born in France, studied at Bologna, taught in Sicily and at Paris, employed in royal and ecclesiastical service in England, archdeacon of London and Bath, died 1204 ; a learned and voluminous writer ; an assiduous and elegant plagiarist ; for bibliography, see de Ghellinck, *L'Essor*, p. 125).

23f. Isa. 49:16.

29ff. The love and unity of the soul and the body are often strongly asserted in the 12th c., no doubt to counter the sharp revival of Manichean ways of thought ; see Introduction, pp. xli, lv. Cp. AW *f.* 50*r* (Salu 82), and Bernard (*PL* 182, cols. 897–8 ; 183, cols. 220–2). Adam the Scot calls body and soul two friends (*socii*) parted by bitter death (*PL* 153, col. 833).

30. etscene [OE *e(a)þ* (' easily ')+*gesyne*]. The same first element, commonly compounded in OE, appears in *eðluke*, ' easy to drag ', SJ 690 ; *sc* is a spelling for *s(s)* in KG texts even in native words.

35. hali chirche oðer cleane sawle. See Introduction, p. xlix ; cp. AW *f.* 89*v* (Salu 146) for the same dual definition.

p. 25

1ff. This paragraph is concerned with how the lover (Christ) can obtain a return of love from the beloved either by (i) looking for a free gift of love, (ii) the beloved selling her affection, or (iii) the lover forcing the beloved to yield what he requires. The passage depends rather remotely on Bernard's division of loves as voluntary, mercenary, and servile in *On the Love of God*, chap. xii ff (*PL* 182, col. 995ff). An exact correspondence is to be found in a tract by a Cistercian, writing about 1240, Gerard of Liège, *Five Incitements to a burning Love of God*, ed. A. Wilmart, *Analecta Reginensia*, Rome (1933), pp. 181–247. Gerard gives the modes of loving God, ' If it is to be given, none is worthier than God, since He is best and most beautiful above all the children of men. . . . Again if our love is for sale, none will buy it at a higher price, and notwithstanding that He has already bought it so dearly with His death, He is still prepared to buy it again. . . . He will give at length in exchange for it the kingdom of heaven, than which nothing greater or more precious can be given. But if our love needs forcing none will use greater violence than He. For he seeks it with an unsheathed sword. Either you will love, or die an eternal death ' (pp. 210–11). If Gerard is following and filling out the Rule as appears, we have here probably the earliest example of its diffusion abroad.

4ff. Secular and divine draw close here ; cp. Andrew the Chaplain, *The Art of Courtly Love*, Book 1, chap. vi, ' The teaching of some people is said to be that there are five means by which [love] may be acquired: a beautiful figure, excellence of character, extreme readiness of speech, great wealth, and the readiness with which one grants that which is sought ' (p. 33), probably referring to the teaching of Hugh of St Victor, *Summa*, Tractate 7, chap. 1 (*PL* 176, col. 155). Cp. also the topics of epideictic discourse, *ad Her.*, III, vi, 10. Rather unsystematically, AW deals with these accepted grounds for the acquisition of love. Celebrations of the attractions of Christ are numerous and fervid at this period : e.g. Ailred, Meditation 10 in the Anselmian *Book of Prayers and Meditations*, ' O benign Jesu, humble Lord, loving Lord, sweet in speech and in loving and listening, unsearchably and ineffably kind, loving and merciful, wise, benign, generous but not spendthrift, entirely sweet and gentle ; thou art the object of desire, beautiful to look upon above all the children of men ' etc. (*PL* 158, col. 762 ; cp. col. 894), and also an extended passage in *Wooing of our Lord*, which must be closely related to these pages of AW. There Christ possesses all that makes a man loved : beauty, wealth, generosity, wisdom, strength, nobility, courtesy, and high kindred (OE Hom I, 269–75). þinge . . . kinge . . . weolie . . . monne . . . are historically genitives [OE -a inflexion], but the genitival force was probably not felt by the 13th c.

7. me seið bi large mon, etc. No proverbial expression of this type implying openhandedness has been found : cp. D.V. Ives, *MLR* 29 (1934), 265. But the insertion into the Anselmian passage found at the end of N *f.* 131*v* speaks of ' His head bent for kissing, His arms extended to embrace, His hands pierced to give, His side open for loving,' etc. (AR N *Introd.* xxii–xxiii). Obviously the idea had currency in devotional writings.

12f. The appropriateness here of this commonplace definition of the supreme worth of virginity is not apparent. It is likely to be an insertion by the reviser of the Rule with the prime interest of the KG texts at heart ; cp. HM 324ff.

14ff. The aposiopesis (here reflecting astonishment at the very idea of buying love) is characteristic of KG texts : cp. AW *f.* 67*r*, ' Edstont ane þe feond & he deð him o fluhte. Edstond ? Þurh hwet strengðe ? ' SJ 181, ' Þu wult aȝeoue me to Eleusium. . . . Aȝef me ? ' The sense of 15–16 would be improved by adopting Tolkien's suggested insertion of *for luue* after 16 . . . *wel luue*, and repunctuating.

21. feor, price [OFr *fuer*, *feur*]. According to *MED*, found in ME elsewhere only once apart from its use in the following passage from *Wooing of our Lord* dependent on AW here, ' Ȝette ȝif þat i mi luue bede for to selle, & sette feor þer upon swa hehe swa ich eauer wile, ȝette þu wult hit habbe & teken al þat he haues ȝiuen—wil tu eke mare, &, ȝif i þe riht luuie, wilt me crune in heuene wið þe self to rixlen. . . .' (OE Hom I, 285–7).

23ff. The basis is chap. xxiv of Anselm, *Proslogion*, a chapter much admired, transcribed, and imitated by devotional writers of the 12th and 13th cs. ' What do you love, my flesh ? What do you desire, my soul ? There [in the state of bliss] is whatever you love ; there, whatever you desire. If beauty . . . or swiftness . . . or strength, . . . or long and lasting life . . . or intoxication . . . or melody . . . or pure delight . . . or wisdom . . . or friendship . . . or concord . . . or honour and riches . . . or true security . . .', the love of God can supply all of these (*PL* 158, cols. 240–1). Anselm is providing a systematic list of the qualities of body and mind which the blessed will possess in heaven ; see G. Shepherd, *MLR* 51 (1956), 161–7.)

25ff. See 4,31 ; cp. SK 1664ff, ' & alle þe burhmen seouen siðes brihtre þen beo þe sunne, gleominde of euch gleo, & a mare iliche glead ? for nawiht ne derueð ham ; ne nawiht ne wonteð ham of al þet ha wilneð ' ; also SW 65ff.

29. Cp. 1 Cor. 2:9 and **30**,25.

31ff. Anselm's account of the bodily and spiritual gifts of the blessed in heaven was taken up and elaborated by Honorius, the recluse of the Rhineland, commonly but erroneously known as Honorius of Autun (*fl.* before 1150), at one time a member of Anselm's circle at Canterbury. His writings are great founts of ecclesiastical lore for the late Middle Ages. In the last chapters of *Elucidarium*, Honorius discusses the beatitudes and provides an exemplary figure for each of the gifts (*PL* 172, cols. 1168–75). This passage was much drawn upon by later writers, and the exemplary names repeated, though often with some variation as in AW : see *MLR* 51, pp. 161–7.

31. Creasuse (for this genitive form see **3**,22 note) does not appear in Honorius's list, but in Richard of St Victor, Sermon lxxxviii (*PL* 177, col. 1177), appears as exemplar of the beatitude of wealth. Croesus, famous in antiquity for his wealth, was the last king of Lydia, 6th c. B.C.

32. Absalom, as for Honorius the type of beauty. On the beauty and value of his hair, see 2 Sam. 14:25–6 ; see also P. E. Beichner, *Medieval Studies* 11 (1950), 222–33.

34. Asahel, as with Honorius the exemplar of the beatitude of swiftness (cp. AW *f.* 24*v* (Salu 31)) ; see 2 Sam. 2:18. The brother of Joab and Abishai, Asahel so pestered Abner by pursuit in battle that Abner reluctantly slew him.

35. Samson, as with Honorius, in reference to the exploit related in Judges 15:14–17, when Samson slew a thousand men with a jaw-bone of an ass.

36. Honorius's treatment of *libertas* (col. 1170) indicates that the type is Caesar Augustus.

37. Alexander, as with Honorius, the exemplar of *potestas*. Moses, Honorius's exemplar of *sanitas*, ' was an hundred and twenty years old when he died ; his eye was not dim, nor his natural force abated ' (Deut. 34:7).

39. bodi. Both Anselm and Honorius distinguish seven gifts of the body from seven gifts of the spirit. A list of bodily gifts (though somewhat altered) is given in AW. Accordingly the reading *bodi* is to be preferred to *bode*, ' offer ' (French text *ofre*). **nelde :** OE *nædl*. On this metathesis see Jordan, § 167 & Anm[1].

p. 26

1ff. þet tu þurh nawt to leosen. See Glossary, *s. þurh*, which here seems to imply both consequence and actual situation ; i.e. blending the meanings ' in consequence of having nothing to lose ' and ' even though you have nothing to lose '. On love taken by violence, see **25**,1ff note.

3. A reminiscence of Ps. 7:11–13.

6. world abuten ende. Cp. *world buten ende*, **8**,27, both traditional formulas for the conclusion of the Lat. doxology, *in secula seculorum* ;

see *NED s.* world, **6.** *abuten* (thus written whenever used in KG texts) is reduced from *á buten*, ' ever without ' (cp. *aa*, 27,26). See Hall, EME II, 335.

13ff. Ps. 19:6. The links of thought in this passage are provided by the gloss on this Psalm, 5:4. ' In them hath He set a tabernacle for the sun ' is taken to refer to Christ's coming down from heaven ' as a Bridegroom ', etc. (5:5). ' His going forth is from the end of the heaven ', etc. (5:6), refers to the ascending again to heaven into the Trinity. The heat of the Word, which is love and also the Holy Ghost, dissolved the shadow of death which none could escape from ; so Peter Lombard, *Commentary on the Psalms* (*PL* 191, cols. 208–10). On Christ as sun, see **4,**31 note.

15. undertid, here the third hour of the day, following Mark 15:25.

19f. Luke 12:49. The Pentecostal fire is usually interpreted as the love of God : cp. Peter of Blois, Sermon xxiv at Whitsun, ' The Holy Ghost is fire ; for love is fire. But as fire cannot help but burn, so the Holy Ghost cannot but inflame and warm. " There is none who can hide from the heat thereof " ' (cp. 13 above) ; and Peter goes on to quote Luke 12:49 as here (*PL* 207, col. 631).

23ff. Rev. 3:15–16. Cp. a passage peculiar to AW, *f.* 29*r* (Salu 48), ' þe wlecche þe Godd speoweð, as is iwriten her efter, etc.' (apparently a forward reference to this passage).

30ff. On how love is to be maintained.

32. See 1 Kings 17:12. **Sarepte.** Sarepta (Zarephath of Luke 4:26), meaning ' smelting-house ', the name of a town on the Phoenician coast between Tyre and Sidon. Hugh of St Victor provides a similar interpretation of this story of Elijah and the widow. ' The widow is the Holy Church, which was a widow for as long as she awaited the coming of the Saviour . . . ; the woman collected two pieces of wood, when the Church received the faith of the Passion . . . ; the widow therefore is the Church ; Elijah, Christ ; the pieces of wood, the Cross ' (*PL* 175, col. 709). This piece of allegorising, deriving from Augustine (*PL* 38, cols. 97–9), seems to have had something of a vogue in academic circles in the late 12th c. It is used by Baldwin of Ford (*PL* 204, col. 523), Peter of Blois (*PL* 207, col. 574), and in the Goliardic poems.

p. 27

2f. Biseoð ofte, etc. A further recommendation to use the crucifix ; see 23,2 note.

4. Of the hermit Bartholomew of Farne it is recorded that in his cell he saw the image on the crucifix come alive and stretch out its arms to him (*Nova Legenda Anglie,* ed. C. Horstman, I, 102). In England the crucified Christ is sometimes represented with bowed head, at least as early as 10th c.

5. cos. In Bernardine devotion, *osculum* usually refers to the culmination of contemplation, the mystical experience itself ; see E. Gilson, *The Mystical Theology of St Bernard,* pp. 110ff ; and this meaning may be hinted at in AW here, recalling *f.* 27*r* (Salu 44).

7, 10. ifinden is found elsewhere with this accusative and infinitive (*gederin*) construction following ; but cp. **4,**14f.

9. as Helie dude. In the miracle of 1 Kings 17:16 ; see 26,32 note.

11ff. Greek fire, a liquid incendiary used by the defence chiefly in siege warfare, is first spoken of as used by the Greeks against the Arabs in the late 7th c. It was encountered by the Western armies in the Third Crusade (1189–92), but had been known, at least by repute, earlier in the century ; see Geoffrey of Monmouth, *History*, Book 1, chap. vi, in his account of the siege of Sparatinum (J. S. P. Tatlock, *The Legendary History of Britain*, pp. 322–3). It was used at the siege of Nottingham in 1194 ; see A. L. Poole, *From Doomsday Book to Magna Carta* (1951), p. 373 and note, p. 480 note, who draws attention to the interest and experimentation in incendiaries stimulated by the *Book of Fires for burning the Enemy* of Mark the Greek. According to Mark, the fire could be extinguished with urine, vinegar, or sand. Such extinguishers were used by the Crusaders at Damietta in 1218 (Matthew Paris, *Chronica Majora*, ed. H. R. Luard, RS III, 38). There were numerous recipes for the manufacture of incendiary mixtures, but naphtha, pitch, and sulphur were the basic ingredients : see M. Mercier, *Le feu grégeois*, Paris (1952); for medieval treatises, Lynn Thorndyke, *A History of Magic and Experimental Science*, II, New York (1929), 785ff. **reades monnes blod.** The masc. genitive inflexion of the adjective is usually retained only in set phrases : cp. **21**,28, **22**,2, **26**,2. Here it may be employed emphatically ; but cp. *reade*, 14. This recipe for Greek fire is not common. But into the narrative of the Lat. *On the Birth of Gawain* (dated second quarter of 13th c.), ed. J. D. Bruce, *PMLA* **13** (1898), 390–432, is inserted without break or stylistic distinction an account of the preparation and qualities of Greek fire, pp. 412–16. This passage, Bruce assumes, was drawn from some undiscovered pseudo-scientific (or early alchemical) treatise. In this recipe the basic ingredients are to be compounded with the bloods of a red man and of a dragon. ' For it is believed that the blood of a red man partakes of the nature of fire which even the colour of hair and also a liveliness of spirit dominant in this type of man demonstrate.' A young man with red hair and freckles is to be fattened in luxurious surroundings for a month, then carefully bled to death and the blood mixed with a dragon's blood. *Red man* (and *dragon's blood*) remains a term in later alchemy.

16. inread cundeliche. The illustration of Greek fire is apt if startling, inasmuch as according to some traditions (which were of course important for illuminators ; see E. de Bruyne, *Études d'esthétique médiévale*, Bruges (1946), I, 286) Christ was thought to have been of sanguine complexion. As a Son of David he preserved David's colouring : v. I Sam. 16:12 & 17:42. The tradition is best known in the influential apocryphal letter (purporting to provide the Roman Senate with an eye-witness account of Christ) of Publius Lentulus, which in fact can be scarcely earlier in date than AW ; see M. R. James, *The Apocryphal New Testament* (1924), p. 477, ' The hair of His head is of the colour of wine. . . . His face free from blemish and somewhat tinged with red.' This does not represent the only tradition concerning Christ's complexion. But the redness of Christ was supported by symbolism. The red heifer sacrificed by Eleazar outside the camp of the Hebrews to expiate their sins (Numb. 19), was taken as a type of Christ ; so Bede, ' The red heifer is the flesh of the Saviour, red with the blood of His passion, and of a perfect age ' (*PL* 91, col. 367). **inread,** ' very red ' : on this intensive prefix see *NED s.* in- *pref.*[4]

17. earre, former, referring to **26**,35ff. Comparative adjective formed by extending an original comparative adverb.

19. Salomon. In Song of Sol. 8:7, ' Many waters cannot quench love, neither can the floods drown it.' The usual interpretation of these many waters is ' threats, persecutions, terrors and temptations ' : so Honorius (*PL* 172, col. 480), following Gregory (*PL* 79, col. 542). Inner and outer temptations have been dealt with in Part 4, *f. 47v* ff. (Salu 78ff).

23ff. With these three, urine as stench of sin, sand as fruitlessness, yinegar for bitterness, cp. AW *f. 20v*, where evil speech is threefold, *attri, ful & idel.*

28f. an neil driueð ut, etc. An ancient and common maxim, found in Aristotle, Augustine, etc., and in many 12th c. writers. Parallel maxims couple or substitute for ' nail ', ' fire ' or ' love ' ; cp. Baldwin of Ford, *PL* 204, col. 419, imitating apparently *PL* 184, col. 624 : see also D. V. Ives, *MLR* 29 (1934), 260.

31ff. From here to **28,15** run reminiscences of earlier passages in AW, notably of *f. 30r* to *f. 31v* (Salu 49–51).

33. John 19:30.

36. (du)den. This reading, which seems certain, illustrates the common causative use of *don* ; see *NED s.* do. B.22. Cp. AW *f. 30r* (Salu 49), ' He seh . . . al his swinc forloren þet he swonc on eorðe ' ; and cp. **28,7.** Underlying the passage is the parable of the Labourers in the Vineyard, Matt. 20.

p. 28

5. piment, spiced drink. Med. Lat. *pigmentum*, originally ' paint ', acquired a number of extended meanings, as a result of the similar methods of preparation of paints, ointments, perfumes, and cordials ; cp. Trevisa quotation, *NED s.* pigment 2. As a drink of sweetness the word was often used of Christ, usually as echo of the famous hymn, ' Jesu the very thought of thee ' (*Dulcis Iesu memoria*—probably of late 12th c. English Cistercian origin), where Jesus is described as *In ore mel mirificum / Corda pigmentum celicum.*

6. Cp. AW *f. 31r* (Salu 50), *drunch of sur galle.*

7f. Cp. *ful pinet* (**27,34**). The greatest suffering of Christ on the cross was considered to be the mental suffering ; cp. C. Brown, *Religious Lyrics of the xivth c.*, rev. G. V. Smithers (1952), Nos. 70 and 77 ; *PL* 184, col. 744.

9. þet ich þus biteo, ' that I give away thus ' (i.e. without obtaining a reward for the labour).

14. Cp. AW *f. 31r* (Salu 51), ' Ant tu, his deore spuse, ne beo þu nawt Giwes make forte birlin [' give drink '] him swa ', etc.

15ff. Here love of our neighbour is considered briefly ; cp. the earlier treatment, f. 49v f (Salu 81f).

17. areareð ow of ei va eani weorre, ' raises up any strife from any foe against you'.

18ff. Prov. 25:21-2, quoted in Rom. 12:20. AW expounds this verse in the usual way : thus Peter Lombard, ' If any hunger, etc. ; that is, help him in the necessities of life. Thus doing, you will heap the fire of love, or of the Holy Ghost, or the smarting coals of penitence on his head, that is, on his mind . . .' (*PL* 191, col. 1503).

22. **efter þin hearm.** Ambiguous. Either, ' after he has harmed thee ', or more likely, *efter* is to be taken with the verbs, ' hungers and thirsts for your downfall '.

27f. Glosses on Rom. 12:20 (cp. 18ff note) usually include this explanation of head.

28ff. This dialogue is based on Matt. 5:46 and Luke 6:32–5.

36ff. Part 7 ends with paragraphs extolling the uniqueness and pre-eminence of the love of God.

p. 29

2f. John 16:7. Similar uses of this text are to be found in Cistercian writers, in Bernard, *Sermons on the Ascension* (*PL* 183, col. 308 and col. 321), Guerricus of Igny (*PL* 185, col. 163), and in Stephen of Grandmont, *Book of Sentences*, chap. viii (*PL* 204, col. 1094) and chap. cxii (col. 1132).

13ff. A commonplace ; so Gregory (*PL* 77, col. 563), John of Fécamp, *Book of Meditations,* ' For there are two loves, one good, one bad, one sweet, one sour, and they cannot be held together in one breast ' (*PL* 40, col. 930) ; *Orison of our Lord,* ' fleshliche loue & gostliche, eorðliche lou & heouenliche, ne maȝen onone wise beddin in a breoste ' (OE Hom I, 185). Cp. AW *f.* 27r (Salu 44), ' For ne schalt tu nanesweis þes ilke twa cunforz, min & te worldes, þe ioie of þe hali gast & ec flesches froure habbe togederes. Cheos nu an of þes twa, for þe oðer þu most leten.'

16ff. Repetition of phrases from **20,**10ff.

20ff. Deut. 11:24. *Pes amoris* is not in the Scripture but is suggested by Deut. 11:22.

24. **þruppe feor.** At AW *f.* 77r (Salu 126) ; see **18,**29 note.

28. This Augustinian idea, as in Sermon xxiii (*PL* 38, cols. 158–9), that the very groping of the mind for God shows that He is already found, was often taken up by 12th c. writers ; so Bernard, *PL* 182, col. 987.

29. After **hauest** *irinen* (*past part.*) is to be understood, ' Extend to Him as much love as thou hast once upon a time extended to some particular man.'

30f. **Ah hwa luueð,** etc. Cp. *Orison of our Lord,* ' Me nis he fol chapmon þe buð deore a wac þing and forsakeþ a deorwurþe þing þet me beodeþ him for naut . . . ? ' (OE Hom I, 185).

32f. **Chearite** is of course etymologically identical with **cherte,** but the author is setting a religious against a commercial meaning.

35. **leaskeð.** AN *lasquier* ; OFr *lascher, laschier,* ' give up, release, let go of ' ; cp. *NED s.* lache, *vb* ; lask, *vb.*

37ff. The idea that God himself is constrained by love is in many 12th c. devotional writings, e.g. Bernard (*PL* 183, col. 1062), Richard of St Victor (*PL* 196, col. 1196).

39f. ' Am I able to prove this ? Yes, assuredly I (can), through His own words.' This use of *ich* unsupported is probably an imitation of Lat. use of *ego* without verb in replying to a suppositious question.

p. 30

2f. Num. 14:20. ' He does not say " thy prayers " ' ; the phrase is added by the author to the scriptural verse to create a distinction between ' word ' and ' prayers ' for his argument's sake.

5ff. **luue binde ð.** A commonplace ; so Augustine, *PL* 40, col. 960, and elsewhere often in writers sacred and profane ; see P. Rousselet, *Pour le problème de l'amour au moyen âge*, *Baeumker Beiträge* 6 (1908), 60, note 1. **luue bint swa ure lauerd.** Bernard, *On the Love of God*, speaks of the law of Charity which binds God (*PL* 182, col. 996), and Hugh of St Victor, *In Praise of Charity*, ' O love, great strength hast thou, that thou alone couldst draw God down from heaven to earth. O how strong is thy bond by which even God could be bound who then as man in bondage broke the bonds of sin ' (*PL* 176, col. 974).

8. Isa. 64:7.

9. **weilawei.** On the etymology of this exclamation, see d'Ardenne, SJ, p. 170.

11ff. Gen. 19:22. etc suppresses Vulgate *et salvare ibi.*

15. **bimong.** A characteristic form in KG texts, a blend of *imong* [OE *gemong*] and *bitweonen*.

16. **Nes þes wið luue ibunden ?** ' Was not such a one compelled by love ?'

17. **chamberleng.** The officer of state (*camerarius*) in Anglo-Norman courts in charge of the royal bedchamber, often employed as confidential agent to the king ; see D. M. Stenton, *English Society in the Early Middle Ages*, pp. 24–5. AW form is adopted from OFr from Med. Lat. *camerlengus*, itself a Germanic form with the Germanic suffix of association : cp. *NED s.* -ling, 1.

18. **heole.** OE *hēlan*, ' conceal ', was used with *wið* as here ; and also with dative of person : so 20. **Abraham,** ' from Abraham '.

19f. Gen. 18:17.

21f. **Nu con þes luuien, etc.** An emphatic assertion, not a question.

25ff. Isa. 64:4, quoted in 1 Cor. 2:9 : cp. **25,29** ; a verse invariably used in accounts of heaven.

28. **elleshwer.** No surviving EME writing is exclusively concerned with this subject, but many touch on it, e.g. *Poema Morale*, *Orison of our Lady*, and in particular SW. But even in SW the treatment is cut short (in comparison with the source, Hugh of St Victor, *On the Soul*). In view of the popularity of the theme of beatitude (see notes on **25,23** and ff) it is likely that here we have a reference to one of the lost works of ME vernacular prose.

29ff. A summary conclusion to the whole Inner Rule, recalling phrases used at the beginning of AW ; cp. *f. 1v* : ' þis makeð þe leafdi riwle, þe riwleð & rihteð & smeðeð þe heorte.'

30ff. Ps. 119:7. *id est in regulatione* are the author's words to strengthen the link with the opening of AW, as quoted Introduction, p. xxxviii.

31. Exprobratio malorum, the reproach of the evil (on the other hand) is that it is ' a generation that set not its heart aright ' (Ps. 78:8).

32f. Alle þe oþre, etc. Cp. AW *f.* 1*v* (Salu 2).

34. for hwon þet. *hwon* here shows the form of the old instrumental *þon* refashioned as a relative (cp. SM, p. 36/25, *to hwon*). *hwon* is distinct from *hwen*, ' when ' (but cp. *MED s.* for-whan), which never appears as *hwon* in this text. The historic meaning of *for hwon þet* should be ' on account of which ', and this is the sense at AW *f.* 85*v* and probably in HM 187. But in the present instance and at AW *f.* 43*r* and in SW 27, there has been a blend of meaning with the temporal relative adverb *hwen*, resulting in a meaning ' in the event that ', ' in cases such that '.

APPENDIX

Translation of St Bernard's Seventh Sermon in Lent
(Text in *PL* 183, cols. 183-6)

1. Happy are those who show themselves as strangers and pilgrims in this present vile world, keeping themselves spotless from it. ' For here we have no abiding city, but seek one to come ' [Heb. 13:14]. Let us abstain therefore as strangers and pilgrims from fleshly desires which fight against the soul [1 Pet. 2:11]. The pilgrim for sure travels along the king's highway ; he turns neither to the right nor to the left. If by chance he sees men quarrelling he pays no attention ; if he sees them marrying or dancing or doing anything else, he nevertheless passes by, because he is a pilgrim and such matters have nothing to do with him. He sighs for his own country and makes towards his own country ; having food and clothing he does not want to be burdened with other things. He is happy indeed who thus knows his own, thus gives up the rest, saying to the Lord, ' For I am a stranger with thee and a pilgrim like all my fathers ' [Ps. 39:12]. This is great indeed, but perhaps another stage is higher. For the pilgrim even as he is not mixed up with the citizens [of this world], yet is sometimes pleased to see what things take place, and either to hear about them from others or himself to tell what he may have seen ; and in such ways, after this fashion, even though he may not be completely held back, yet is he detained and delayed in as much as he is the while less mindful of his own country and hastens on with less desire. For he may be so greatly pleased with these things that indeed he may be not only delayed and come home less quickly, but even stay altogether and not even arrive late.

2. Who therefore is more a stranger to the doings of the world than the pilgrim ? Surely those to whom the Apostle says, ' For ye are dead and your life is hid with Christ in God ' [Col. 3:3]. The pilgrim, beyond question, can easily by reason of his journey be both detained through curiosity, and overburdened with things to carry, more than is proper ; the dead man does not even notice if he lacks a grave itself. So praise as well as blame, flattery as well as detraction he hears, yet indeed he does not hear, because he is dead. How entirely happy a death which thus keeps a man spotless ; it makes him completely a stranger to this world. But it must be that Christ live in him who does not live in himself. For this is what the Apostle says : ' Nevertheless I live ; yet not I, but Christ liveth in me ' [Gal. 2:20]. As if he had said : ' To all other things indeed I am dead ; I do not feel, I pay no attention, I do not care ; but if any things be of Christ, these find me fully alive and ready. For if I can do nothing else, at least I feel ; what I see rightfully done in His honour pleases ; what ever is done otherwise, displeases.' Very exalted is this stage.

3. But perhaps something higher is to be found. Where shall we look for it ? Where do you think, unless in him of whom we spoke just now, who was caught up into the third heaven ? [2 Cor. 12:2]. For who forbids the third heaven to be spoken of, if you shall be able to find some stage which is above those others ? Hear him therefore on the subject of this great exaltation, not boasting, but merely saying : ' But

God forbid that I should boast, save in the cross of our Lord Jesus Christ, by whom the world is crucified unto me, and I unto the world ' [Gal. 6:14]. He does not only say ' dead ' to the world, but even ' crucified '—which is a shameful kind of death. I to it, as much as it to me. All the things which the world loves are to me a cross : delight of the flesh, honours, riches, the empty praises of men. But what the world reckons a cross, to those things am I fixed, to those I cling, I embrace them with all my heart. Is not this greater than the second and the first stages ? The pilgrim if he is careful and does not forget his pilgrimage, journeys on although with difficulty, and is not greatly entangled with affairs of this world. The dead man spurns the pleasant things of this world equally with the harsh. But to him who is caught up to the third heaven everything which the world clings to is a crosss ; and he clings to those things which to the world seem to be a cross. Although from the words of the Apostle it may not be unreasonably understood that he considers that it is the world which is crucified, yet he himself is crucified in compassion with the world. For he saw the world crucified in the bonds of vices, and was himself crucified for it through the eagerness of compassion.

4. Let us now think individually in what stage each of us may be placed and let us strive to advance from day to day, since in going from strength to strength the God of Gods shall be seen in Zion [Ps. 84:7]. But I implore you, let us strive to live in all purity especially at this holy time, of which a fixed as well as a limited number of days is set, lest human frailty despair. For if we were told, ' Be careful to preserve the purity of your way of life completely all the time ', who would not despair ? But now we are reminded to make good in a small number of days all the careless acts of other times, so that we may thus surely taste the sweetness of perfect purity, and that henceforth for all time the bright tokens of this our holy Lent may shine in our lives. Let us strive therefore, brothers, to pass this holy time with a full devotion, and to refurbish our spiritual armour now more completely. For at this time the Saviour fights with a kind of mass levy of the whole world against the devil ; blessed are they who shall have fought vigorously under such a leader. Although the king's own household is fighting throughout the year, and is constantly in readiness for war, yet at one particular and certain time the whole kingdom is gathered into a general army. Happy are you who have deserved to be of the household, to whom the Apostle says, ' Now therefore ye are no more strangers and foreigners but fellow-citizens with the saints and of the household of God ' [Eph. 2:19]. What therefore shall be done by those who have undertaken to fight the whole year when even the ignorant with shouts first snatch up their spiritual armour ? Surely they must prosecute their usual war more than usual so that a great victory may result in glory for our king and in salvation for us.

BIBLIOGRAPHY

For full bibliography on *Ancrene Riwle*, see Charlotte D'Evelyn, *A Manual of the Writings in Middle English 1050-1500* (gen. ed. J. Burke Severs), vol. 2, Connecticut Academy of Arts & Sciences (1970), pp. 650-4. Only such titles as are of interest in reading Parts 6 and 7 of AW are listed below.

Editions and translations of texts
(i) The Rule

The English Text of the Ancrene Riwle : Ancrene Wisse (Corpus Christi College, Cambridge, MS 402), ed. J. R. R. Tolkien, EETS 249 (1962).

The Ancren Riwle, ed. James Morton ; Camden Society LVII (1853). With translation of N.

The English Text of the Ancrene Riwle (BM Cotton MS Nero A. xiv), ed. Mabel Day, EETS 225 (1952).

The English Text of the Ancrene Riwle (Gonville and Caius College, Cambridge, MS 234/120), ed. R. M. Wilson, EETS 229 (1954).

The English Text of the Ancrene Riwie (BM Cotton MS Titus D. xviii), ed. Frances M. Mack, EETS 252 (1963).

The French Text of the Ancrene Riwle (BM Cotton MS Vitellius F. vii), ed. J. A. Herbert, EETS 219 (1944).

The Latin Text of the Ancrene Riwle (Merton College MS 44 and BM Cotton MS Vitellius E. vii), ed. Charlotte D'Evelyn, EETS 216 (1944).

The Nun's Rule. AR modernised by James Morton, with Introduction by (Cardinal) F. A. Gasquet, London (1926).

The Recluse, ed. Joel Påhlsson, Lund (1911, reissued 1918).

The Ancrene Riwle (Corpus MS : *Ancrene Wisse*), trans. M. B. Salu, with Introduction by Dom Gerard Sitwell and Preface by Professor J. R. R. Tolkien, London (1955). Good translation.

(ii) Other texts

The Early-English Life of St Katherine, ed. E. Einenkel, EETS 80 (1884). (SK)

Hali Meiðhad (MS Bodley 34 and MS Cotton Titus D. xviii), ed. A. F. Colborn, Copenhagen (1940). (HM)

Þe Liflade ant te Passiun of Seinte Iuliene, ed. S. T. R. O. d'Ardenne, Bibliothèque de la Faculté de philosophie et lettres de l'Université de Liège LXIV (1936) ; reprinted as EETS 248 (1962). (SJ)

Old English Homilies (1st series), ed. Richard Morris, EETS 29 and 34 (1867–8). Minor KG texts with translations.

Þe Wohunge of ure Lauerd, and other pieces, ed. W. Meredith Thompson, EETS 241 (1958).

Sawles Warde (Bodley, Royal, and Cotton MSS), ed. R. M· Wilson, Leeds School of English Language : Texts and Monographs III (1938). (SW)

Seinte Marherete, þe Meiden ant Martyr, ed. Frances M. Mack, EETS 193 (1934). (SM)

Tretyse of Loue, ed. J. H. Fisher, EETS 223 (1951).

(iii) Extracts

First Middle-English Primer, ed. Henry Sweet, Oxford (1884). Extracts from N include part of Part 7.

Selections from Early Middle English 1130–1250, ed. J. Hall ; I Text, II Notes, Oxford (1920). Parts 6 and 7 of AW not represented in extracts, but notes on KG texts valuable.

Early Middle English Verse & Prose, ed. J. A. W. Bennett & G. V. Smithers, with glossary by N. Davis, Oxford (1966), pp. 222–45 and notes.

Studies of the Rule

ALLEN, HOPE EMILY. ' The Mystical Lyrics of the *Manuel des Pechiez* ', *Romanic Review*, **9** (1918), 154–93. Useful survey of post-Conquest devotional writing in England.

ALLEN, HOPE EMILY. ' The Origin of the AR ', *PMLA* **33** (1918), 474–546.

ALLEN, HOPE EMILY. ' On the Author of the AR ', *PMLA* **44** (1929), 635–80. Both articles remain important.

ALLEN, HOPE EMILY. ' Some Fourteenth Century Borrowings from the AR ', *MLR* **18** (1923), 1–8 ; a correction *MLR* **19** (1924), 95.

ALLEN, HOPE EMILY. 'Further Borrowings from the AR', *MLR* **24** (1929), 1–15.

ALLEN, HOPE EMILY. 'The Localisation of MS Bodley 34', *MLR* **28** (1933), 485–7.

BETHURUM, DOROTHY. 'The connection of the Katherine Group with OE Prose', *JEGP* **34** (1935), 553–64. Good points but lightly urged.

CHAMBERS, R. W. 'Recent Research upon the AR', *RES* **1** (1925), 4–23. Still illuminating.

CHAMBERS, R. W., McNABB, V., and THURSTON, H. 'Further Research upon the AR', *RES* **2** (1926), 82–9, 197–201.

COOPER, SISTER ETHELBERT. 'Latin Elements of the AR' (unpublished thesis, University of Birmingham, 1956).

D'EVELYN, CHARLOTTE. 'Inter-relations between the Latin and the English Texts of the AR', *PMLA* **64** (1949), 1164–79.

DOBSON, E. J. 'The Affiliations of the MSS of AW' in *Studies presented to J. R. R. Tolkien*, ed. N. Davis & C. L. Wrenn, London (1962), pp. 128–63.

DOBSON, E. J. 'The Date & Composition of AW', Proceedings of British Academy **52** (1967), 181–208.

HULBERT, J. R. 'A Thirteenth-Century English Literary Standard', *JEGP* **45** (1946), 411–14.

HUMBERT, SISTER AGNES MARGARET. *Verbal Repetition in the AR*, Catholic University of America, Washington (1944).

IVES, D. V. 'The Proverbs in the AR', *MLR* **29** (1934), 257–66 (supplemented by B. J. Whiting, 'Proverbs in the AR and *The Recluse*', *MLR* **30** (1935), 502–5).

KIRCHBERGER, CLARE. 'Some Notes on the AR', *Dominican Studies* **7** (1954), 215–38. Main argument unconvincing; informative.

MACAULAY, G. C. 'The AR', *MLR* **9** (1914), 63–78, 145–60, 324–31, 463–74. Important. On MSS, collations (full but not complete), revisions and insertions.

SAMUELS, M. L. 'AR Studies', *MÆ* **22** (1953), 1–9.

SERJEANTSON, M. S. 'The Dialect of the Corpus MS of the AR', *LMS*, **1/2** (1938), 225–48. Phonology and accidence studied in first 50 folios.

TALBOT, C. H.   'Some Notes on the Dating of AR',
  Neophilologus **40** (1956), 38–50.

TOLKIEN, J. R. R.   'AW and *Hali Meiðhad*', *E&S* **14**
  (1929), 104–26.

TRETHEWEY, W. H.   'The Seven Deadly Sins & the Devil's
  Court in the Trinity College Cambridge French Text of
  AR', *PMLA* **65** (1950), 1233–46.

Literary background

CAPLAN, HARRY.   'Classical Rhetoric and the Medieval
  Theory of Preaching', *Classical Philology* **28** (1933), 73–96.

CAPLAN, HARRY, ed. and trans. [Cicero], *Ad C. Herennium,
  de ratione dicendi* (*Rhetorica ad Herennium*), London and
  Cambridge (Mass.), 1954 (Loeb Classical Library).

CHAMBERS, R. W.   'On the Continuity of English Prose
  from Alfred to More and his School', in Harpsfield's *Life
  of More*, ed. E. V. Hitchchock, EETS 186 (1932), reprinted separately (Oxford, 1933).

CHARLAND, T. M.   *Artes Praedicandi*, Publications de
  l'Institut d'Études Médiévales d'Ottawa, VII (1936).

CLEMOES, PETER.   *Liturgical Influence on Punctuation in LOE
  and EME MSS*, Occasional Paper 1 (Dept. of Anglo-
  Saxon), Cambridge (1952).

DE BRUYNE, EDGAR.   *Études d'esthétique médiévale*, vol. ii,
  Bruges (1946).

DE GHELLINCK, J.   *L'Essor de la littérature latine au XII*e
  siècle, 2nd ed., Brussels-Bruges-Paris (1954).   Brilliant
  and comprehensive.

GILSON, E.   'Michel Menot et la technique du sermon
  médiéval', in *Les Idées et les Lettres*, Paris (1932), pp. 93–154.

PARÉ, G., BRUNET, A., and TREMBLAY, P.   *La Renaissance du
  XII*e *siècle: les écoles et l'enseignement*, Publications de
  l'Institut d'Études Médiévales d'Ottawa, III (1933).

SMALLEY, BERYL.   *The Study of the Bible in the Middle Ages*,
  2nd ed., Oxford (1952).

SPICQ, C.   *Esquisse d'une histoire de l'exégèse latine au moyen
  âge*, Paris (1944).

WILSON, R. M. *Early Middle English Literature*, London (1939).

Historical and religious background

Bernard of Clairvaux. Commission d'histoire de l'ordre de Cîteaux, III, Abbaye d'Aigubelle, Paris (1953).

BERNARDS, MATTHÄUS. *Speculum Virginum : Geistigkeit und Seelenleben der Frau im Hochmittelalter*, Cologne-Graz (1955).

BUTLER, CUTHBERT. *Western Mysticism*, 2nd ed., London (1927).

CLAY, R. M. *The Hermits and Anchorites of England*, London (1914). Comprehensive.

DARWIN, F. D. *The English Medieval Recluse*, London (1944). Brief, unsympathetic, scholarly.

ECKENSTEIN, LINA. *Woman under Monasticism*, Cambridge (1896).

GILSON, E. *The Mystical Theology of St Bernard*, English trans., London (1940).

GOUGAUD, LOUIS. *Dévotions et practiques ascétiques du moyen âge*, Collection Pax, XXI, Maredsous (1925).

GOUGAUD, LOUIS. *Ermites et reclus*, Ligugé, Vienne (1928).

KIRK, KENNETH E. *The Vision of God*, 2nd ed., London (1946).

KNOWLES, D. *The Monastic Order in England*, corr. ed., Cambridge (1949). Indispensable.

POWICKE, SIR F. M. Ed. and trans., *The Life of Ailred of Rievaulx by Walter Daniel*, Nelson's Medieval Classics (1950).

WILLIAMS, WATKIN. *Saint Bernard of Clairvaux*, Manchester (1935).

WILMART, A. *Auteurs spirituels et textes dévots de moyen âge latin*, Paris (1932). Important. Specialised articles providing general illumination.

GLOSSARY

GLOSSARY

The Glossary is intended to provide a complete list of forms found in the text. No form is entered under a head-word which does not occur in the text. Words are parsed where parsing is useful for the discrimination of form or meaning. *preposit.* is used to indicate the indeterminate inflected form of a noun after a preposition. No further indication of meaning may follow a form which is no more than a grammatical variant of the head-word.

ʒ follows *g* ; *ð*, *þ* follow *t* ; the prefix *i-* is ignored in head-words. † is attached to emended forms.

a, *interj.* ah, **5,**20

a (*before cons.*), **an** (*before vowels and h*), *indef. art.* a, an, **5,**3,13, **7,**16, etc. : *num. adj.* one, **13,**32, **14,**36, **22,**13, etc. ; **ane,** **4,**12 ; *in adv. phrases,* **a dei** (< OE on (*prep.*) + dæg/deg), one day, **13,**4n ; **ane hwile,** for a while, **15,**26 ; *pron.* one. **10,**18, **12,**10,36, etc. ; **anes,** *gen.* **13,**9 ; **þe ane,** *pl.* the first sort, **3,**20

aa, *adv.* always, ever, **27,**26

abbat, *n.* abbot, **12,**9, **19,**15

abit, 3 *sg. pres.* awaits, **8,**1 ; **abide,** *pres. pl. subj. as imper.* **8,**30

abute(n), *adv.* around, on every side, **7,**1, **17,**2, **21,**9, etc. ; *prep.* around, about, **16,**32, **23,**32

abuten, *prep.* (ever) without, **26,**6n

acemin, *infin.* adorn, **8,**29,31

acourin, *infin.* recover, **10,**20

acwenchen, *infin.* extinguish, **27,** 13,21 ; **acwencheð,** 3 *sg. pres.* **27,**23,25, **28,**11, etc.

acwitin (ut), *infin.* deliver, ransom, **23,**14,16

aga ð, *pl. pres.* pass away, go by, **7,**4

agras, *pret. impers.* : **him agras,** he was terrified, **11,**5

aʒein, *adv.* again, back, as a defence against, **10,**21, **11,**24, **14,**26, etc. ; *prep.* (set) against,

in contrast with, instead of, in spite of, **3,**28, **6,**24, **7,**22, etc. : **a ʒein hire ʒeincume,** to meet her returning, **23,**31

a ʒeines, *prep.* against, in comparison with, **14,**21, **19,**3

a ʒeinewardes, *adv.* backwards, **17,**5

ah, *conj.* but, and, **3,**31, **4,**6,9, etc.

ah, 3 *sg. pres.* owes, ought (to), should, **3,**15, **20,**37, **25,**10, **28,**34, etc.; **ahen,** *pl. pres.* **4,**10, **11,**33, **17,**8, etc.; **ahte,** *pret.* possessed, **21,**24, **25,**38 ; owed, **28,**33 ; **ahtest,** 2 *sg. pret.* **28,**31

ahne, *adj.* own, **7,**25,27,30, etc.

ahonget, *past. part.* hanged, **5,**20, **6,**1

ahte, ahtest, *see* **ah,** *v.*

ake, *pres. subj.* ache, **9,**11, **12,**27; **akinde,** *pres. part.* **9,**3

akeldeð, 3 *sg. pres.* cools, **27,**25

al, *adj.* all, **3,**14, **5,**39, **7,**21,38, etc.; **alle,** *sg. accus.* **17,**38, **19,**12,28,32; *sg. gen. in* **alles cunnes,** of all kinds, **26,**2 ; **alle,** *pl.* **4,**14, **6,**15,21, etc.: **al,** *pron.* all, everything, **3,**4,5,6, etc.; **alle,** *pl.* **3,**23, **8,**37, **24,**35, etc.; **alre,** *pl. gen.* **25,**9 ; *in adv. phrases,* **alle to gederes,** altogether, **6,**21 ; **mid alle,** entirely, completely, **4,**22; **ouer alle,** supremely, **8,**12: **al,** *adv.* all, entirely, **11,**13, **12,**8,

81

17,20, etc.; **over al**, completely, **13**,26

al, *conj. with inversion and subj.* although, **4**,19

alde, *adj.* old, **9**,28, **10**,4,6, etc.; **alde feader**, ancestor, first father, **9**,29n, **20**,25

allegate, *adv.* in all ways, all the time, **4**,19

alle, alles, *see* **al**, *adj.* and *pron.*

allunge, *adv.* wholly, altogether, **3**,16, **12**,5, **25**,1, etc.

almeast, *adv.* almost ; **almeast is**, it is more or less, **3**,17

almihti, *adj.* almighty, **10**,34, **23**,14, **27**,6

aloes, *n.* aloes, **13**,33

alre, *see* **al**, *pron.*

alswa, *adv.* in the same way, also, likewise, **12**,1, **16**,28, **22**,34, etc.: *in compound conj.* **alswa as . . . ne**, just as . . . so not, **7**,27 ; **as . . . alswa (as)**, as . . . so, **14**,7, **30**,24; **alswa as . . . alswa**, just as . . . so, **19**,20,21

am, 1 *sg. pres.* am, **5**,19,23 ; **nam**, am not, **25**,4,5,9, etc.

an, *see* **a, an**

anan, *adv.* at once, straightway, **14**,36, **23**,32

ancre, *n.* anchorite anchoress, **16**,16 ; *attributively*, **5**,21n, **16**,24,28 ; **ancren**, *pl.* **16**,25 ; **ancres**, *pl.* **5**,38

ancreful, *adj.* anxious, devoted, **13**,14n

ane, *adv.* alone, only, **4**,1, **5**,38, **7**,9, etc. *See also* **a, an**

anes, *see* **a, an**

anewil, *adj.* obstinate, **26**,1

anlepi, *adj.* single, only, **11**,14

ant, *conj.* and, **3**,2,4,12, etc.; **&**, **3**,7,17,27, etc.: *adv.* even (*rendering* Lat. &), **4**,36

Apocalipse, *n.* Book of Revelation, **24**,17, **26**,23

apostle, *n.* apostle, **4**,5,30, **5**,6

aras, *see* **arisen**

are, *n.* grace, mercy, **11**,5, **28**,24

arearen, *infin.* raise (up), erect, **9**,20, **21**,21; **areareð**, 3 *sg. pres.* **28**,17

arisen, *infin.* arise, **8**,19 ; **aras**, 3 *sg. pret.* **22**,1

ariste, *n.* resurrection, **8**,17,24,26, etc.

aromaz, *n. pl.* spices, **14**,8n, **15**,15, **16**,1, etc.

art, 2 *sg. pres.* art, **15**,32, **21**,27, **26**,27

arudde, *infin.* set free, deliver, **21**,31; **arudde**, 3 *sg. pret.* **21**,37; **arud**, *past part.* redeemed, **22**,27

as, *adv.* as, **3**,8,9,27, etc.; *conj.* **3**,31, **4**,9,19, etc. ; **ase**, **6**,35, **11**,19, **14**,32, etc.; **ase** forþ **as**, as fully as, **13**,36 ; **as** þ**ah** (*with subj.*), as if, **5**,9, **7**,32, **13**,7, etc. *See* **alswa**

asailin, *infin.* attack, **10**,5

asprete, *n.* harshness, rigour, bitterness, **6**,12

attri, *adj.* poisonous, **10**,25

aþ**et**, *prep.* until, **26**,17 : *conj.* (*with subj.*) until, **17**,27

awakeneð, *sg. pres.* awakens, **is** produced, **14**,4

awei, *adv.* away, **6**,28

axe, *n.* axe, **19**,18

ba, *adj.* both (*sometimes post-positive*), **6**,25, **7**,34, **10**,18, etc.: **ba twa his honden**, both of His hands, **24**,28; *pron.* **16**,27

baldeliche, *adv.* boldly, **6**,18, **10**,11

banere, *n.* banner, **10**,14; **baneres**, *pl.* **10**,12

banes, *n. pl.* bones, relics, **4**,12

baðe, *adj.* both, **6**,11, **24**,33, **29**,9; *adv.* **21**,14

bead, *see* **beoden**, *infin.*

bearnde, 3 *sg. pret. intrans.* burned, **12**,21 ; **bearninde**, *pres. part. as adj.* **26**,21, **28**,26

beast, *n.* beast, **17**,3; **beastes**, *pl.* beasts, cattle, **16**,37, **20**,26

beate(n), *infin.* beat, **10**,31, **11**,21; **beatest**, 2 *sg. pres.* **11**,14; **beot**, 3 *sg. pret.* **10**,34, **11**,15 ; **beote**, *sg. pret. subj.* **10**,32

beatunge, *n.* beating, chastisement, 11,17

baðe, *n.* bath, 24,6,7,11, etc.; **beaðes,** *pl.* 24,11

beawbelez, *n. pl.* splendid gifts, 21,13n

bed, *see* **bit**

beggin, *infin.* beg, 7,16n

beoden, *infin.* offer, 27,5 ; **beodeð,** *pl. pres.* 28,10 ; **bead,** 3 *sg. pret.* 21,23

beoden, *n. pl.* prayers, 28,23

beodes mon, *n.* bedesman, 7,17n

beo(n), *infin.* be ; live, 3,8,14,16, etc.; **beoð,** *pl. pres.* 3,7,22, 4,2, etc. ; **beoð bi þe leaste,** (they) make do with the least, 4,7n; **beo,** *sg. subj.* (*often with future sense*), 5,25, 6,4, 11,23, etc.; **beon,** *pl. subj.* 4,2,8, 13,26, etc.: **beo ȝe,** 16,21, 17,16; **ibeo,** *sg. imper.* 15,30; **beoð,** *pl. imper.* 20,1 ; **ibeon,** *past part.* 22,16

beot, beote, *see* **beate(n)**

bereð, 3 *sg. pres.* bears, carries, wears, 3,32, 18,11, 28,13; **beoreð,** *pl. pres.* 10,37n; **beoren,** *pl. pres. subj.* may bear, 17,39; **ber,** 3 *sg. pret.* 10,36, 13,7; **beren,** *pl. pret.* 6,32

best, *adj., adv.* best, 3,23, 13,16

betere, *adj.* better, 3,22, 4,18,29, etc.: *adv.* 9,10, 11,37, 25,4, etc.

bi, *prep.* by (means of), along, on, 3,30, 4,7,21, 6,16,29, etc.; about, 7,7, 8,14, 15,27, 18,25, etc.; towards, 18,22; in respect of, 6,34, 23,10

bichearren, *infin.* deceive, 12,7

bicluset, *past part.* enclosed, 16,23

bicoruen, *past part.* **heafdes bicoruen,** beheaded, 9,25n

bicumen, *pl. pres. subj.* become, 4,20

biginnen, *infin.* begin, 3,16 ; **bigon,** 3 *sg. pret.* 11,11

biginnunge, *n.* beginning, 15,9

bigurd, 3 *sg. pres.* surrounds, 16,37; **bigurde,** *past part.* 17,8

bi ȝete, *n.* profit, advantage, 8,35, 26,2

bihalden, *infin.* look upon, 21,19; **bihalde,** *sg. pres. subj.* 23,4; **bihald,** *sg. imper.* look, observe, 6,20,25 ; **biheold,** 3 *sg. pret.* beheld, 13,12

bihaten, *past part.* promised, 20,23

biheue, *adj. used as n.* profit, advantage, 19,30, 20,30, 26,8

bihinde, *prep.* behind, 6,27

bihofde, *pret. impers.* was necessary, 24,6

bileaue, *n.* faith, 24,3

bilimeð, 3 *sg. pres.* dismembers: **bilimeð him of him seolf,** cuts himself off as a member from Him, 9,11

bimong, *prep.* among, 30,15n.

bindeð, 3 *sg. pres.* binds, compels, 30,5 ; **bint,** 3 *sg. pres.* 30,6 ; **ibunden,** *past part.* 16,21, 18,12, 30,16

bineomen, *infin.* deprive (*with double object*), 22,28

bineoðen, *adv.* beneath, at the bottom, 22,13

bireowsunge, *n.* repentance, 12,30, 14,12,15

biseche, 1 *sg. pres.* seek, beseech, 21,34 ; **bisecheð,** *pl. pres.* 4,17

bisenchen, *infin.* submerge, plunge, 26,4, 30,14

biseoð, *pl. imper.* look, 27,2

biset, *past part.* surrounded, besieged, 17,2, 21,9, 22,5

bisie, *adj. pl.* busy: **beoð bisie,** exert yourselves, 20,1

bisiliche, *adv.* diligently, 27,7

bisischipe, *n.* exercise, effort, 19,5

bit, 3 *sg. pres.* prays, asks, 18,16; **bed,** 3 *sg. pret.* 11,5

bitacneð, 3 *sg. pres.* signifies, denotes, 27,25, 28,38; **bitacnið,** *pl. pres.* 13,33, 14,9, 26,36 ; **bitacnede,** 3 *sg. pret.* 27,35 ; **bitacnet,** *past part.* 6,36, 7,12, 8,10, etc.

bitacnunge, *n.* signification: **for bitacnunge,** as a sign, 22,15

bitellunge, *n.* excuse, 22,29

biten, *infin.* bite, taste, 10,25 ; **biten o(n),** bite at, 15,33, 17,4

biteon, *infin.* bestow, give away, 25,4; **biteo,** 1 *sg. pres.* 28,9

bitter, *adj.* bitter, **10**,20, **14**,23,31, etc.; *as n.* what is bitter, **15**,26; **bittres,** *gen.*: nawt bittres, nothing bitter, **10**,25; **bittre,** *wk. adj. as n.* **15**,33; **bittre,** *pl. adj.* **13**,33 (2)

bitterliche, *adv.* bitterly, cruelly, 10,34

bitternesse, *n.* bitterness, **14**,2,3,11, etc. ; **bitternesses,** *pl.* **14**,4,10, 16,11

bituhhen, *prep.* between, among, 7,33 ; **bituhen,** 21,32. Cp. **bitweone(n)**

biturn, *sg. imper. reflex.* turn, 23,29 ; **biturnd up on,** *past. part.* set upon, directed towards, 21,11

bitweone(n), *prep.* between, among, 6,14, **11**,18,20, etc.: swa muchel is bitweonen . . . the difference between . . . is so great, 23,36

biuore(n), *prep.* before, in front of, **6**,37, **13**,29, 21,22, 29,19; *adv.* in the first place, beforehand, **16**,2, 21,2

biuoren hond, *adv.* beforehand, 8,30

bleasie, 3 *sg. pres. subj.* blaze, burst into flame, 26,22

i-blescet, *past part.,* blessed, **15**,29, 24,11

blikien, *infin.* shine, 9,31

blisful, *adj.* blessed, glorious, 8,17,26; **blisfule,** *pl. adj. or adv.* in blessedness, 8,19

blisse, *n.* bliss, joy, glory, beatitude, 3,10,14,15, etc.; **blissen,** *pl.* 7,22, 30,24,28

blissin, *infin.* rejoice, glory, 6,6 (*reflex.*), 8,32; **blissi,** 1 *sg. pres.* (*subj.*) *reflex.* 5,22; **blissi ð,** *pl. imper. reflex.* 7,21; **iblisset,** *past part.*; **meast iblisset,** greatest in glory, 20,17

bli ðe, *adj.* glad, joyful, 3,8, **15**,31: *or adv.* joyfully, 6,2 : **bli ðe iheortet,** glad at heart, 17,14

bli ðeliche, *adv.* joyfully, 12,19

blod, *n.* blood, 7,5, **8**,37, 21,6, etc.; **blodes,** *gen.* 9,6

boc, *n.* book: þet luue boc, the book of love, *scil.* Song of Solomon, 15,38, 17,17

bodi, *n.* 8,26,30 (*with pl. sense*) body, 13,39, etc., 25,39

i-boht, bohte, bohten, *see* **buggen**

bondes, *n. pl.* bands, 18,13

bone, *n.* petition, 15,19, 20

bote, *see* dead bote

botte, *n.* cudgel, 11,29

brad, *adj.* wide, broad, **22**,12 ; **brade,** *pl.* 18,13

bredde, 3 *sg. pret.* engendered, nourished, 12,20

breoste, *n. preposit.* breast, heart, 28,13

briht, *adj.* bright, clear, 8,27, 19,24 ; **brihtre,** *comp.* brighter, 25,26; *or adv.* more brightly, 10,8

brihte ð, 3 *sg. pres.* makes bright, 19,3

bringen, *infin.* bring, 26,20; **brohte,** 3 *sg. pret.* 12,33, **13**,31, 14,6, etc.

brondes, *n. pl.* brands, the fire, 12,23

bruche, *n.* breaking, fracture, 16,28,30

brune, *n.* burning, fire, **12**,25, 13,22, 27,27, etc.

brunie, *n.* corslet, coat of mail, 18,12

buggen, *infin.* buy, purchase, pay for, 9,22, **16**,6, 25,15, etc.; **bu ð,** 3 *sg. pres.* 15,13, 22,30; **bugge ð,** *pl. pres.* 15,17; **bugge,** 3 *sg. pres. subj.* 25,14 ; **bohte,** 3 *sg. pret.* 22,30,31, 23,5, etc.; **bohten,** *pl. pret.* 9,22, 14,7, 15,14; **iboht,** *past part.* 25,18

buhe ð, 3 *sg. pres.* bends, 27,5

buhsum, *adj.* obedient, 7,9

bulten, *infin.* recoil, rebound, 11,25; **bulte ð,** 3 *sg. pres.*: **bulte ð** a ʒein, reverberates, 11,24n

bultunge, *n.* recoil, repercussion, reverberation, 11,27

i-bunden, *see* **bindeð**

bune, *n.* buying, purchase, expense, 9,21, 12,16

burh, *n.* town, city, 4,20. 26,33

burhen, *infin.* save, redeem, 11,29

burhmen, *n. pl.* citizens, 4,20

bute(n), *prep.* without, except, but, only, 4,1, 5,18,23, etc.: **buten ende**, everlasting, 4,15, 7,23, 8,27, etc.: **nis bute**, is only, 6,10, 8,14, 9,9, etc.: **bute þe an**, only one (of them), 12,36: **bute ane þet**, only because, 10,35: *conj.* unless, 20,10, 26,29, 29,3

buð, *see* **buggen**

buuen, *prep.* above, 5,1, 9,18: *adv.* at the top, 22,12

cader, *n.* cradle, 16,22n

cald, *adj.* cold, 12,22, 26,26,28; **calde**, *wk.* 12,37

cang, *adj.* foolish, silly, 7,36n

canges, *n. pl.* fools, ninnies, 9,21

castel, *n.* castle, 10,11,12, 16,32, etc.; **castles**, *pl.* 25,23

chamberleng, *n.* chamberlain, 30,17n

chap, *n.* bargain, price: **se liht chap**, so cheap a price, 25,20

chaste, *adj.* chaste, 12,20, 25,11

chastete, *n.* chastity, 12,8,16

chearite, *n.* charity, 29,32

chearre, *n.* time: **sum chearre**, *adv.* at some time, once, 4,21, 29,30

cheose, *infin.* choose, 13,30: *sg. pres. subj. as imper.* 29,13; **icorene**, *past part. as n. pl.* chosen ones, elect, 3,19

cherte, *n.* dearness, holding precious, 29,33

cherubines, *n. gen.* cherubin's, 6,36

child, *n.* child, 11,20, 13,24, 23,11, etc.; **children**, *pl.* 9,27

chirche, *n.* church, 3,12, 6,2, 23,1, etc.

chulle, *see* **wulle**

cla ð, *n.* clothing, 20,6; **claðes**, *pl.* clothes, 4,1, 9,28

cleane, *adj.* pure, clean, 12,8, 15,6, 24,13, etc.

cleannesse, *n.* purity, cleanness, 12,16, 25,11

cleansin, *infin.* cleanse, 24,9

clearkes, *n. pl.* clerics, 8,9

cleopie, 1 *sg. pres.* call, count, 7,15; **cleopeð**, 3 *sg. pres.* 9,38; **cleopieð**, *pl. pres.* 13,27

climbeð, *pl. pres.* climb, 6,16; **clomb**, 3 *sg. pret.* 6,18

clowes de gilofre, *n. pl.* clove-gillyflowers, cloves, 13,4

cluppunges, *n. pl.* embraces, 24,14

(i-)cnawen, *infin.* know, recognise, acknowledge, 18,28, 19,27

cneaue, *n.* boy, 17,15

cniht, *n.* knight, soldier, 7,36, 22,10; **cnihtes**, *gen.* 22,37; *pl.* 8,9, 22,8

cnihtschipe, *n.* chivalry, valour, 22,7; feat of arms, 23,3

cnut, 3 *sg. pres.* knots, 24,26

cokes, *n. gen.* cook's, 17,15

con, 3 *sg. pres.* is able, 25,7, 29,35; 30,22; **const**, 2 *sg. pres.* 26,6; **cuðe**, *sg. pret. subj.* knew, 19,10

conseiler, *n.* counsellor, 30,17

i-corene, *see* **cheose**

cos, *n.* kiss, 27,5

costnede, 3 *sg. pret.* cost, 22,32

cote, *n.* cottage, 9,20

crucifix, *n.* crucifix, 23,2

cruneð, 3 *sg. pres.* crowns, 22,21; **icrunet**, *past part.* 22,23

cuchene, *n.* kitchen, 17,15

i-cud, *see* **cuðe**

cumen, *infin.* come, 23,21,25, 29,5: **aȝein cumen**, return, 23,21; **kimeð**, 3 *sg. pres.* 4,24, 27, 7,1, etc.: **kimeð up**, develops, 13,20; **cume**, *sg. pres. subj.* 13,20; **cum**, *sg. imper.* 23,29; **cuminde**, *pres. part.* 16, 12 (2; *second use as verbal noun, see note*); **com**, *sg. pret.* 8,17, 13,6, 12,4, etc.; **come**, *sg. pret. subj.* 11,4,34; **icumen**, *past part.* 18,32

cunde, *n.* kind, birth, **22**,2

cundeliche, *adv.* by nature, **27**,16

cunnes, *n. gen.* of kin : **of uueles cunnes cunde,** from the stock of a wicked race, **22**,2: **alles cunnes selhôe,** happiness of every sort, **26**,2n ; **cunne,** *n. pl. gen.* of kinds : **twauald cunne mede,** rewards of two kinds, **7**,31n, **on alle cunne wise,** in all kinds of ways, **20**,22

i-cunnet, *past part.* born, **25**,5

curtel, *n.* tunic, **9**,28, **10**,6 ; **curtles,** *pl.* **9**,33

cuôe, 1 *sg. pres.* make known, show, **21**,35 ; **cuô,** *sg. imper.* **18**,3; **icud,** *past part.* **25**,19

cuôe, *see* con

i-cweme, *adj.* pleasant, **13**,15

cwemeô, 3 *sg. pres.* pleases, **9**,11

cwen, *n.* queen, **13**,6, **21**,23, **25**,25

cwic, *adj.* living, **5**,3,4,12

cwicliche, *adv.* actively, **27**,26

cwicnesse, *n.* life: **i cwicnesse,** in lively fashion, **5**,11

dahes, *see* dei

dahunge, *n.* dawn, daybreak, **4**,35

dale, *n.* part, section, **3**,2, **18**,32, **30**,35

dame, *n.* (*as form of address*) my lady, **21**,27

danger, *n.* lordliness, arrogance, ungracious treatment, **7**,18n, **17**,14

dead, *adj.* dead, **5**,5,12: (when I am) dead, **21**,36; **deade,** *oblique, as n.,* **4**,38n, **5**,10,29, etc.; *pl.* **4**,33,37 : *as n.* **3**,21, **5**,39, **17**,13, etc.

dead bote, *n.* penance, act of satisfaction, **3**,1n, **14**,12

deadliche, *adj.* deadly ; mortal, **10**,7, **23**,34

deadlicnesse, *n.* mortality: **Cristes deadlicnesse,** the likeness of Christ's death, **18**,1

dealen, *infin.* separate, **26**,4 ; **dealeô,** 3 *sg. pres.* shares, **12**,25; **lo deale,** *sg. imper.* distinguish then, **9**,16n

dear, 1 *sg. pres.* dare, **29**,37

deaô, *n.* death, **5**,3, **7**,9,10, etc.; **deaôes,** *gen.* : **deaôes dunt,** deathblow, **11**,22, **deaôes wunde,** deathwound, **21**,33; **deaôe,** *preposit.* **22**,1

deboneirte, *n.* graciousness, loving-kindness, **21**,26

deciples, *n. pl.* disciples, **22**,15, **29**,2,6. *Cp.* desciples

dede, *n.* deed: **ful dede,** a completed action, **13**,35; **wiô dede,** in deed, **17**,12; **efter þe ilke dede,** on account of that very deed, **21**,36

dei, *n.* day, **8**,19, **26**,17: *in adv. phrases,* **niht & dei,** **3**,7, a dei, one day, **13**,4n, al dei, all day, **23**,28; **deies,** *gen.* **28**,4; **dahes,** *pl.* **23**,24

deieô, 3 *sg. pres.* dies, **7**,14 ; **deide,** 3 *sg. pret.* **8**,26

delit, *n.* delight, pleasure, **7**,23, **11**,36; **delices,** *pl.* **12**,1,19

deme(n), *infin.* judge, give judgment, **8**,7,8,11; **demeô ow seoluen,** *pl. imper.* judge for yourselves, **29**,9; **idemet,** *past part.* **8**,8

deoflen, deofles, *see* deouel

deore, *adj.* dear, beloved, precious, expensive, **7**,13, **11**,34, **15**,35, etc., **29**,33 : *adv.* dear, **9**,23: **se deore,** at such a (high) price, **22**,29, **29**,22 ; **deorre,** *ádj. comp.* dearer, **22**,31

deorewurôe, *adj.* precious, **7**,5. **10**,34, **11**,10, etc.

deorewurôliche, *adv.* honourably, preciously, scrupulously, **30**,34

deorling, *n.* beloved, **6**,26

deorre, *see* deore

deouel, *n.* devil, **14**,32, **23**,25 ; **deofles,** *gen.* **10**,9, **11**,29, **14**,25, etc.; **deoflen,** *pl.* **22**,5

depeint, *past part.* painted, **24**,24

derf, *adj.* cruel, hard, austere, **3**,7n

derf, *n.* suffering, pain, **19**,22

deruen, *infin.* torment, mortify, **18**,17 ; **derueô,** *sg. pres.* **28**,8 desciples, *n. pl.* disciples, 13,15n. *Cp.* deciples

dest, *see* don

destruet, *past part.* laid waste, devastated, 21,10

deð, *see* don

deuleset, *interj.* God knows, 9,8, 18,18

deuociun, *n.* devoutness, earnestness, 12,13

deuot, *adj.* pious, devout, 15,16

disceplines, *n. pl.* scourgings, 12,11

disches, *n. pl.* dishes, 17,15

do, *see* don

dom, *n.* judgment, 8,11; domes, *gen.*: domes dei, Day of Judgment, 8,19, 9,31; dome, *preposit.* 28,29

do(n), *infin.* do (*often replacing verb already used*), make, 13,13, 28,36, etc.: **don se wa him seoluen**, so to mortify himself, 10,16; **ful do . . . pine**, mortify completely, 13,36; donne, *infin.* 22,9, 30,21; **do of ham,** 1 *sg. pres.* attach to them, 30,34; dest, 2 *sg. pres.* 19,29,30; deð, 3 *sg. pres.* 7,34, 10,12, puts, 11,19, etc.; doð, *pl. pres.* 3,5,31, 4,28, etc.; do, *sg. pres. subj.* 24,22, may show, 28,24 ; don, *pl. pres. subj.* 4,22, put, 21,29 ; do, *sg. imper.* 19,29,32 : **do scheome,** maltreat, 5,2 ; dude, 1 *sg. pret.* inflicted, 19,11: **dude ich me,** I applied to myself, I made use of, 12,35 ; 3 *sg. pret.* 11,21, 12,31, 16,28, etc.; put, 11,18, 13,8; gave, 20,32, 23,15; made, 24,27; **dude him i,** entered, 22,9; duden, *pl. pret.* caused, 27,36†n, 28,32; idon, *past part.* 17,10, 20,23, 28,9, etc.; behaved, 23,29

dred, *n.* fear, 10,14

dredeð, *pl. pres.* fear, 13,19

dreheð, 3 *sg. pres.* endures, suffers, 6,24, 15,21; *pl. pres.* 3,5, 7,26; droh, 3 *sg. pret.* 6,7

drinken, *infin.* drink, 13,2, 27,36; drinkeð, 3 *sg. pres.* 10,19; dronc, 3 *sg. pret.* 10,24

driueð, 3 *sg. pres.* drives, 27,28,29
(2,055)

droh, *see* dreheð

dronc, *see* drinken

drunch, *n.* drink, 10,25, 12,38, 28,21, etc.; drunches, *pl.* 10,19, 12,24

dude, duden, *see* don,

duhen, *infin.* be good for: **ah wel mei duhen,** but it can serve the purpose, 6,34n

dulue, *sg. pret. subj.* digged, 19,19

dun, *n.* mountain, 15,36; dunes, *pl.* 17,16,19,23, etc.

duneward, *adv.* downwards, 27,5

dunt, *n.* blow, 11,23,25,28, etc.: **deaðes dunt,** deathblow, 11,22

dweole, *n.* deceit, vanity, 6,5

eadeaweð, 3 *sg. pres.* appears again, 4,35

eadi, *adj.* blessed, 7,19

eadmodliche, *adv.* humbly, 17,35, 18,28

eadmodnesse, *n.* humility, 6,20, 23,24, etc.

eahtuðe, *adj.* eighth, 30,35

eani, *adj.* any, 5,17,25, 8,38, etc.

ear, *adv.* before, previously, sooner, 4,19, 6,3, 11,4, etc.: *conj.* (*with subj.*) before, 20,26, 24,6: **ear þen,** sooner than, before, 13,20,30

eard, *n.* country, 7,33

earmes, *n. pl.* arms, 18,13, 22,13, 23,31, etc.

earre, *adj. comp.* former, previously mentioned, 19,32, 27,17; earste, *adj. superl.* 14,12,14, 24,14

earst, *adv.* first, 7,10, 14,13, 15,9, etc.

eaðe, *adv.* easily, without difficulty, 27,3

eauer, *adv.* ever, always, 3,4,5,29, etc.: **eaure,** 24,11: **hwil eauer,** all the time that, 14,28

eawt, *n.* anything, 20,10

ec, *adv.* also, 6,36,17,12,18,26, etc.

eche, *n.* ache, 9,3, 13,22

eche, *adj.* eternal, 4,37, 9,22

ed, *prep.* at, 7,35, 8,2, 11,9, etc., from, 12,16

11

edfleon, *infin.* escape, 21,29

edhalden, *infin.* withhold, hold back, 25,8; edhalt, 3 *sg. pres.* 15,7, 20,19

edlutien, *infin.* hide away, 26,14

edstearten, *infin.* spring away from, avoid, 13,21

edstuteð, *pl. pres.* remain, linger, 4,22n

edstont, 3 *sg. pres.* stands still, stops, 3,31

eft, *adv.* again, later, furthermore, 8,35, 10,29, 13,39, etc.

efter, *adv.* afterwards, 14,34, 16,3, 24,23 ; *prep.* after, 3,1, 4,35, 7,38, etc., according to, 22,13, on account of 21,35, after the fashion of, 8,31, for, 11,35

ehnen, *n. pl.* eyes, 19,26

ehsihðe, *n.* eyesight, eyes, 21,22

ei, *adj. pron.* any, 15,1n, 18,24, 28,17, etc.

eileð, 3 *sg. pres.* troubles, afflicts, 4,38, 6,34

eise, *n.* ease, 7,37, 8,10, 9,18, etc.

eisil, *n.* vinegar, 27,12,23,30, etc.

elheowet, *adj.* pallid, 11,37n

elles, *adv.* else, otherwise, 20,20, 25,16,17, etc.

elleshwer, *adv.* elsewhere, 30,28

elne, *n.* strength, comfort, 29,14

elþeodie, *n. pl.* foreigners, strangers, 3,27n

ende, *n.* end, 4,16, 7,24, 8,27, etc.: on ende, finally, 16,30, 21,4,18 etc.

englene, *n. pl. gen.* of angels, 19,11

ennu, *n.* weariness, 14,37

ententes, *n. pl.* intentions, 19,31

eode, 3 *sg. pret.* went, 17,33, 26,36 ; eoden, *pl. pret.* 13,9: *see* gan

eorneð, 3 *sg. pres.* runs, 23,31; *pl. pres.* 8,30

eorðe, *n.* earth, ground, 3,10,19, 5,1, etc.

eorðene, *adj.* made of earth, 21,10

eorðlich, *adj.* earthly, 19,25, 26,21, 29,14

eoten, *infin.* eat, 13,2

epistle, *n.* epistle, 4,31

erede, 3 *sg. pret. subj.* ploughed, 19,19

essample, *n.* illustration, 11,33

este, *n.* pleasure, comfort, 10,9,28, 12,20, etc.

etscene, *adj.* easily seen, manifest, 24,30n

euch, *adj.* every, all, 5,9,12, 6,33, etc.: on euche half, on all sides, 22,10: euch an, each one, 29,13

euene, *n.* nature; fashion, 13,36, 18,19†n

i-euenet, *past part.* likened, 3,20

euening, *n.* peer, equal, 29,37

euentid, *n.* evening, 28,4

euesede, 3 *sg. pret.* trimmed, 25,32

euesunge, *n.* clippings, trimmings, 25,33

fa, *n.* foe, 28,21; va, 28,17; fan, *pl.* 21,9, 25,36; van, 21,28,37

failede, 3 *sg. pret.* failed, was unsuccessful : failede . . . of his hure, missed his reward, 27,37

fallen, *infin.* fall, 14,18 ; falleð, 3 *sg. pres.* (it) is necessary, 3,1; is comprised, 19,31; hangs, 21,7: falleð to, befalls, 4,23; feol, 3 *sg. pret.* fell, 11,17

fals, *adj.* false, 18,8

famen, *n. pl.* enemies, 28,16

fan, *see* fa

feader, *n.* father, 7,9, 9,30, 10,34, etc.; feaderes, *gen.* 29,4; *pl.* 9,27: ure alde feader, our first father, 9,29, 20,25

i-fearen, *past part.* travelled, 11,34

fearlac, *n.* terror, something frightful, 10,1

fearlich, *adj.* terrible, 9,36

feasten, *n. pl.* fasts, 12,10

feasteð, 3 *sg. pres.* fasts, 18,14

feblesce, *n.* weakness, 17,26

febli, 3· *sg. pres. subj.* grow weak, 12,27

fecchen, *infin.* fetch, 12,4

fed, *sg. imper.* feed, 28,21

feherest, *superl. adj.* fairest, 21,19, 25,4

feht, *n.* warfare, fight, struggle, 7,37,38, 8,1, etc.

fehteð, *pl. pres.* fight, 8,1

feier, *adj.* fair, 24,13; **feire,** *wk., pl.* 21,14,18

feieð, 3 *sg. pres.* joins, 6,22; **ifeiet,** *past part.* 6,30, 14,19. *See also* veien.

feire, *adv.* fair, 22,36. *See also* feier

fel, *n.* skin, 10,4,7

feleð, 3 *sg. pres.* feels, 5,30; **felde,** 3 *sg. pret.* 15,22

feol, *see* fallen

feolahe, *n.* companion, 8,34; **feolahes,** *pl.* 16,20

feole, *adj.* many, 21,14,21, 22,6, etc.

feond, *n.* enemy, devil, 10,1, 23,23

feor, *adv.* far, afar, 11,34, 29,24; **of feor,** apart, at a distance, 13,11n

feor, *n.* price: sete feor o, set a price on, 25,22n

feorðe, *adj.* fourth, 24,29

feorlich, *adj.* strange, unnatural; **na feorlich,** nothing strange, 7,32n

feorrene, *adj.* distant, 21,2

ferd, *n.* army, 14,29

fere, *n.* friend, 23,13,14,16, etc.; **iferen,** *pl.* 23,10

i-festnet, *past part.* fastened, 6,15

fet, *see* fot

fifte, *adj.* fifth, 3,2

(i-)finden, *infin.* find, discover, reveal, 4,14, 15,23, 17,22, etc.; **ifind,** 3 *sg. pres.* 23,9, 24,36, **ifint,** 3 *sg. pres.* (*with infin.*), 27,7; **ifindeð,** *pl. pres.* 4,16, 5,10; **ifond,** 3 *sg. pret.* (*with infin.*) 27,10; **ifunde,** *sg. pret. subj.* 10,32

finger, *n.* finger, 9,10

fisiciens, *n. pl.* physicians, 12,31

fleoð, *pl. pres.* fly (from), 8,37; **flih,** *sg. imper.* 14,33; **fleah,** 3 *sg. pret.* fled, 14,30; **fluhen,** *pl. pret.* fled, 22,16

flesch, *n.* flesh, 6,34, 9,29,31, etc.;

flesches, *gen.* of the flesh, carnal, bodily, 6,5,8, 8,38, etc.

fleschlich, *adj.* physical, carnal, 12,34; **fleschliche,** *pl. adj.* 3,28

fleschliche, *adv.* in the flesh, 29,7,11

fleschwise, *adj.* carnal-minded, solicitous about the body, 12,26

flih, fluhen, *see* fleoð

fode, *n.* food, 28,23

folc, *n.* people, nation, 9,35,36,37, etc.

i-folen, *past part.* entered: ifolen o slepe, fallen asleep, 13,5n

foles, *n. pl.* fools, 3,31

folhere, *n.* follower, 10,26

folhin, *infin.* follow, 10,27, 14,34; **folheð,** 3 *sg. pres.* 10,20

i-fond, *see* (i-)finden

fondunge, *n.* temptation, 13,31; **fondunges,** *pl.* 14,21,25,35

for, *prep.* for, on account of, for the sake of, instead of, 5,28,36, 8,37, etc.; **forte,** (in order) to (*before infin.*), 5,17, 6,1, 7,5, etc.; **for hwi,** *see* hwi; **for hwon,** *see* hwon; **for þe,** for those who, 14,24; **for þi,** and so, therefore, on this account, for this purpose, 3,11, 5,30,33, etc., **nawt for þi,** nevertheless, 18,11; **for þi þet,** because, 6,16, 10,2, 14,17, etc.; **bute for þi þet,** only to the extent that, 19,22; **for,** *conj.* for, because, 3,7,8,17, etc.

forbereð, 3 *sg. pres.* avoids, passes over, 17,27; **forber,** 3 *sg. pret.* *reflex.* desisted, 11,10

forbuheð, 3 *sg. pres.* turns aside, 17,27

forbisne, *n.* example, 21,8

fordede, *n.* an act of service, a favour, 23,17n

fordeð, 3 *sg. pres.* fulfils, promotes 10,21n; **iuorðet,** *past part.* fulfilled, 11,9; **iforðet,** 30,5

foreoden, *see* forgeað

foreword, *n.* agreement, bargain, 8,33

forgeað, 3 *sg. pres.* does without,

forgoes, 10,19; foreoden,*pl. pret.* 29,7

forgulte, *past part.* convicted of sin, 20,26

for ʒef, *sg. imper.* forgive, 6,21

for ʒeme, 3 *sg. pres. subj.* neglect, 13,39

for ʒeoten, *infin.* forget, 24,22,23, 27; for ʒet, 3 *sg. pres.* 18,19

forhorin, *infin. reflex.* commit adultery, 23,20; forhori, 3 *sg. pres. subj. reflex,* 23,22; forhoret, *past part.* defiled, made unchaste, 23,33

forkeoruen, *infin.* cut off, 9,9

forlorene, *past part. as n. pl.* damned, lost, 18,22

forme, *adj. superl.* first, 24,15 ; þe forme, *pl.* the first sort, 3,22,24

forsakest, 2 *sg. pres.* dost deny, repudiate, 26,2

forte, *see* for

for ð, *adv.* forth, onwards, on, advanced, 3,31, 14,24; ase for ð as, as fully as, 13,36; se for ð as, so completely as, 18,10 ; for ðre, *comp. adv.* further, next, 13,9

i-for ðet, *see* forde ð

for ð ʒong, *n.* course, continuance, 15,10

for ðre, *see* for ð

for ðriht, *adv.* straightway, promptly, 13,2

for ðward, *adv.* forward, onwards, 3,29, 4,20, 5,26

forwarpe, *past part.* abandoned, 11,13

forwur ðe ð, *pl. pres.* degenerate into, 12,31n

fot, *n.* foot, 22,13; fet, *pl.* 20,26

fowr, *num.* 16,22, 23,9,12, etc.

fremede, *adj. as n. pl.* strangers 22,17

freo, *adj.* free-born, free, 13,24; freoest, *superl.* most generous, 25,7

freolec, *n.* liberality, generosity, 20,19n, 25,37

freond, *n.* friend, 10,23, 30,14 ; *pl.* 24,31

freoten, *pl. pres. subj.* devour, feed on, 16,37

from, *prep.* from, away from, 3,28, 6,28, 14,30, etc.

frommard, *prep.* away from, 16,8

froure, *n.* comfort, 4,8, 29,13

fuheles, *n. pl.* birds, 20,26

ful, *adj.* full ; completed, 10,36, 13,34,35; *adv.* full, completely, 13,35, 27,34 ; ful wel, well enough 12,2; (*as intensive*) very, 14,23, 22,27; ful for ð, far advanced, 14,24

ful, *adj.* filthy, unclean, 18,8, 27,29

fulle ð, 3 *sg. pres.* fulfils, 20,13

fulluht, *n.* baptism, 24,14

fultohe, *past part. as adj.* ill-disciplined, 12,24

i-funde, *see* (i-)finden

fur, *n.* fire, 6,32, 12,21, 26,4, etc.

furene, *adj.* fiery, made of fire, 6,31, 7,2

galle, *n.* gall, 28,6

galnesses, *n. gen.* of lust, 13,22

gan, *infin.* go, 15,35; gea ð, 3 *sg. pres.* 10,11, 16,8; ga ð, *pl. pres.* 4,3,11,13, etc.; ga, 3 *sg. pres. subj.* 5,26; gan, *pl. pres. subj.* 4,19; ga, *sg. imper.* 13,11: *see* eode

gast, *n.* spirit, 12,28, 14,1, 16,29: þe hali gast, the Holy Ghost, 29,4,8; þe hali gastes, the Holy Ghost's, 29,13: i gast, in the spirit, spiritual, 13,39

gastelich, *adj.* spiritual, 28,37

ga ð, gea ð, *see* gan

gederes, *see* togederes

gederin, *infin.* gather, 27,7,10 ; gederi, 1 *sg. pres.* 26,35; gederi ð, *pl. imper.* 26,32

geine ð, 3 *sg. pres.*: ne geine ð me nawt, it profits me nothing, 10,5

gentil, *adj.* of good family, noble, 7,34, 21,1

gersum, *n.* treasure, 3,32

gestnin, *infin.* lodge, 27,8 ; gestnede, 3 *sg. pret.* 27,9

gilofre, *see* clowes de gilofre

gingiure, *n.* ginger, 13,3

giste, *n.* (place of) lodging, 3,32

Giwes, *n. gen.* Jew's, 28,14 ; Giws, *pl.* 27,31; Giwene, *pl. gen.* 23,16

Giwerie, *n.* Jewry, 23,14n,15

gleade, *adj.* content, 17,5: gleade iheortet, glad at heart, 5,34

gleadfulre, *comp. adj.* more joyful, 23,33

gleadien, *infin.* rejoice, be glad: gleadien of, rejoice in, 19,27; gleadieð, *pl. imper.* 7,21

gleadliche, *adv.* gladly, 8,14

gleames, *n. pl.* rays, 26,17

gleden, *n. pl.* coals, 28,26

gleowde, 3 *sg. pret.* revelled, made merry, 11,38

gloire, *n.* glory, 8,17, 12,5

gnedeliche, *adv.* frugally, barely, 4,1

god, *adj.* good, 4,3, 8,33,34, etc.; gode, *wk.* 3,21,29, 17,34, etc.; *fem. accus.* 3,17; *pl.* 3,20,22, 4,18, etc.; þe gode, the good man, 14,35; *pl.* 7,28, 20,30

god, *n.* good (thing), 4,21, 11,32, 13,13, etc.: al . . . of god, all the good, whatever good, 3,6

Godd, *n. nom., oblique,* God, to God, etc., 4,29, 5,5,14, etc.; Godes, *gen.* 3,7,16,19, etc.; Godd seolf, God Himself, 4,14n, 8,14

goddeden, *n. pl.* acts of kindness, 22,6n

Goddhead, *n.* Godhead, 22,11

i-godet, *past part.*: igodet of, provided with, 20,7

godspel, *n.* gospel, 15,14, 16,9, 21,5, etc.

gold, *n.* gold, 13,8

gomenes, *n. pl.* games, jests, 3,30

gomnede, 3 *sg. pret.* played, dallied, 11,38

grace, *n.* grace, 5,8, 8,20, 12,4, etc.

i-gracet, *past part.* thanked, blessed, 11,23

grapeð, 3 *sg. pres. reflex.* handles, treats, 16,36; grapi, 3 *sg. pres. subj. as imper.*: ne grapi hire nan, let none treat herself, 12,6

greden, *infin.* cry out, wail, 11,11 ; gredeð, 3 *sg. pres.* 3,24

gref, *n.* pain, 22,27

greiðede, 3 *sg. pret.* prepared, 24,12; igreiðet, *past part.* 6,10

gretunge, *n.* salutation, 21,6

greueð, 3 *sg. pres.* gives pain, 18,15

grickisch, *adj.* Greek, 27,11,13,19, etc.

gridil, *n.* gridiron, 9,24

grimliche, *adv.* savagely, fiercely, 11,16

griðful, *adj.* peaceful, 29,18

groweð, 3 *sg. pres.* grows, 27,24

grucchunge, *n.* grumbling, complaining, 13,23

grulleð, *impers. pres.*: sare . . . me grulleð aʒein, I am sorely afraid of, 11,7

gultes, *n. pl.* offences, 6,28

gurdel, *n.* girdle, 24,26

ʒape, *adj.* sly, cunning, 9,26

ʒarkeð, 3 *sg. pres.* prepares, 30,23; iʒarket, *past part.* 7,22

ʒarow, *adj.* ready, available, 23,24

ʒe, *adv.* yes, 10,30, 16,26,27, etc., 25,28

ʒe, *pron. pl. nom.,* you, 3,4,5,6, etc.; ow, *acc., dat., preposit.,* you, yourselves, to you, for you, 3,6,27,28, etc.; ow seoluen, for yourselves, 29,9; ower, *adj. poss.* your, 4,34, 7,19, 27,2, etc.

ʒef, *conj.* if (*with indic.*), 6,10, 7,16, 8,1, etc.; (*with subj.*) 8,18, 18,24, 19,18, etc.

ʒef, *see* ʒeoue(n)

ʒeiʒeð, 3 *sg. pres.* cries, shouts, 23,28

ʒeincume, *n.* return, 23,31

ʒeld, *n.* payment, recompense, 15,27

ȝelden, *infin.* repay, pay, give in return, 28,31,35 ; ȝeldest, 2 *sg. pres.* 15,31; ȝeit, 3 *sg. pres.* 28,4 ; ȝeld, *sg. imper.* 10,17 ; ȝulde, 2 *sg. pret.* 28,30; ȝulden, *pl. pret.* 28,5

ȝeme, *n.* heed, attention, 3,17, 11,33, 13,1, etc.

ȝeoi, *adv.* yes (*emphatic*), 22,27n

ȝeornliche, *adv.* earnestly, diligently, 4,17

ȝeoue(n), *infin.* give, 10,4, 25,10, 23, etc.; *with passive sense*, 25,1,3, to ȝeouene, 25,14; ȝeueð, 3 *sg. pres.* 18,27, 20,19; ȝeoueð, *pl. pres.* give away, 4,27; ȝef, *sg. imper.* 28,21,23,24; ȝef, 3 *sg. pret.* 20,24,31,35; ȝeue, *sg. pret. subj.* 19,13; iȝeuen, *past part.* 20,33, 22,18, 28,34

ȝeoue, *n.* gift, 12,4,15,17, etc.

ȝer, *n. pl.* (*after numeral*), years, 28,1; ȝeres, *pl.*: feole ȝeres & dahes, for many a full year, 23,23n

ȝet, *adv.* yet, still, even now, even so, 4,18, 5,13,38, etc.; ah ȝet is þah, but yet there is still, 5,13

ȝeten, *n. pl.* gates, 6,37, 15,2

ȝette, *sg. imper.* grant, 26,7

ȝette(n), *adv.* still, even now, 6,32, 9,7, 24,37, 25,21

ȝeue, iȝeuen, ȝeueð, *see* ȝeouen

ȝirne, 1 *sg. pres.* long for, 26,7,22; ȝirne, *sg. pres. subj.* 29,11

ȝulde, ȝulden, *see* ȝelden

ȝunge, *adj.* young, 16,36,38

ha, *pron. fem.* she, 5,21, 7,14, 11,38, etc.; it, 12,25 (*with ref. wombe*), 19,26, 30,24; heo, she, 11,35, 20,19, 21,25, etc.; hire, *accus., dat., preposit., reflex.*, her, to her, for her, herself, etc., 11,19, 12,3,6, etc.; it, 22,36 (*with ref. rode*), 5,19 (*with ref. world*); hire seolf, hire seoluen, herself, 5,5, 12,6, 17,25, etc.; hire (*gen.*), *adj. poss.* her, 5,6, 7,17 11,20 etc.; hiren, *disjunctive*, hers, 20,21

ha, *pron. pl.* they, 4,2,3,7, etc.;

heo, 9,26, 27,35; ham, *accus., dat., preposit., reflex.*, them, to them, for them, themselves, etc., 4,20,23,28, etc.; heom, 8,37; ham seolf, 19,20, ham seoluen, 8,38, 20,5, etc., themselves; hare (*gen.*), *adj. poss.* of them, their, 3,21, 4,9,37, etc.

habbe(n), *infin.* have (*often as auxiliary*), 4,10, 5,17,37, etc.; habbe, 1 *sg. pres.* 6,26, 16,19,33, etc.: nabbe, have not, 28,31; hauest, 2 *sg. pres.* 11,13, 22,23, 23,28, etc.; haueð, 3 *sg. pres.* 5,32, 10,14, 13,12, etc.: naueð, has not, 9,3, 22,14; habbeð, *pl. pres.* 3,2, 4,9,26, etc.: nabbeð, have not, 7,27,28; nabbe, 4,6, 12,35 ; haue, *sg. imper.* 19,30, 32,33 ; habbeð, *pl. imper.* receive, 30,35; hefde, 1 & 3 *sg. pret.* 6,17, 10,33, 19,13, etc.: nefde, had not, 10,35, 11,2,36, etc.; hefden, *pl. pret.* 22,5

hal, *adj.* wholesome, 13,1

halden, *infin.* hold, control, keep, preserve, 12,8,18, 13,30, etc. ; halde, 1 *sg. pres.* 26,3; halt, 3 *sg. pres.* 3,29: halt forð(ward), keeps on, 3,29,31; haldeð, *pl. pres.*: ne haldeð na tale of, take no account of, 4,8; halde, *sg. pres. subj.* 25,12, 30,10; heold, 3 *sg. pret.* availed, was of use, 21,24n; ihalden, *past part.* observed, 30,35

i-hale, *adj.* intact, unblemished, 16,29

half, *n.* side, 22,10: o Godes half, on God's side, 15,11, in God's name, 12,33

halflunge, *adv.* partially, halfway, 6,10

halhen, *n. pl.* saints, 4,14, 9,22

halheð, 3 *sg. pres.* sanctifies, 24,16

hali, *adj.* holy, 3,12, 4,2,14, etc.

halsi, 1 *sg. pres,* adjure, implore, 3,27

halt, *see* halden

ham, *n.* home, 5,26 ; *adverbially,* 4,24, 23,25: ed hame, at home, 7,36, 8,2

ham, hare, *see* ha, *pron. pl.*

hat, *adj.* hot, **6,33, 7,2, 26,26,** etc.; **hate,** *pl.* **12,37, 26,17**

hat, 3 *sg. pres.* commands, **29,38, 30,33**

hattre, *adj. comp.* hotter, **26,29**

hauest, haueð, *see* **habbe(n)**

he, *pron. masc. nom.* he, **3,27, 30,31,** etc.; it, **9,10** *(with ref. finger)*, **12,22** *(with ref. pot)*; **him,** *accus., dat., preposit., reflex.* him, to him, for him, himself, etc., **3,9,10, 4,2,15,** etc.; itself, **18,4** *(with ref. luue)*: **him seolf,** him himself, **7,5,7, 9,12,** etc.: **of him seolf,** from (God) Himself, **9,12:** **him seoluen,** to oneself, **10,17:** **of him seoluen,** His very own, **17,32; his,** *(gen.) adj. poss.,* of him, his, **3,10, 29,31,** etc.; its, **9,9** *(with ref. lim),* **16,30: of his,** of His possessions, **20,32**

heafdes, *see* **heaued**

heale, *n.* health, vigour, **10,20, 12,28, 13,16,** etc.

healen, *infin.* heal, **12,33, 24,9; ihealet,** *past part.* **24,6**

healent, *n.* saviour, **8,30**

heard, *adj.* hard, rough, **9,38, 12,11, 18,6,** etc.: *as n.* the rough, **5,29;** **al þet heard,** all the hardship, **19,16: heard iheortet, 21,16, 26,9**

hearde, *adv.* hard, tight, **11,14, 18,12**

heardest, *adj. superl.* hardest, **20,17**

heardschipe, *n.* hardship, austerity, **6,8, 10,14 ; heardschipes,** *pl.* **17,1,5, 19,1**

hearlot, *n.* vagabond, rogue, mendicant, **7,16**

hearm, *n.* injury, **12,26, 28,22: þet mare hearm is,** which is the greater pity, **4,24**

heastes, *n. pl.* commandments, **20,14**

heate, *n.* heat, **6,33, 12,25**

heatel, *adj.* angry, hostile, cruel, **26,3**

heaten, *infin.* warm, heat, **27,26**

heateð, 3 *sg. pres.* hates, detests, **10,31**

heatunge, *n.* hatred: **for muchel heatunge,** because he hated it so much, **10,32**

heaued, *n.* head, **9,1,2,4,** etc.: **heaued eche,** headache, **13,22; heafdes,** *gen. adverbially:* **heafdes bicoruen,** beheaded, **9,25n;** *adjectivally,* **heaued sunne,** capital sin, **17,9, 23,23; heaued luuen,** chief kinds of love, **23,9**

hefde, hefden, *see* **habbe(n)**

heh, *adj.* high, noble, supreme, **5,13, 12,18, 14,20,** etc.: **on heh,** aloft, **26,16;** **of se heh as,** of one so high as, **26,12; hehe,** *wk., pl., predicatively,* **9,18, 15,1, 17,23,** etc.

hehe, *adv.* high, on high, aloft, **5,20, 12,2, 22,37**

i-hehet, *past part.* exalted, **17,16**

hehnesse, *n.* height, altitude, **14,19**

hehschipe, *n.* eminence, high dignity, **8,11**

helle, *n.* hell, **11,29, 17,3, 18,23,** etc.

help, *n.* help, assistance, **21,14**

helpeð, *pl. pres.* help, **20,4**

hendest, *adj. superl.* most courteous, **25,6**

heo, *see* **ha,** *sg. and pl.*

heold, *see* **halden**

heole(n), *infin.* **heolen Abraham þing,** conceal the matter from Abraham, **30,20;** **heole wið,** conceal from, **30,18**

heom, *see* **ha,** *pron. pl.*

heorte, *n.* heart, **4,10** *(requiring pl. sense),* **5,6, 14,16,** etc.; of the heart, **12,12,30, 15,1,** etc.: **heorte blod,** heart's blood, **22,31**

heortes, *n. pl.* harts, **25,35**

heorteliche, *adv.* eagerly, in good heart, **21,33**

i-heortet, *adj.:* **bliðe iheortet,** joyful in heart, **17,14;** **gleade iheortet,** glad at heart, **5,34;** **heard iheortet, 21,16, 26,9**

heouene, *n. oblique cases* (of) heaven, **3,11, 4,4,10,** etc.; **of heouene,** heavenly, **5,26**

heouenlich, *adj.* heavenly, **29,14**

heoueriche, *n.* kingdom of heaven, 8,2n, 25,25

heowede, 3 *sg. pret.* coloured, 22,36; iheowet, *past part.* 7,7

her, *n.* hair, 25,33

her, *adv.* here, 4,6, 6,35, 7,16, 23,32 etc.: her efter, after this, 22,3

here, *n.* hairshirt, 18,12n

here, 1 *sg. pres.* hear, 5,11; 3 *sg. pres. subj.* 3,30; hereð, 3 *sg. pres.* 5,27; iherd, *past part.* 12,35, 26,30

hereword, *n.* renown, prowess, 25,37

herre, *adj. comp.* higher, more exalted, 4,38, 5,13,25, etc.; *adv. comp.* higher, 3,16

herto, *adv.* to this, in this connection, 3,17, 21,7

hest, *adv. superl.* most highly, 25,5

heste, *adj. superl. as n.* highest, 25,13

hetefeste, *adv.* cruelly (tight), 16,23

heui, *adj.* heavy, 11,25,28, 18,12

heuinesse, *n.* burden, 6,29

hihin, *infin.* make haste, 12,3; hiheð, 3 *sg. pres.* 3,32; hihe, *sg. imper. reflex.* 30,14

him, *see* he

hird, *n.* army, 21,15

hire, hiren, *see* ha, *pron. fem.*

his, *see* he

hit, *pron. neut. nom., accus.* (often as formal object or subject or antecedent to *þet* clause), 4,27, 6,31, 7,7, etc., 14,30 (*with ref. Israles folc*), 27,22 (*accus., with ref. luue*)

hoker, *n.* contempt, disdain, 21,24

hond, *n.* hand ; power, 8,30, 14,29 ; ed hond, at hand, 13,12; honden, *pl.* 21,29, 23,16, 24,25, etc.

hondlin, *infin.* handle, 16,15

hongeð, 3 *sg. pres.* hangs, 22,37; ihongede, *past part. as n. pl.* hanged men, 3,21

hope, *n.* hope, 14,19

hore, *n.* whore, 26,5

hu, *adv. interrog.* how, in what way, 5,24, 8,3 10,30, etc.

i-lud, *past part.* hidden, 4,34

hul, *n.* hill, 15,36; hulles, *pl.* 17,24,28

hundret, *num.* hundred, 13,32,34, 25,34

hunger, *n.* hunger, 28,23

hungreð, 3 *sg. pres.* is hungry, 28,21

huni, *n.* honey : *adjectivally*, huni luue, love as sweet as honey, 28,5

hure, *n.* wage, reward, 28,1,5,10, etc.: hure ouer hure, outstanding reward, 5,33n; to hure, as payment, 28,3

hurt, *n.* injury, 13,30

hurte, 3 *sg. pres. subj. reflex.* hurt, 17,4

hus, *n.* house, dwelling, 16,31; huses, *pl.* 16,24,28,30

hwa, *pron. interrog., rel.,* who, 4,25,29, 5,13, etc.; hwa se, whoever, 5,5,36, 7,13, etc.; hwas, *gen. used as rel.,* whose, 3,15; hwam, *preposit.:* þurh hwam, *as rel.* through whom, 5,18

hweat, *see* hwet

hwen, *adv. interrog., rel.* when, 4,34, 5,34, 8,6, etc.

hweoles, *n. pl.* wheels, 6,31,35, 7,3, etc.

hweolinde, *pres. part.* wheeling, revolving, fugitive, 6,35n,37

hwer, *adv. interrog., rel.,* where, 17,33, 25,3: hwer se, wherever, 10,32, 11,23; hwer þurh, through which, by means of which, 4,23

hwerto, *adv. interrog.* to what end, 22,26

hwet, *pron. interrog.* what, 13,1, 20,1, 21,17, etc.; hweat, 11,30, 13,1, 18,7, etc.; *adj.* what, 28,38; *rel.* that which, what, hwet, 9,16, 13,38, hweat, 25,21 : wið hwet, with which, 18,16 : hwet se, whatever, 6,4, 13,2

hweðer, *pron. interrog.* which (of two), 10,18,22,23, etc.

hwi, *adv. interrog., rel.,* why,

14,34, 25,10, **28**,29, etc.; **for hwi**, why, 20,37, 22,28, 26,30

hwil, *conj.* while, 16,37, **17**,29, **30**,15; **hwil eauer,** all the time that, **14**,28; **hwil þet,** while, **29**,7

hwile, *n. in adv. phrases*: **ane hwile,** for a while, 15,26 ; **nane hwile,** for not a moment, for only a moment, 6,36

hwit, *adj.* white, 24,13

hwon, *adv. rel.*: **for hwon þet,** in cases when, 30,34n

hwuch, *adj. interrog.* what, which, what sort of, of what sort, 15,36, 17,32,33, etc.: **hwuch selhðe þet,** happiness such that, **25**,29 ; **hwucche,** *preposit.* 6,16, 8,25

i, *see* **ich, in,** *prep.*

i(-), *for forms thus prefixed, see under simplex*

ich, *pron.* I, 3,16,26, 4,9, etc.; *reduced form* **i,** 30,4; **me,** *accus., dat., preposit., reflex.,* me, to me, for me, myself, etc. 5,8,10,17, **etc.**; **min,** *adj. poss. (before vowel or h),* of me, mine, my, 6,20, **11**,9, 29,4 : **mi,** *adj. poss. (before cons.),* 5,18, 6,21, 11,8, **etc.** ; **mines,** *adj. gen.* 29,4 ; **mine,** *pl.* 3,5, 6,21,28, etc.

ichulle, *see* **wulle**

idel, *adj.* idle, empty: *as n.* idleness, 27,25; **idele,** *adj. pl.* 3,30

ilke, *adj.* same, very, 7,21, 11,2, 15,38, etc.: **þis ilke,** this very thing, 6,36; **al þis ilke,** the whole affair, 13,12

impen, *n. pl.* young shoots, saplings, graftlings, 16,36,38

i-impet, *past part.* planted, engrafted, 8,23

in, *n.* house, inn, 4,16

in, *prep.* in, 3,11, 4,30, 6,25, etc.; *usual reduced form before cons.* **i,** 3,6,14,16, etc. ; **ine,** 7,14 ; **i,** in respect of, 18,27 : **i,** upon, 30,4; **in to,** into, to, 3,2, 4,37, 5,33, etc.

inʒong, *n.* entry, way in, transition (*of argument*), 3,2, 9,15,16

inne, *adv.* within, living (in), 30,14

inoh, inoh reaðe, *see* **i-noh, i-noh-reaðe**

inre, *adj.* inner, inward, 24,15, 27,21

inread, very red, ruddy, 27,16n

inwardliche, *adv.* inwardly, fervently, from the heart, 3,24, 23,7, 30,23

inwit, *n.* conscience, 15,6

inwið, *prep.* within, inside, 12,21, 16,21, 21,10, etc.; *adv.* within, 14,3

inwuniende, *pres. part. as adj.* indwelling, 5,8

irn, *n.* iron, 18,13

is, 3 *sg. pres.* is, 3,1,4,6, etc.: **þet al penitence is in,** in which the whole of penance consists, 7,21; **nis,** is not, 7,7,36, 8,17, etc.: **nis bute,** is only, 6,10, 8,14, 9,9, etc.; **nis þer nawiht þrof,** there is nothing right about that, 10,26; **þe deade nis noht of,** it is nothing to the dead man, **5**,1; **þe deade nis namare of scheome,** the dead man cares no more for the shame, 5,29

jurnee, *n.* day's march, journey, 5,28

kearf, 3 *sg. pret.*: **kearf of,** cut off, 25,33 ; **kurue,** 3 *sg. pret. subj.* 19,18

keisers, *n. pl.* emperors, 8,9

kene, *adj.* brave, valiant, 22,10,37

i-kepe, 3 *sg. pres. subj.* let him look out for, 14,36; **kepte,** 3 *sg. pret.* took notice of, 20,20, 23,21; 3 *sg. pret. subj.* would care, 19,19 ; **ikepte,** 3 *sg. pret.* received, 11,22,25

kimeð, *see* **cumen**

kinedom, *n.* kingdom, 21,23 ; **kinedomes,** *pl.* 25,23

king, *n.* king, 6,17, 21,1,36, etc.; **kinges,** *gen.* 21,11 ; *pl.* 8,9 ; **kinge,** *pl. gen.* 25,5,31

kurue, *see* **kearf**

lah, *adj.* low, base : **se lah,** one so low, 26,13; **lahe,** *pl.* 20,33

lahe, *n.* law, 20,13

lahre, *adj. comp.* lower, 17,24

lahschipe, *n.* lowliness, abjectness, 8,12

lanhure, *adv.* at least, notwithstanding, 17,29n, 21,35

large, *adj.* liberal, 25,7, ample, 16,22

laste, *sg. imper.* blame, 5,2

la ð, *adj.* hateful, loathsome, 26,23

la ðlese, *adj.* innocent, 9,24

lauerd, *n.* Lord, 5,18,20, 6,18, etc.: ure lauerd seolf, our Lord Himself, 8,3 ; lauerdes, *gen.* 12,32, 18,18

leaddre, *n.* ladder, 6,17,30; *gen.* 6,14,26

leade ð, *pl. pres.* lead, 20,17; leadde, 3 *sg. pret.* 14,29, 17,34

leaf, leafde, leafden, *see* leaue ð

leafdi, *n.* lady, 13,8,10, 17,17, etc.: *adjectivally*, þe leafdi riwle, the mistress *or* supreme rule, 30,32

leane, *adj.* emaciated, wasted, 11,36

leape ð, 3 *sg. pres.* leaps, 17,27,29; leapinde, *pres. part.* 17,19

i-learet, *past part.* instructed, 13,17

leaske ð, 3 *sg. pres.*: of his luue leaske ð, relinquishes His love, 29,35n

leasse, *adj. comp.* less, 22,27, 29,31; *adv.* 18,24,26, 20,9

leaste, *adj. superl.* least: beo ð bi þe leaste, (they) manage with the least, 4,7

leaste, *adj. superl.* last, 15,10

leaste ð, *pl. pres.* remain in one place, stop, 6,36

leate, *adv.* late, 4,24

leatere, *adj. comp.* latter, second, 19,31

leattres, *n. pl.* letters, 21,4,5

leaue, *n.* permission, 30,7

leaue ð, 3 *sg. pres.* leaves, remains, 9,9, 29,31; leaf, *sg. imper.* 16,29: leaf bihinde, put behind, 6,27; leafde, 3 *sg. pret.* 14,16; leafden, *pl. pret.* 22,17

leche, *n.* healer, doctor, 12,31, 13,11

lechecreft, *n.* art of medicine, 13,15,17

lechnin, *infin.* (give) physic (to), 12,29

ledene, *n.* language, tongue, 19,11n

lei, *n.* flame, 6,37

lei, leien, *see* ligge ð

leitinde, *pres. part.* flaming, 7,2

lei ð, 3 *sg. pres.* lays, puts, 17,30, 23,13; leide, 3 *sg. pret.* 11,11, 23,14; ileid, *past. part.* 20,15

leof, *adj.* dear, beloved, welcome, precious, 5,3 ; leoue, *wk.*, *pl.*, 3,5, 5,24, 7,18, etc.: leof, *as n.* beloved, love, 17,18, 23,33; leoues, *gen.* beloved's, 22,9, 26,18

leofmon, *n.* beloved, 20,35, 21,6, 23,4, etc.

leohe, *n.* shelter, 12,11n

leosen, *infin.* lose, 26,2; leose ð, 3 *sg. pres.* 10,21; *pl. pres.* 29,27

leote, leten, *infin.* let, leave, 23,25, 25,20, 29,15; let, *sg. imper.* (*with infin.*), 8,29 ; lette, 3 *sg. pret.* desisted, 11,15 : lette þurlin, allowed to be pierced, had pierced, 23,5

leoue, leoues, *see* leof

leste, *conj.* lest, 12,27, 16,37

let, leten, lette, *see* leote

letten (of), *infin.* hinder (from), 5,28; ilette, *past part.* 4,23

letuaire, *n.* electuary, syrup, 13,7,9

le ðer, *n.* leather, skin, 22,34,35

leue ð, *pl. pres.* believe (in), 30,23

libbe ð, *see* liuien

i-lich, *adj.* like, 9,26, 10,36 : ilich as þah, just as if, 27,36 ; iliche, *pl.*: iliche his blisful ariste, like Him in His glorious resurrection, 8,26

i-liche, *adv.* alike, equally, 5,3

(i-)licnesse, *n.* likeness, 8,23, 10,33, 17,30

licome, *n.* body, 12,27, 16,31,

18,17, etc.; **licomes**, *gen.* of the body, physical, **12**,31, **13**,16,30, etc.

licomlich, *adj.* bodily, **19**,5 ; **licomliche**, *pl.* **19**,2

licunge, *n.* enjoyment : flesches licunge, sensuality, **6**,5, **8**,38

lif, *n.* life, **4**,34, **7**,38, **10**,14, etc.: for hire lif, on any account, **12**,7; **liue**, *preposit.* **21**,21, **22**,1 ; **liues**, *gen. as adv.* alive, **21**,36

liflade, *n.* manner of life, **4**,4,38, **9**,38, etc.

liggeð, *pl. pres.* lie, **9**,7; **ligge**, 3 *sg. pres. subj.* **5**,1; **lei**, 3 *sg. pret.* **13**,5; **leien on**, *pl. pret.* lay sick with, **9**,7

liht, *adj.* light, easy, cheap, **11**,27, **25**,20; **lihte**, *pl.* (*or adv.*), **4**,28

lihten, *infin.* come down, **3**,17

lihteð, 3 *sg. pres.* lightens, relieves, **18**,6 ; **ilihtet**, *past part.* **6**,28

lihtleapes, *n.*: wið lihtleapes, with easy steps, **9**,21n

lihtliche, *adv.* easily, cheaply, **6**,29, **22**,28,30

likin, *infin. impers.* please, **11**,37

lim, *n.* limb, member, **9**,2,4,7, etc.; **limen**, *pl.* **9**,1

limpeð, 3 *sg. pres.* belongs, applies, **3**,15, **5**,10 ; *pl. pres.* **16**,16

litunge, *n.* paint, colouring, **22**, 34,35

liue, **liues**, *see* lif

liueneð, *n.* (means of) living, provisions, **7**,17, **21**,14, **27**,9

liuien, *infin.* live, **4**,15; **liuie**, 1 *sg. pres.* **5**,7; **liueð**, 3 *sg. pres.* **5**,5,5,8, **6**,32; **liuieð**, **libbeð**, *pres. pl.* **3**,19, **8**,25n; **liuede**, 3 *sg. pret.* **12**,1; **liuiende**, *pres. part. as adj.* **4**,15

lo, *interj.* look, **15**,36, **17**,16, **26**,3, etc.; þus lo, see then, **5**,37, **15**,8, **24**,34; lo deale, *see* deale

loki, 3 *sg. pres. subj.* may look, **19**,23; **loke**, *sg. imper.* **10**,30, **28**,5; **lokið**, *pl. imper.* **5**,24, **8**,2, **29**,27; **iloket**, *past part.*: ouer al iloket, thoroughly considered, **13**,26

lomen, *n. pl.* tools, **19**,17,20

lond, *n.* land, country, **7**,25,27,30, etc. ; **londe**, *preposit.* **21**,2 ; **londes**, *pl.* **9**,7

londuuel, *n.* epidemic disease, plague, **9**,6

long, *adj.* long, **27**,37

longe, *adv.* long, for a long time, **11**,15, **23**,20, **27**,37

longeð, *sg. pres. impers.*: ham longeð to, they long for, **15**,7

longunge, *n.* longing, **14**,37

lot, *n.* share, **7**,28

lure, *n.* loss, **8**,34

lustes, *n. pl.* lusts, desires, **3**,28, **10**,21

lutel, *adj.* little, **9**,20, **17**,6, **19**,6, etc.; *adv.* **18**,26, **22**,30

luðerliche, *adv.* viciously, **11**,11

luue, *n.* love, **5**,37, **8**,13,25, etc.; *gen.* **15**,38, **17**,17, **21**,6, **26**,17; **luues**, *gen.* Love's, **30**,7; **luuen**, *pl.* loves, **23**,9, **24**,36, **25**,19

luuewurðe, *adj.* worthy of love, **22**,8

luuien, *infin.* love, **18**,24, **20**,37, **26**,15, etc.; **luuie**, **25**,12, **28**,27; **luuien**, *infin. with passive sense*, be loved, **19**,22, **26**,31, **30**,33; **luuest**, 2 *sg. pres.* **18**,3, **25**,11, **29**,24; **luueð**, 3 *sg. pres.* **10**,19, 23, **19**,20, etc.; **luuieð**, *pl. pres.* **4**,27, **15**,8, **20**,9, etc.; **luuie**, 2 *sg. pres. subj.* **21**,35; *pl. pres. subj.* **18**,28 ; **luuien**, *pl. pres. subj.* **20**,3,5,10; **luuede**, 1 *and* 3 *sg. pret.* **20**,35, **21**,1, **22**,2, etc. ; **luuedest**, 2 *sg. pret.* **28**,29 ; **luueden**, *pl. pret.* **28**,30, **29**,7

mahe, *n.* stomach, **12**,37

mahe, **mahen**, **maht**, **mahte**, **mahten**, *see* mei

make, *n.* partner, companion, **28**,14

makie(n), *infin.* make, put, do, **9**,36, **21**,23, **24**,7, etc.; **makest**, 2 *sg. pres.* **15**,30, **26**,28, **29**,25; **makeð**, 3 *sg. pres.* **5**,3, **16**,2,14, etc.; **makieð**, *pl. pres.* **12**,18, **19**,28 ; **makie**, 3 *sg. pres. subj.* **14**,1; **makeden**, *pl. pret.*: ne makeden . . . strengôe of, put no trust in, 13,3n; imaket, *past. part.* 27,11

manere, *n.* kind: þreo manere men, three kinds of men, 3,19n

mare, *adj. comp.* more, greater, 4,24, 12,26, 18,9, etc.; *as n.* 16,34, 18,8, 20,23, etc.; *adv.* 4,25, 10,23, 16,34, etc.; neauer mare, never at all, 4,24

martirdom, *n.* martyrdom, 3,6

mat, *adj.* overcome, confounded, 18,25n

me, *adv. (introducing objection)*, but, 10,16n,29, 12,14, etc.

me, *pron. indef. (reduced from mon)* one, 6,16, 7,35,36, etc. *(often best rendered by passive construction)*

me, *see* ich

i-meane, *adj.* in common, 16,26

meanen, *infin. reflex.* complain, 11,26, meaneô, 3 *sg. pres.* 16,4, 18,15; meande, 3 *sg. pret.* 10,2

mearci, *n.* mercy, 14,20, 23,24: *as interj.* 9,14

mearewe, *adj.* tender, 16,38

mearke, *n.* mark, target, banner, 24,27; mearken, *pl.* 10,9,10,13

meast, *adv.* most, chiefly, 14,2, 20,16,17, etc.

measte, *adj. superl., pl., wk.,* greatest, chief, 24,36, 25,18,19

mede, *n.* reward, 7,31

medecine, *n.* medicine, 12,35

mei, 1 *and* 3 *sg. pres.* can, is able, may, 5,28,36, 6,34, etc.; maht, 2 *sg. pres.* 21,28, 25,3,10, etc.; mahe(n), *pl. pres.* 3,8,20, 4,7, etc.; mahe, *sg. pres. subj.* 13,38, 26,14; mahte, 1 *and* 3 *sg. pret.* 6,9, 14,17, 17,26, etc.: mahte beon, may have been, 7,19; mahte(n), *pl. pret.* 17,26 *(with subject hulles),* 21,20, 29,8

meiden, *n.* maiden, virgin, 23,35, 24,2; meidnes, *pl.* 9,24, 13,6,9

meidenhad, *n.* maidenhood, virginity, 25,13

meistre, *n.* master, sovereign, 29,38

meistrie, *n.* authority, 29,19; meistries, *pl.* works of power, 21,22

meistrin, *infin.* master, 18,10

meiôhad, *n.* maidenhood, virginity, 24,4

men, *see* mon

menske, *n.* honour, honourable estate, 5,29,32, 7,23, etc.

menskeful, *adj.* honourable, 8,11

meosure, *n.* moderation, 13,26,37

meraht, merariht, *forms of Hebrew* mar, ' bitter ', 14,10,11n

messagers, *n. pl.* messengers, 22,6

mete, *n.* food, meat, 12,37, 20,6; metes, *pl.* 10,19, 12,24

mi, min, mine, mines, *see* ich

mid, *prep.* with, 4,34, 18,13, 19,23, etc.; mid alle, entirely, 4,22, 26,26, as well, indeed, 29,34: swiôe mid alle, very much indeed, 24,29

middel, *n.* waist, 18,13

midleste, *adj.* midmost: *as n.* one in the middle, 13,10

migge, *n.* urine, 27,12,23,24, etc.

mihte, *n.* power, 21,22

mihti, *adj.* mighty, 21,11

milce, *n.* mercy, 11,23, 23,32

mildeliche, *adv.* meekly, patiently, 8,13

min(e), mines, *see* ich

miracle, *n.* miracle, 21,38

mirre, *n.* myrrh, 13,32. *Cp.* myrre

misseô, 3 *sg. pres.* fails to find, 10,13

mistohe, *past part. as adj.* disordered, 13,23

misþoht, *n.* evil thought, 17,11

moder, *n.* mother, 11,19, 13,27, 24,7, etc.

mon, *n.* man, 5,4, 6,24, 7,35, etc.; *reduced form* me, *which see*; monnes, *gen.* 24,1, 27,11,14, etc.; men, *pl.* 3,19, 4,2,17, etc.; monne, *gen. pl.* 19,11, 25,6, 30,1

moni, *adj.* many *(with sg. n.),* 4,22, 5,28, 7,34, etc.; monie, *pl.* 9,7, 21,13, 22,6, etc.; moni, *pron. sg.*

many, **6**,7; monies, *gen.* **22**,14; monie, *pl.* **12**,26, **14**,24

monifalden, *infin.* multiply, **27**,8

monihwet, *pron. sg.* many things (*as subject*), **4**,38

mong, *n.* mixture, traffic, **19**,26

monglunge, *n.* mingling, **19**,24n, **29**,15

most, 2 *sg. pres.* must, **15**,33 ; mot, 3 *sg. pres.* **3**,14, **7**,14,35, etc. ; moten, **14**,26 ; mote, **6**,6, *pres. pl.*; moste, 3 *sg. pret.* **9**,14: moste nede, had (to) of necessity, **29**,38

muche, *adj.* much, great, **4**,11, 10,14, **14**,17, etc.; muches, *gen.* : nawt muches, nothing much, **28**,31

muchel, *adj.* great, mighty, much, **10**,32, **11**,23, **18**,20, etc.; muchele, *wk., pl.* **11**,8, **12**,12, **20**,18, etc.; muchel, *as n.* much, **20**,23, **23**,36; *adv.* much, greatly, **9**,19, **24**,6, **25**,22; mucheles, *gen. as adv.* by far, **12**,4

mungunge, *n.* memory, **23**,1: in ure munegunge, to remember us, **24**,28

munt, *n.* mount, **17**,23

i-munt, *past part.* intended, **30**,3

murhðes, *n. pl.* delights, joys, **15**,31

murie, *adj.* pleasant, **21**,20

murneð (efter), 3 *sg. pres.* mourns (for), **12**,3; murnede, 3 *sg. pret.* **11**,35

muð, *n.* mouth, **13**,9

myrre, *n.* myrrh, **15**,36,37, **16**,2, etc. *Cp.* mirre

na, *adj.* (*with other negative*) no, **3**,32, **4**,6,8, etc.: na þing, nothing, **5**,22, **11**,36, **16**,26, etc.; nan (*before vowels or disjunctively*) **13**,28, **25**,26; nanes, *gen. in* nanesweis, *which see*; nane, *accus. fem.* : nane hwile, for not a moment, **6**,36; *pl.* **27**,19, 20 ; nan, *pron.* no-one, none, **7**,1, **10**,27, **12**,6, etc.

na, *adv* not, nothing, **7**,32 : nan

oðerweis, in no other way, **9**,17. *See* namare

nabbe, nabbeð, *see* habbe(n)

nahhi, *infin.* approach, come near, **25**,27

nai, *adv.* no, **13**,10, **30**,21

nalde, naldest, *see* wulle

nam, *see* am

namare, *adv.* (*after negative*), any more, **15**,22 ; *n.* nothing more, **5**,29

nan, *see* na

nanesweis, *adv.* (*after negative*), in anyway, **21**,28

naueð, *see* habbe(n)

nawiht, *n.* nothing, **10**,26 (*see* is), **28**,8; nawt, *with gen. or partitive construction*; nawt bittres, nothing bitter, **10**,25, nawt muches, nothing much, **28**,31, nawt of sunne, nothing sinful, **11**,2 ; nawiht, *adv.* (*after negative*), in the least, at all, **16**,6; nawt, *adv.* (*usually with other negative*), not (at all), **3**,31, **4**,27, **5**,7, etc.: nawt for þi, nevertheless, **18**,11

ne, *adv.* (*preceding verb, usually with other negative, but not in* **4**,20,22, etc.), not **3**,31,32, **4**,7, etc.: nor (*in negative sequence*), **4**,1,7, **8**,34, etc.

nearow, *adj.* narrow, confined, **16**,17,20,22, etc.

nearowðe, *n.* constraint, repression, **16**,17

neauer, *adv.* (*with other negative*), never, **5**,34, **10**,35, **11**,26, etc.: neaure, **12**,35; neauer mare, never at all, never again, **4**,24, **29**,16

neb, *n.* face, **21**,18

nede, *n.* used adverbially, necessarily, of necessity, **6**,6, **29**,38

nefde, *see* habbe(n)

neh, *adj.* near, **12**,24 : when He was near, **29**,7 ; *adv.* **11**,24 ; *prepositionally*, **11**,25,27

nehbur, *n.* neighbour, **12**,24

neil, *n.* nail, **27**,28

i-neilet, *past part.* nailed, **16**,22

nelde, *n.* needle, **25**,39

nempne, *sg. imper.* declare, 25,21

neoces, *n. pl.* wedding, marriage feast, 15,19

neod, *n.* need, 7,17: *adjectivally,* necessary, 14,31; ow is neoð, it is necessary for you, 17,2n

neodeð, 3 *sg. pres.*: þet him to neodeð, that are necessary to him, 4,2

neodful, *adj.* earnest, eager, 26,17

neoleachunge, *n.* approach, 23,36, 24,1

neome(n), *infin.* take, receive, 21,31,33; *with passive sense,* 25,2; nim, *sg. imper.* 11,33, understand, 15,18; neomeð, *pl. imper.* 3,17, 14,8, 15,12, etc.; nom, 3 *sg. pret.* 13,8; nomen, *pl. pret.* 13,1,2; inumen, *past part.* captured, 18,25

neorre, *adj. comp. used pre-positionally,* nearer, 21,17

neoð, *see* neod

neowe, *adj.* new, 9,28,30, 10,4, etc.: neowe meiden, virgin afresh, 23,35

nere, nes, *see* wes

nesche, *adj.* soft, tender, 16,15: *as n.* the smooth, 5,30

niht, *n.* night: *adverbially* niht & dei, (by) night and day, 3,7; nihtes, *gen.* 4,35

nim, *see* neome(n)

nis, *see* is

nið, *n.* envy, spite, 27,30,35, 28,6

niðfule, *adj. pl.* envious, malicious, 27,31

noble, *adj.* noble, 22,6

i-noh, *adv.* enough, 14,34

i-nohreaðe, *adv.* promptly enough, 16,35n

noht, *n.* nothing: þe deade nis noht of, it is nothing to the dead man, 5,1

nom, nomen, *see* neome(n)

nome, *n.* name, 14,10, 15,18

nomeliche, *adv.* especially, above all, 3,15, 13,14, 25,11

notien, *infin.* make use of, 13,13

noteð, 3 *sg. pres.* denotes, signifies,

13,34; notið, *pl. imper.* observe, mark, 6,22

noðeles, *adv.* nonetheless, 1636,

nowðer, *adv.* neither: nowðer . . . ne, neither . . . nor, 26,27; ne . . . nowðer . . . ne, nor . . . either . . . or, 5,31, 27,20; *pron.* (*with ne*) neither, 5,30, 16,24

nu, *adv.* now, 3,17, 4,18,37, etc.

nule, nulleð, nult, *see* wulle

i-numen, *see* neome(n)

nurrice, *n.* nurse, 13,27

nutten, *infin.* make use of, 12,37

O, *interj.* O, 28,6

o, *see* on

of, *prep.* of, from, off, out of, among, 3,19, 4,4, 5,25, etc.; concerning, about, 3,1, 4,8,9, etc.; *partitive,* 3,6, 4,21, 5,29, etc.: of þe letuaire, some of the electuary, 13,9; made of, 6,37; with respect to, in, at, 3,9,10, 6,4, etc.; ut of, out of, from, 3,2, 4,25, 5,4, etc.; of feor, apart, at a distance, 13,11; *adv.* off, 9,25, 25,33: *cp.* offe

ofdrahen, *infin.* attract, extract, 22,32, 23,7; ofdraheð, 3 *sg. pres.* 20,24

ofdred, *past part.* frightened, 12,27

ofearneð, 3 *sg. pres.* earns, deserves, 5,31,33

offe, *adv.* off, 9,10. Cp. of, *adv.*

offearet, *past part.* terrified, 10,1

offreð, 3 *sg. pres.* offers, 28,14; offreden, *pl. pret.* 27,31

offruht, *past part.* afraid, 10,1

ofgan, *infin.* make claim to, obtain, 21,34; *past part.*claimed, earned, 20,22

ofhungret, *past part.* hungry, famished, 15,32

ofte, *adv.* often, 7,18, 13,19,28, etc.

on, *prep.* on, upon, 3,10,19, 5,35, etc.; *reduced to* o *before cons. other than* h, 3,7,21, 5,24, etc.: on hire on oþre, about her among others, 17,12n; in, 5,20, 9,7, 19,16, etc.; *reduced form con-*

fused with article in a dei, 13,4: *see* a

onde, *n.* hatred, spite, 27,30, 28,6

ondfule, *adj. wk.* malicious, 27,35; ontfule, *adj. pl. as n.* 29,27

ondswere, *n.* answer, 10 17

ondswerian, *infin.* answer, 28,32; ondswerest, 2 *sg. pres.* 12,14, 16,27 ; ondswere, *sg. imper.* 26,6; ondswerede, *sg. pret.* 12,32

onont, *prep.* in respect of, 15,1n: onont hire, as far as she is concerned, 28,15

ontende(n), *infin.* set fire to, kindle, 26,18,31, 27,2, etc.

ontendunge, *n.* kindling, 26,33

ontfule, *see* ondfule

openin, *infin. (here with passive sense),* be opened, 23,5; iopenet, *past part.* 21,5n

openliche, *adv.* openly, 23,6

orchard, *n.* orchard, 17,1

ordre, *n.* (religious) order, 3,7n, 29,18; ordres, *pl.* 20,12

ornre, *adj. comp.* more fastidious, 12,37

ortrowi, 3 *sg. pres. subj.* suspect, 18,24

oðer, *adj.* other, (the) second, 4,11, 14,20,22, etc. ; oþre, *pl.* 11,38, 23,30; þe oþre, the second class, 3,20,22

oþer, *pron.* other, another, 4,7, 10,20, 12,12, etc.; oþre, *preposit.* 17,12, 18,10; oþres, *gen.* 6,6, 7,17, 18,30, etc.; oþre, *pl.* 4,18, 5,25, 6,4†, 7,13, etc.

oðer, *conj.* or, 3,30, 4,12, 5,4, etc.: unless, 12,22; oðer . . . oðer, either . . . or, 9,21, 19,29, 25,15, etc.

oðerhwile, *adv.* at some time or other, on occasion, 7,19, 16,34; oðerhwiles, at times, 14,26

oðerweis, *adv.:* nan oðerweis, in no other way 9,17

ouer, *prep.* above, over, beyond, 5,33, 7,13, 8,12, etc.: ouer al, completely, utterly, everywhere, 13,26, 26,16, ouer alle, supremely 8,12

ouergeað, 3 *sg. pres.* surpasses ; passes over and beyond, 17,29, 23,12

ouerkimeð, 3 *sg. pres.* overcomes, triumphs over, 24,36, 28,16; ouercumen, vanquished, 14,36, 21,26

ouerleapeð, 3 *sg. pres.* leaps over, 17,25

ouerleden, *past part.* overbrimmed, 12,22n

ouerswiðe, *adv.* exceedingly, extravagantly, 12,26, 13,38, 29,36

ouerturneð, *pl. pres.* revolve, 6,35, 7,3

ouerweieð, 3 *sg. pres.* outweighs, 20,18

ow, ower, *see* ȝe

i-paiet, *past part.* pleased, 12,2, 17,6

parais, *n.* paradise, 6,32, 7,1: paraise, *gen.* 6,37

parti, 1 *sg. pres.* depart, 29,3

passeð, 3 *sg. pres.* goes beyond, surpasses, 23,12, 24,35

passiun, *n.* suffering, torment, 9,15, 18,14, 19,12

patriarches, *n. pl.* patriarchs, 21,3

penitence, *n.* spiritual discipline, penitence, 3,1,4, 7,21, etc.

perfectiun, *n.* completeness, perfection, 13,34

pes, *n.* peace, 15,5

pilche, *n.* (leather) garment, 10,6

pilegrim, *n.* pilgrim, 3,29, 4,9,38, etc. ; pilegrimes, *pl.* 3,20,27, 4,3, etc.

piment, *n.* spiced drink, nectar, 28,5n

pine, *n.* punishment, suffering, 3,10, 6,13,23, etc.: do pine, mortify, 13,36

pinful, *adj.* painful, 7,13

pini, 1 *sg. pres. reflex.* torment, mortify myself, 11,31; pinið, *pl. pres. reflex.* 8,38; ipinet, *past part.* tormented, 11,3: ful pinet, completely mortified, 27,34

pinsunge, *n.* mortification, 12,10,

30, **16**,33 ; pinsunges, *pl.* **13**,34, **19**,2

place, *n.* place of battle, field, **7**,37n

pot, *n.* pot, **12**,21,23

poure, *adj.* poor, **21**,1,10, **26**,32, etc.: *as n.* **19**,13

preise, *sg. imper.* praise, **5**,2

preoue, *n.* proof, **11**,27, **30**,7

present, *n.* present, **9**,37, **27**,32

pris, *n.* price, **20**,36, **22**,31

prophete, *n.* prophet, **26**,35; prophes, *pl.* **21**,3

pruuien, *infin.* give proof of, demonstrate, **22**,7, **29**,39; pruuieð, *pl. pres.* **18**,2

quoð, 3 *sg. pret.* said, **6**,20,25,27, etc.

read, *adj.* red, **6**,33, **7**,2, **24**,25; reade, *gen.* **27**,14; *wk.* **22**,36; *as n.* þe reade, the redness, **6**,34; reades, *adj. gen.* **27**,11n

i-readet, *past part.* reddened, **7**,5, **27**,15

reaðere, *adv.* sooner, **19**,22

reauin, *infin.* take by force: (*with passive sense*) hit is to reauin hire, it is to be taken from her by force, **25**,2

rechles, *n.* incense, **16**,2,3; rechleses, *gen.* **15**,36,37

reclus, *adj.* shut up, **16**,16: (*or as n.* recluse) **16**,18,21; recluses, *n.pl.* **3**,15

rede, *infin.* read, **16**,35

reisun, *n.* reason, **22**,37 ; resun, **24**,23; reisuns, *pl.* **25**,10

religiuns, *n. pl.* religious professions, **20**,11, **29**,17

religius, *adj. as n.* (a) religious, person in religion, **5**,12, **13**,14

reowfulnesse, *n.* compassion, pitifulness, **12**,13

reowðful, *adj.* full of pity, **11**,19; reowðfule, *preposit.*, *wk.*, piteous, **11**,12, **27**,33

reste, *n.* rest, **7**,23,37, **8**,1, etc.: heorte reste, peace of heart, **15**,1

resten, *infin.* rest, **7**,36

resun, *see* reisun

riche, *n.* kingdom, **4**,4, **9**,15,16

riche, *adj.* rich, **9**,27†,30; richest, *superl.* richest, most powerful, **25**,5,32

riht, *adj.* right, true, **12**,13; rihte, *pl.* **5**,37; *wk. sg.* direct, **3**,29; riht, *adv.* right, just, properly, **12**,8, **14**,6, **29**,35, etc.: þus riht, to this extent, **5**,12

i-riht, *past part.* raised, **6**,14, **10**,11,13

rihte, *n.*: bi god rihte, with good reason, **14**,15

rihtliche, *adv.* properly, justifiably, **17**,10

rineð, 3 *sg. pres.* touches, **29**,20; rine, 3 *sg. pres. subj.* **29**,23; rin, *sg. imper.* **29**,29

rinunge, *n.* touch, **29**,25

riwle, *n.* rule, **30**,29,32

riwleð, 3 *sg. pres.* rules, **30**,29

rixleð, 3 *sg. pres.* rules, **15**,8

rode, *n.* cross, **3**,8,14,16, etc.

rotie, 3 *sg. pres. subj.* rot, **5**,1

i-rotet, *past part.* rooted, **20**,15

i-ruded, *past part.* made red, encrimsoned, **7**,5

rukelin, *infin.* heap, **28**,25

rute, *n.* way, route, **3**,32

sabraz, *n.* decoction, **10**,20n

sahe, *n.* saying, maxim, **8**,22

sahtneð, 3 *sg. pres.* is reconciled, **15**,9

sake, *n.* sake, **30**,33

salde, *see* sulle(n)

salmwruhte, *n.* psalmist, **26**,13

salue, *n.* ointment, **12**,33

saluz, *n. pl.* greetings, **21**,6n

sar, *adj.* sore, grievous, painful, **9**,2,10 : *adverbially*, sorely, **9**,3; sare, *wk.* **28**,2; sarest, *superl.* bitterest, **18**,19

sar, *n.* suffering, mortification, grief, **6**,23, **7**,3,6, etc.

sare, *adv.* bitterly, heavily, **11**,7, **22**,33

sari, *adj.* sorry, miserable, **24**,31

sariliche, *adv.* painfully, in anguish 6,1

sauur, *n.* savour, 15,22

sawle, *n.* soul, 3,29, 12,30, 13,18; *gen.* of the soul, spiritual, 12,1, 13,15,20, etc.

scandle, *n.* scandal, 17,9n

schadewe, *n.* shadow, 10,33, 11,2,3, etc.

schal, 1 *sg. pres.* shall, must, 30,4; schalt, 2 *sg. pres.* 23,30, 25,22,25, etc.; schal, 3 *sg. pres.* 8,8, 9,31, 36, etc. : is wont to, 7,36; schule(n). *pl. pres,* 3,10, 4,15,36, etc.; schule, 3 *sg. pres. subj.* 25,21; schulden, *pl. pret.* 7,6, 10,37, 12,29, etc.

scharp, *adj.* sharp, 17,7

scharpschipe, *n.* sharpness, 17,4

schawin, *infin.* show, manifest, reveal, 7,5, 13,35, 16,25, etc.; schaweð, 3 *sg. pres.* 17,21,22 ; *pl. pres.* 17,32 ; schawde, 3 *sg. pret.* 21,18,22, 22,7

schedde, 3 *sg. pret.* shed, 8,36; isched, *past part.* 27,17

scheld, *n.* shield, 22,10,11,12, etc.

schendlac, *n.* ignominy, 7,12

schene, *adj.* bright, 25,32; schenre, *comp.* 4,36, 9,32

schentful, *adj.* shameful, 7,13, 8,16

schentfulliche, *adv.* shamefully, 26,5

scheome, *n.* shame, 5,2,29,32, etc.: *gen.* scheome deað, death of shame, 21,30

scheomeliche, *adv.* shamefully, in shame, 6,1, 11,3

scheortliche, *adv.* briefly, 30,35

scheos, *n. pl.* shoes, 9,20

schilden, *infin.* shield, 11,22 ; schilt, 3 *sg. pres.* 22,20 ; schilde, 3 *sg. pres. subj.*: me schilde forte habben, keep me from having, 5,17

schine, *infin.* shine, 10,8

schir, *adj.* bright, pure, 18,33, 19,6,23, etc.

schireð, 3 *sg. pres.* makes pure, 19,3

schirnesse, *n.* clearness, purity, 20,10, 29,16

schrift, *n.* confession, 3,1

schulden, schule, schulen, *see* schal

schunche, 3 *sg. pres. subj.*: schunche a ȝeinwardes, may be frightened back again, 17,4n

scotti(n), *infin.* share, 3,10, 8,34; scottið, *pl. pres.* 3,9

se, *adv.* so, such a, 3,6, 8,22, 9,3, etc.; hwa se, whoever, 5,5,36, 7,13, etc.; hwet se, whatever, 6,4, 13,2: sone se, *see* sone

sea, *n.* sea, 20,31

i-sealet, *past part.* sealed, 21,4n

sec (of), *adj.* sick, ill (from), 10,24, 13,12 ; seke, *pl.* 10,18, 12,38, 24,8

sechen, *infin.* seek, 4,11 ; secheð, 3 *sg. pres.* 7,36; *pl. pres.* 4,7,21, 32

secleð, 3 *sg. pres.* sickens, 12,29

secnesse, *n.* sickness, disease, 9,6,9, 10,21, etc.

seggen, *infin.* say, tell, speak (of), 4,26, 8,24, 25,22, etc.; segge, 29,37 ; segge, 1 *sg. pres.* 13,25, 20,5, 27,6 ; seist, 2 *sg. pres.* 22,26, 25,20, 30,4; seið, 3 *sg. pres.* 3,8,11,27, etc.; seggeð, *pl. pres.* 4,4; segge, 3 *sg. pres. subj.* 5,21; segge we, *pl. pres. subj.* let us say, 14,3; sei him scheome, *sg. imper.* revile him, 5,2; seide, 1 *and* 3 *sg. pret.* (*subj.*) 4,9,19, 5,9, etc.; seiden, *pl. pret.* 29,17 ; iseid, *past part.* 14,2,34, 16,19, etc.

sein, *adj.* saint, 3,18, 4,12,16, etc.; seint, 12,9, 14,27, 20,7, etc.; seinte, 3,8,11,24,etc.

seist, seið, *see* seggen

seke, *see* sec

selcuð, *n.* wonder, 8,17

selhðe, *n.* happiness, bliss, 5,36, 17,39, 25,29, etc.

seli, *adj.* happy, blessed, 5,3

senden, *infin.* send, 29,6 ; sent, 3 *sg. pres.* 18,20 ; sende, 3 *sg. pret.* 13,3, 21,2,12,etc.

sentence, *n.* way of thinking, matter, 3,18

12

seo, 1 sg. pres. see, 5,11; sið, 3 sg. pres. 5,27, 10,10,11, etc.; seoð, pl. pres. 4,21; seo, 3 sg. pres. subj. 3,30, 23,3; sih, sg. imper. 6,20

seolf, seoluen in combination, see Godd, ȝe, ha, he, lauerd, þing, þu, we, etc.

seoluer, n. silver, 25,34

seoð, see seo

seoueðe, adj. seventh, 18,32

seoueuald, adv. seven times, 10,8, 25,26

serueð, 3 sg. pres. serves, 20,30; seruið, pl. pres. 20,31, 30,32

seste, adj. sixth, 3,3

sete, n. seat, 8,9

set, 3 sg. pres. sets, 16,2 ; sete, sg. imper. 25,21; iset, past part. 16,38, 23,2

set, 22,14 ; see sitten

sicles, n. pl. shekels, 25,34

side, n. side, 23,6 ; siden, pl. 22,15,16

sih, see seo

sihðe, n. sight, vision, 5,9, 19,24: his sihðe, the sight of him, 19,27, 29,11

siker, adj. secure, stable, 18,9

sikerliche, adv. certainly, assuredly, 5,5, 10,26, 27,5

singen, infin. sing, 6,2 ; singeð, 3 sg. pres. 3,13

sire, n. (as form of address), sir, lord, 10,16,29, 12,14, etc.

sitten, infin. sit, 8,7; sitte, 1 sg. pres. 8,6; sit, 3 sg. pres. affects, 19,33n; sitte, sg. pres. subj. 12,2; set, 3 sg. pret. was placed, 22,14

sið, see seo

sker, adj. purified: sker of, free from, 14,35; skerre, comp. holier, 4,25

i-slein, see sloh

slepe, n. sleep, 13,5

sloh, 3 sg. pret. slew, 11,1, 25,35; islein, past part. 21,38

smeallinde, pres. part. as adj. smelling, 15,15

smech, n. flavour, taste, 15,23

smechles, adj. tasteless, 15,21

smirien, infin. anoint, 13,32, 14,8, 15,15, etc.; ismired, past part. 16,14

smirles, n. ointment, 14,6

smiten, infin. strike, 11,19, 30,9,11

snakereð, 3 sg. pres. creeps, sneaks, 17,3n

softe, adj. soft, 16,15; adv. softly, 16,36

softeliche, adv. gently, 12,6

softeð, 3 sg. pres. softens, 18,6

somet, adv. together, 6,22, 13,30, 21,13, etc.

sond, n. sand, 27,12,23,24

sonde, n. messenger, 12,32; sonden pl. 21,2,12

sone, adv. soon, quickly, 6,35, 7,4, 10,22; sone se, as soon as, 14,35, 23,34 ; sonest, superl. most readily, 23,3

sontes, n. gen. saint's, 4,12n

i-sontet, past part.: to beon isontet, to be made saints, 4,14

sorhe, n. grief, pain, 6,23, 7,6,31, etc.

sorhfulliche, adv. miserably, grievously, 11,3, 26,5

sotschipe, n. folly, 9,26

soð, adj. true, 13,28, 18,6; soðe, wk. 26,15, 27,6 ; to soðe, in truth, 21,32

soðliche, adv. truly, assuredly, 11,24

spealeð, 3 sg. pres. means, 14,11, 18,23, etc.

speare, sg. imper. spare, 11,8; ispearet, past part. 10,37

speces, n. pl. spices, 12,37, 13,33

speche, n. speech, conversation, 5,9, 29,12

speoken, infin. speak, 3,1; spekeð, 3 sg. pres. 4,30, 5,27, 17,17, etc.; spek, spec, 1 & 3 sg. pret. 5,20, 14,11, 17,35, etc.; speken, pl. pret. 13,15; ispeken, past part. 17,2

speonse, n. expenses, 4,1

speowe, infin. spew, 26,28

i-spillet, *past part.* destroyed, 19,14

spitelsteaf, *n.* spittle, spud, small spade, 19,18

spreaden, *infin.* spread, 26,16 ; **ispread,** *past part.* 22,12

springen, *infin.* rise, 4,36; **springeð,** 3 *sg. pres.* 4,35

spus, *n.* husband, bridegroom, 12,1

spuse, *n.* wife, bride, 11,35, 15,35, 23,22, etc.

spushad, *n.* the marriage state, wifehood, 25,13

stanene, *adj.* (made) of stone, 16,23

stat, *n.* condition, 15,8

stearf, 3 *sg. pret.* died, 11,16

steire, *n.* step, degree, grade, 5,13,21,24

stench, *n.* stench, 27,24

steolen, *n. pl.* sides, uprights, 6,14, 15,17, etc.

steuene, *n.* voice, 11,12

sticke, sticcke, *n.* stick, spoon, 13,8

stihen, *infin.* go up, mount, 9,18, 10,28 ; **stihe,** 1 *sg. pres. (subj.),* may mount, 6,29; **istihen,** *past part.* 26,16

stille, *n.* calm, 15,30

stinkinde, *pres. part. as adj.* stinking, 28,37

stiward, *n.* steward, 20,18n

stonden, *infin.* stand, 22,16; **stont,** 3 *sg. pres.* 11,27 ; **stondeð,** *pl. pres.* 11,24, 12,17 ; **stod,** 3 *sg. pret.* 5,14,20, 13,11, etc.

storm, *n.* storm, 15,30

straf, 3 *sg. pret.* strove, 25,35

strecheð, 3 *sg. pres.* stretches, extends, 16,14 ; **streche,** *sg. imper.* 29,28; **istraht,** *past part.* 9,24; **istrahte,** *as adj. pl.* 22,13

strengðe, *n.* strength, power, (military) force, 14,30, 18,27,30, etc. ; importance, 30,33 : **ne makeden ... strengðe of,** put no trust in, 13,3n

strong, *adj.* strong, severe, hard,

3,4, 9,38, 13,31, etc.; **stronge,** *pl.* 21,28

stude, *n.* place, 16,20, 23,2

sturieð, *pl. imper. reflex.* bestir, 27,26

sturne, *adj.* severe, strict, 11,20

sucurs, *n.* help, reinforcements, 21,14,29

suleð, 3 *sg. pres. reflex.* soils, 24,16 ; **isulet,** *past part.* 24,9

suleð, *see* **sulle(n)**

sulh, *n.* ploughshare, 19,19

sulle(n), *infin.* sell, 25,16 : *in passive sense,* 25,2,17 ; **suleð,** 3 *sg. pres.* 12,14, 25,16 ; **salde,** 3 *sg. pret.* 25,33

sum, *adj.* certain, some, 5,35, 16,7, 17,30, etc.; *(in adverbial combinations)* **sum chearre,** once, at some time, 4,21, 29,29; **sumdeal, sumhwile,** *which see*; *gen. in* **summes weis,** in some way, 6,8; *pron.* (a certain) one, someone, 4,24, 10,16,29, etc.; **summe,** *pl.* 6,4,5

sumdeal, *adv.* somewhat, a little, 4,22

sumhweat, *pron.* something, 14,3, 25,15 : **sumhwet wið hwet,** some means by which, 18,16

sumhwile, *adv.* formerly, 22,8

sune, *n.* son, 10,35, 11,14, 22,4; *gen.* 10,37

sunegin, *infin.* sin, 17,11n; **sungin,** 17,12

sunfule, *adj.* sinful; *as n.* sinner, 14,13; *pl.* 8,18, 9,17

sunne, *n.* sin, 10,24,30,35, etc.; **sunne,** *gen.* 14,12; **sunnen,** *pl.* 6,21, 14,16, 23,34

sunne, *n.* sun, 4,37, 9,32, 10,8, etc.

sur, *adj.* sour, 27,30, 28,6,11; **sure,** *wk.* 27,32, 28,10

suster, *n.* sister, 12,9; **sustren,** *pl.* 3,5, 5,24, 7,18, etc.

sutel, *adj.* manifest, apparent, 9,26

suteli, 3 *sg. pres. subj.* may manifest, 18,1

swa, *adv.* so, thus, like this, 3,2,17, 4,23, etc.

swat, *n.* sweat, 9,6, 18,14

sweameð, 3 sg. pres. afflicts, grieves, 28,8

sweaten, infin. sweat, 9,12; sweat, 3 sg. pres. 9,4,8; swet, 9,4; sweatte, 3 sg. pret. 9,5

swenges, n. pl. blows, catches, 14,25

sweord, n. sword, 6,37, 7,2, 26,3

swete, adj. sweet, 15,23, 17,17, 18,10, etc.; as n. þet swete, what is sweet, 15,33; swetest, superl. 25,9

sweteð, 3 sg. pres. sweetens, 18,6

swetnesse, n. sweetness, 14,4, 15,13n, 16,5. etc.

swiftschipe, n. speed, 25,34

swinc, n. labour, toil, exertion, 4,11, 6,21,22, etc.; swinkes, pl. 12,12, 13,33, 19,2

swincful, adj. arduous, distressing, 9,8

swinken, infin. work (hard), labour, 7,35; swinkeð, 3 sg. pres. 18,15; iswunken, past part. 27,37

swire, n. neck, 23,32

swiðe, adv. very (as intensive), exceedingly, violently, 9,19, 10,31, 11,15, etc.: to swiðe, too much, 12,28, 29,10,11; swa unimete swiðe, so extravagantly, 21,12; swiðe mid alle, very specially, 24,29; swiðere, comp. more quickly, 12,4

swote, adj. sweet, 15,16, 19,6; adv., 15,14; swotest, adj. superl. 25,9

swoteliche, adv. agreeably, 21,20

swotnesse, n. sweetness, 15,16n, 18,37, etc.

swuch, adj. such (a), 7,12, 17,26, 18,24, etc.: swuch wummon, a woman very like, 18,26; pron. swuch . . . þe, such a one . . . who, 7,18; swuch þet, a (particular) man who, 18,11; swucche, preposit., pl., 10,1,12, 19,17: of the same sort, 12,14

i-swunken, see swinken

tacne, n. sign, symptom, 9,5

i-tald, talde, see tellen

tale, n. reckoning, number, story, 13,34, 21,7: haldeð na tale of, set no store by, 4,8

talie, 1 sg. pres.: of talie, talk about, 7,20

te, see to, þe, þu; also for

teachen, infin. teach, 18,16; teacheð, 3 sg. pres. 28,18

teares, n. pl. tears, 24,15, 28,24

tellen, infin. tell, relate, account, 12,35; teleð, 3 sg. pres. 6,32, 15,14, 23,13, etc.; talde, 3 sg. pret. 21,23; subj. 11,34; itald, past part. accounted, held, 5,23, 6,9,25, etc.

temptatiuns, n. pl. temptations, 22,19, 27,20

tendre, adj. tender, solicitous, 13,39

teone, n. hurt, annoyance, 5,37

tereð, 3 sg. pres. tears, 10,6; itoren, past part. 9,25

tes, see þis

testament, n. testament, 21,3

tet, see þe

tidliche, adv. promptly, 7,4

tilie, infin. labour, cultivate, 19,18; tilede, 3 sg. pret. 28,2

time, n. time, 11,9, 25,36

tindes, n. pl. rungs, 6,15

tis, see þis

tittes, n. pl. breasts, 9,25, 12,33

to, prep. to, 3,15,20,21, etc.: to his þurst, to him thirsting, 28,21; with infin. to, often in combination forte, which see under for; towards, 3,24, 6,16; into, 5,32, 15,19; for, 19,6; to lutel wurð, of little account, 19,5; in to, see in ; to gederes, see togederes

to, adv. too, 12,6,27, 13,30, etc.

tofuleð, 3 sg. pres. defiles, disfigures, 17,19

togederes, adv. together, 24,33, 29,9; to gederes, 6,21,31, 18,12, etc.

to ȝeines, see under þer

tohwiðeret, past part. whirled to pieces, 9,25

tolaimet, past part. mutilated, 9,36n, 37

i-toren, *see* tereð

torendeð, 3 *sg. pres.* pulls to pieces, 10,6

tospreat, 3 *sg. pres.* stretches out, 27,4

toteoreð, *pl. pres.* tear apart, 9,28,33; **totore(n),** *past part.* 9,32,36,38, etc.

totret, 3 *sg. pres.* treads down, 17,19; **totreode,** 3 *sg. pres. subj.* 17,20; **totreden,** *past part.* 17,22

totreodunge, *n.* treading down, trampling, 17,26

totweamde, 3 *sg. pret.* separated, 24,32

toward, *prep.* towards, for, 3,32, 4,4,10, etc.; **towart,** 27,3

treo, *n.* (piece of) wood, 22,33,34, 26,36; **treon,** *pl.* 26,35, 27,1,7, etc.

treowe, *adj.* true, faithful, 8,34, 18,9, 24,3

tribulatiuns, *n. pl.* tribulations, 27,20

trode, *n.* footprint, 17,22; **troden,** *pl.* 17,21,32

trudde, 3 *sg. pres. subj.*: trudde him in ham, may follow His track in them, 17,21n

trukeð, 3 *sg. pres.* fails, will fail, 7,20

trust, 3 *sg. pres.* trusts, has confidence in, 17,25

tu, *see* þu

tuke, 3 *sg. pres. subj.* ill-treat, 17,20; **ituket,** *past part.* 11,3, 21,38

tungen, *n. pl.* tongues, 30,25

tures, *n. gen.* of a tower, 14,18

turnen, *infin.* turn, 9,6, 17,10, 26,10; **turneð,** 3 *sg. pres.* 29,20; **turninde,** *pres. part.* 7,1; **turnde,** 3 *sg. pret.* 14,16; **iturnd,** *past. part.* 14,13

turneiment, *n.* tournament, 22,9

twa, *num.* two, 6,12,13,17, etc.; **tweie, tweien,** *masc.* 10,18, 12,38; **tweire,** *gen.* of the two, 29,15

twauald, twafald, *adj.* (of) two (sorts), double, 7,22,26,31

twinnin, *infin.* separate, part, 24,31

twinnunge, *n.* separation, 24,30

þa, *adv.* then, 28,7: þa . . . þa, when . . . then, 14,30, 27,31

þah, *adv.* yet, nevertheless, still, however, 5,12,13, 11,9, etc.; *conj. with subj.* although, 3,30, 4,2,8, etc.; even if, 11,30; **as þah,** as if, 5,9, 7,32, 10,4, etc.: as þah hit were, as it might appear, 13,7

þe, *def. art., adj. demons.*, the, this, that, 3,3,20,21, etc.; *after dental,* te, 4,4, 5,6,26, etc.; **þen,** *masc. accus.* 23,25, 27,28; **þes,** *masc. gen.* 10,9; **þet,** *def. art., adj. demons.* 7,19, 9,4,6, etc.; *after dental,* tet, 18,14, 27,35; *neut. art.* 10,31, 12,24, 22,35, 26,36; **þeo,** *pl. as determinative in relative constructions,* the, those . . . who, 4,12,26,30, etc.

þe, *pron. (in conjunction with rel. þe or þet),* þe þe, (he) who, 5,14,31, etc.; one who, 21,19; **þet,** *neut. (anticipatory subject)* 3,1, 4,6,26, etc.; þet te, that which, 5,10; þet tet, that which, 11,33; **þeo,** *pron. pl.*: þeo þe, those who, those which, 4,30, 5,34, 9,21, etc. : þe *(with omission of þeo),* 14,25 ; þeo þet, 4,1; þeo, which, 17,24

þe, *adv. with comparative,* the, 11,30, 12,4 ; te, 19,22

þe, *rel.* who, which, 3,28, 4,2,13, etc.; te, 5,10

þe, *see* þu

þeawes, *n. pl.* moral qualities, 12,12, 13,27: gode þeawes, virtues, 6,15

þeh, *n.* thigh, 18,13

þen, *conj.* than, 4,25,26,36, etc.; þene, 4,29

þen, *see* þe, *def. art.*

þenchen, *infin.* think (of), consider, intend, 23,3, 25,29 ; þenche, 1 *sg. pres.* 30,21; þencheð, 3 *sg. pres.* 26,11, 30,19; þencheð, *pl. imper.* 27,3

þenne, *adv.* then, accordingly, 4,25, 8,14,18, etc.

þeo, *see* þe, *def. art., pron.*

þeof, *n.* thief, 18,25

þeofðe, *n.* theft, 18,25

þeos, þeose, *see* þis

þeosternesse, *n.* darkness, 4,35

þeowe, *n.* slave, 14,2

þer, *adv.* there, 8,14, 9,9, 10,26, etc.; *rel.* where, 6,32, 10,11, 16,18, etc.; *in adv. combinations,* **þer aȝein,** on that account, 11,5; **þer toȝeines,** against it, 12,17; **þer þurh,** by reason of it, 17,11

þerbi, *adv.* thereby, thus, 23,3

þerto, *adv.* to it; for that purpose, 10,33, 11,4, 26,32

þeruore, *adv.* for it, for that reason, 9,23, 12,19

þerwið, *adv.* with it, against it, as well, 11,22, 12,25, 19,13, etc.

þes, *see* þe, *art., þis, adj., pron.*

þet, *conj.* that, so that, in order that (*with indic.*), 7,6, 11,5, 12,21, etc.; (*with subj.*) 3,27, 6,28, 17,3, etc.; in that, 5,23, 10,36; in so far as, 5,21, 17,39; se, swa . . . **þet,** so . . . (with the result) that, 11.11,16,35, etc.; for þi **þet,** *see* for

þet, *rel.* that, who, which, what, that which, 3,4,5,6, etc., 18,21 (*both*), 21,3, etc.

þet, *see* þe, *art., pron.*

þi, *see under* for

þi, þin, *see* þu

þicke, *adj.* thick, 18,13

þiderward, *adv.* in that direction, 19,22

þing, *n.* thing, something, possession, 5,10, 10,31, 12,18, etc.; *with pl. sense,* 4,23,27, 5,28, etc.; *pl.* 7,21, 16,16, 28,11; na **þing,** nothing, 5,22, 16,26, 24,9, etc.; **þet þing seolf,** the thing itself, 10,31; **þinges,** *pl.* 6,30, 12,9, 15,3, etc.; **þinge,** *pl. gen.* of things, 25,4,6,9

þis, *adj. demons.* this, 3,2,14, 5,18, etc.; *after dental,* tis, 11,9, 15,3,

16,18, etc.; **þes,** *masc.* 21,36, 22,4; *after dental,* tes, 26,17; **þeos,** *fem.* 6,29, 22,1; *gen. in* **þisses weis,** in this way, 16,10; *preposit. in* o **þisse wise,** in this way, 5,20, 9,33, 22,4, *but cp.* 24,37; **þes,** *pl.* these, 6,22, 10,22, 13,5, etc.; **þeos,** *pl.* 5,39, 6,12,26, etc.; **þeose,** *pl.* (*usually oblique*), 6,15, 9,26, 16,11, etc.

þis, *pron.* this, 5,3,6,13, etc.; *as subject to pl. verb,* 4,2, 5,33, 17,23, etc.; **þes,** *masc.* this person (*scil.* God), 30,16,22; **þeos,** *fem.* 14,14,22, 30,34; **þeos,** *pron. pl.* these, 4,18,29, 6,2, etc.

þoht, *n.* thought, reminder, 11,36, 24,26

þolemode, *adj. wk.* patient, long suffering: *as n.* 15,25

þolien, *infin.* suffer, endure, allow, 6,8,9,11, etc.: **þolie,** 9,14; **þolie,** 1 *sg. pres* (*subj.*), 5,23; **þoleð,** 3 *sg. pres.* 16,13, 17,20, 18,26; **þolieð,** *pl. pres.* 3,6, 5,35, 7,18, etc.; **þolie,** 3 *sg. pres. subj.* 15,26; **þolien,** *pl. pres. subj.* 8,18; **þolede,** 3 *sg. pret.* 22,24; **þoleden,** *pl. pret.* 8,13

þonc, *n.* thought, acknowledgment, 28,11

þoncki, *infin.* thank, 18,27

þorn, *n.* thorn, 17,7; **þornes,** *pl.* 16,37, 17,1

þreal, *n.* serf, slave, 7,19, 13,25

þreatte, 3 *sg. pret.* threatened, 11,18

þreatunge, *n.* threat, 11,4

þrefter, *adv.* after that, after them, for it, afterwards, 7,11, 13,14, 14,31, etc.

þreo, *num.* three, 3,19, 12,36, 13,4, etc.

þreouald, *adv.* of three kinds, 25,12

þridde, *adj.* third, 14,36, 15,3,4, etc.; *as n.* 13,5,11; third sort, 3,21,23, 5,39

þrin, *adv.* in it, therein, 4,3, 5,14, 12,23, etc.

þritti, *num.* thirty, 28,1

þrof, *adv.* of it, from it, in that,

on that account, 3,8, 5,32, 10,15, etc.

þron, *adv.* on it, thereby, 23,4, 25,20; against them, 14,29

þrowunge, *n.* suffering, 13,31

þruh, *n.* sepulchre, 16,23,24

þruppe, *adv.* higher up, previously, 5,17, 14,11,34, etc.

þu, *pron.* thou, 12,14, 15,30,32, etc.; *after dentals*, tu, 10,17, 11,13, 16,27, etc.; þe, *accus.*, *dat.*, *preposit.*, *reflex.*, thee, to thee, for thee, thyself, etc., 21,29,31,34, etc.; *after dentals*, te, 24,24, 25,19, 30,10; te seolf, thyself, 25,25 ; þin, *adj. poss.* (*before vowel or h*), of thee, thine, thy, 11,14, 21,34, 25,17 ; þi (*before cons.*), 11,9, 21,31, 25,1, etc.; þine, *pl.* 16,28, 21,27, 28,23

þuften, *n.* handmaid, 21,25

þulli, þullich, *adj.* such, like this, 10,2, 26,10, 28,28; þulliche, *pl.* 17,34

þuncheð, *sg. pres. impers.* it seems (*with dat.*), 4,21, 15,2, 18,18, etc.: Godd þuncheð god of ure god, God is concerned with our good, 11,32; þunche, *sg. pres. subj.* 9,10: *as imper.* 7,32, 29,12

þurh, *prep.* through(out), by, 5,8,18, 7,1, etc.: þurh nawt to leosen, with meanwhile nothing to lose, 26,1n; þurh hwet, by which, 14,19; þurh þet, because, by reason that, 7,10,11, 9,12, etc.; hwer þurh, through which, 4,23

þurhfulleð, 3 *sg. pres.* consummates, completes, 28,10,14

þurhwuniende, *pres. part. as adj.* permanent, enduring, 12,5

þurlin, *infin.* pierce : *in passive sense*, 23,5 ; iþurlet, *past part.* 22,10, 25,8

þurlunge, *n.* piercing, 24,27

þurst, *n.* thirst, 28,21,23

þus, *adv.* thus, in this way, then, 4,37, 5,4,5, etc.: þus riht, to this extent, 5,11; þus lo, *see* lo

þusent, *num.* thousand, 25,36

þwertouer, *adv.* crosswise, 27,1

þwongede, *past part. as adj.* laced, 9,20

uertuz, *n. pl.* virtues, 12,13

umbehwile, *adv.* at times, 5,27

unburiet, *past part.* unburied, 5,1

uncuð, *adj.* unknown, strange, 7,33,35

uncuððe, *n.* strange land, 7,35

undeadlich, *adj.* immortal, 10,7

undeore, *adj.* inexpensive, 29,33

under, *prep.* beneath, under (the power of), in, 9,3, 13,25, 14,29, etc.

underfeng, *see* underuon

understonden, *infin.* understand : *in passive sense*, 6,33, 7,10, 8,12, etc. ; understondeð, *pl. imper.* 27,31; understonden, *past part.* 14,14, 15,4,16

undertid, *n.* third hour of the day, 26,15n

underuon, *infin.* receive, 9,30 ; underuoð, *pl. pres.* 17,31; underueng, 3 *sg. pret.* 11,28 : underfeng, 21,15

unendeliche, *adv.* infinitely, 25,31

uneuenlich (to), *adj.* not to be compared (with), 30,24 ; *adv.* incomparably, 29,32 : vneuenliche, 25,30

ungraciuse, *adv.* ungratefully, 12,17n

unhal, *adj.* unwholesome, 13,1

unhope, *n.* despair, 14,18

unimete, *adv.* immeasurably: swa unimete swiðe, so extravagantly, 21,12

unmeteliche, *adv.* immeasurably, 25,30

unnen, *infin.* permit, 17,8,13

unnet, *n.* what is unprofitable, foolishness, 5,27

unrecheles, *adj. or n.*: on unrecheles, in carelessness, without thought, 21,16n

unstrengeð, 3 *sg. pres.* weakens, 12,28

untalelich (to), *adj.* not to be uttered (by), 30,25

untohen, *past part.* undisciplined, 14,1

untrusset, *past part.* unburdened, 4,28

unþeawes, *n. pl.* bad habits, vices, 15,2, 19,25

unþeode, *n.* foreign people, 7,34

unwreast, *adj.* bad, wicked, 23,19; unwreaste, *adv.* wickedly, 23,29

unwurð, *adj.* worthless, unworthy, of no account, cheap, 5,19,23, 6,9, etc. ; unwurðe, *pl.* 12,18, 17,6

i-uorðet, *see* fordeð

up, *adv.* up, upwards, 10,11,13, 13,20, etc.; up on, *prep.* upon, 21,11: up o, 3,7, 6,10, 10,30, etc.; up to, up to, 6,14,29,32, etc.

uppard, *adv.* up, 6,18

upriht, *adv.* upright, 26,36

ure, us, *see* we

urn, *n.*: of urn, in running, 25,35

ut, ute, *adv.* out, abroad, away from home, 7,35: ut of, *prep.* out of, apart from, 3,2, 4,25, 5,4, etc.

utewið, *adv.* without, outwardly, 14,2

uttre, *adj. comp.* outer, external, 16,31, 18,4, 19,1, etc.

utward, *adv.* away from here, 30,15

uuel, *adj.* bad, evil, 9,5, 17,8,11, etc.; uueles, *gen.* 22,2; uuele, vuele, *pl. as n.* wicked (men), 7,27, 20,30

uuel, *n.* evil, harm, disease, 6,6, 12,11, 13,19, etc.; uuele, *preposit.* 17,10; uueles, *pl.* 22,21

uuele, *adv.* evilly, hurtfully, uncomfortably, 18,22, 19,33

va, van, *see* fa

veien, *infin.* join, 24,33: *see also* feieð

vilte, *n.* dishonour, abjectness, 6,12, 17,33

vndeore, *see* undeore

vnderstondeð, *see* understonden

vneuenliche, *see* uneuenlich

vngraciuse, *see* ungraciuse

vre, *see* we

vuele, *see* uuel, *adj.*

wa, *n.* pain, grief, 5,23,31,33, etc.: don se wa, treat so painfully, 10,17

wacnesse, *n.* frailty, 18,28

waggið, *pl. pres.* shake, are agitated, 14,25

wah, *n.* wall, 16,32 ; wahes, *pl.* 16,22

wakeð, 3 *sg. pres.* keeps vigil, stays awake, 18,14

walde, walden, *see* wulle

waldes, *n. gen. as adv.* deliberately, of set purpose, 9,27

walleð, 3 *sg. pres.* boils, is boiling, 12,21,23

warliche, *adv.* warily, 27,22

warpen, *infin.* throw, cast, 28,18; warpeð, 3 *sg. pres.* 23,31, 28,15; warp, *sg. imper.* 6,28 ; weorp, 3 *sg. pret.* 20,25 ; wurpe, 3 *sg. pret. subj.* 18,23 ; iwarpe, *past part.* 12,22

wat, 1 *and* 3 *sg. pres.* knows, 10,10, 18,11,26, etc.: *in asseverations :* wat Crist, let Christ witness, 8,33 ; Godd (hit) wat, 4,29n, 5,14, 18,2,20

waxen, *pl. pres. subj.* grow, 17,28

we, *pron. pl. nom.* we, 3,2, 4,6, 6,6, etc.; us, *acc., dat., preposit., reflex.*, us, ourselves, to us, for us, etc., 6,6, 8,1, 10,37, etc.: us seolf, ourselves, 8,20: us seoluen, 10,26; ure, vre, *adj. poss.* our, ours, 3,14, 6,18, 8,2, etc.

wealden, *infin.* rule, hold, enjoy, win power over, 7,25,31, 21,7, etc.

weane, *n.* misery, woe, 9,33n, 21,30

weari, *n.* felon, 5,19

wearnen, *infin.* refuse to allow, forbid, 30,11

weater, *n.* water, 12,22, 15,19, 22, etc.; weattres, *pl.* 15,31, 27,19

weattri, *adj.* watery, 15,21

wecchen, *n. pl.* vigils, night watches, 12,10

wed, *n.* pledge, 23,13

wedde, 3 *sg. pret.* went wild, wantoned, 11,38n

i-weddet, *past part.* wedded to, 23,19

wei, *n.* way, road, route, 3,29, 4,9, 5,26, etc.; weie, *preposit.* 3,31, 4,21; *gen. in* þisses weis, thus, in this way, 16,10; summes weis, in some way, 6,8

weie, 3 *sg. pres.. subj.* (may) measure, assess, 13,38; iweiet, *past. part.* in measure, 25,34

weie, *n.* balance, measure, 13,37, 20,16; weies, *pl.* 13,32

weifearinde, *pres. part. as adj.* wayfaring, 4,16

weilawei, *interj.* alas, 30,9

wel, *adv.* well, 4,10, 6,22,34, etc.

welcume, *adj.* welcome, 23,29

wem, *n.* blemish, injury, 16,30

wendeð, 3 *sg. pres.* turns, passes, goes, 5,32: went, 16,29; went, *sg. imper.* 16,27; wende, 3 *sg. pret.* 16,27, 14,30; iwent, *past part.* 15,19,23

wene, *n.* opinion, belief, 22,14

weneð, 3 *sg. pres.* thinks, expects, 27,17; *pl. pres.* 9,21; wene, 3 *sg. pres. subj. as imper.* 10,27

i-went, *see* wendeð

weohes, *see* woh

weole, *n.* good fortune, riches, 25,31

weolie, *adj. pl. as n. in gen.* of rich men, 25,6

weorp, *see* warpen

weorre, *n.* war, strife, 15,2, 28,17

weorrið, *pl. pres.* wage war, 3,28; iweorret, *past part.* beleaguered, 21,27

wepeð, 3 *sg. pres.* weeps, 18,19; wep, *sg. imper.* 28,24

wepne, *n.* weapon, 11,1

wercmen, *n. pl.* workmen, 28,4

were, *sg. imper. reflex.*: were þe, defend thyself, 26,6

were, weren, *see* wes

werkes, *n. pl.* works, 18,4, 24,3, 27,26

werunge, *n.* (kind of) clothing, habit, 12,11

wes, 3 *sg. pret.* was, 5,24, 6,37, 7,9, etc.; nes, was not, 7,4, 9,23, 16,15, etc.; weren, *pl. pret.* 6,31, 9,26, 13,5, etc.; *subj.* 12,38 ; were, *sg. pret. subj.* 6,18, 11,34, 36, etc.: as þah it were, as it might appear, 13,7 ; nere, *sg. pret. subj.* were not, 22,1

weschen, *infin.* wash, 24,12; wescheð, 3 *sg. pres.* 17,15

widewehad, *n.* widowhood, 25,13

wif, *n.* (married) woman, 23,10, 24,2

wil, *n.* desire, inclination, will, 10,21, 11,9, 22,23, etc.: wið hare gode wil, voluntarily, 3,21; willes, *gen. as adv.* freely, 22,24: willes & waldes, wantonly and of set purpose, 9,27

wil ȝeoue, *n.* voluntary gift, 12,15n

willeliche, *adv.* willingly, 24,32

wilnest, 2 *sg. pres.* desirest, 29,30; wilneð, 3 *sg. pres.* 15,11; wilnin, *pl. pres. subj.* 20,3 ; wilnede, 3 *sg. pret.* 28,2

wine, *n.* wine, 15,20,23 ; wines, *pl.* 15,24

wipeð, 3 *sg. pres.* wipes, 17,15

i-wis, *adv.* surely, 4,16 ; iwiss, 22,27

wisdom, *n.* wisdom, sense, discretion, 10,16, 13,17,26, etc.

wise, *n.* manner : o þisse wise, thus, in this way, 5,21, 9,34, 22,4: o þis wise, 24,37; o þulli wise, in such fashion as this, 28,28; o nane wise, in no way, 30,21; alle cunne wise, all sorts of ways, 20,22

wise, *adj.* wise: *as n.* þe wise, *scil.* the Preacher, 15,24 ; wisre, *adj. comp.* wiser, 10,18,22 ; wisest, *adj. superl.* wisest, 25,6

i-wiss, *see* iwis

wit, *n.* mind, senses, 26,1

witen, *infin.* guard, look after, keep, 12,7, 27,22 ; witeð, *pl. pres.* 12,28

witerliche, *adv.* certainly, 8,3, 15,33, 29,39, etc.

witneð, 3 sg. pres. testifies, bears witness to, 7,38, 8,3,27, etc.

wið, prep. with, in company with, by means of, 3,9,10,21, etc. against, 27,22; in, 4,3, 10,28. 18,25; adverbially, from, 30,18; wið innen, inwardly, within herself, 16,5; wið ute(n), prep. without, lacking, 9,19, 11,35, etc.; wið uten, adv. from without, 16,7

wiðdrahene, past part. as adj. pl. withdrawn, 12,23

wiðhalden, pl. pres. subj. refrain 3,27

wleatien, infin. feel disgust, 26,28

wlech, adj. lukewarm, 26,22,27

wlite, n. beauty, appearance, 25,32

wod, adj. mad, 29,9

woh, n. wrong, injury, 6,24; weohes, pl. 5,28

wohere, n. wooer, 22,6, 26,10

wohin, infin. woo, 21,7; woheð, 3 sg. pres. 21,1, 24,37, 26,9; wohede, 3 sg. pret. 22,5

wohlech, n.; for wohlech, in courtship, 21,12

wombe, n. belly, womb, 12,23, 13,23, 16,16, etc.

wonti, infin. (with dat.) be lacking, 25,27; wonti, sg. pres. subj.: hire wonti, she lacks, 29,12

wontreaðe, n. misery, adversity, 9,32

wopi, adj. tearful, of tears, 15,31

word, n. word, saying, report, 3,15, 16,18, 17,6, etc.; wordes, pl. 21,20, 30,1; word, pl. 6,22

woreð, 3 sg. pres. destroys, confuses, harasses, 19,26n

wori, adj. troubled, confused, 19,33

world, n. world, 4,3,25, 5,18, etc.; worldes, gen. 4,20, 5,25†, 6,5; worlde, preposit. 5,4,12

worltlich, adj. worldly, earthly, of the world, secular, 4,8,9,26, etc.; worltliche, pl. 15,3, 19,25; worldliche, pl. 27,20, 30,25

wracfulliche, adv. vengefully, savagely, 10,29

wrag(e)lunge,n.struggling,14,21,26

i-wraht, wrahte, see wurche

wrat, 3 sg. pret. wrote, 12,9, 21,5; iwriten, past part. 7,7, 8,15, 16,10: as n. something written, 30,28

wraðe, adj. angry, 11,20

wreah, see wrið

wreastlere, n. wrestler, 14,23

wreastlin, infin. wrestle: wreastlin a ʒein, fight back, 14,26

wreastlunge, n. wrestling, 14,21,23

wreaðeð, 3 sg. pres. reflex. becomes angry, 5,27

wreaððe, n. anger, 30,4

wrecche, n. pl. exiles, wretches, 8,18; wrecches, pl. 9,17, 20,33†

wreoke(n), infin. take vengeance, 10,30, 30,3

wrihe, see wrið

writ, n. scripture, 28,27

i-writen, see wrat

wrið, 3 sg. pres. covers, conceals, 17,29; wreah, 3 sg. pret. 22,11; wrihe, past part. as adj. with a hidden meaning, 21,8

wude, n. wood, pieces of wood, 26,32

wulle, 1 sg. pres. desire, am willing, think, will, intend, often suggesting future (sometimes followed by subj.) 21,33, 26,28: with cons. assimilated, ich chulle, 3,16, 15,35, 21,30, etc.: nule, will not, 25,23; wult, 2 sg. pres. 19,33, 21,17, 25,14, etc.: nult, wilt not, 25,20; wule, 3 sg. pres. 10,3,29, 11,21, etc.: nule, will not, 8,34, 9,12, 11,26, etc.; wulleð, pres. pl. 8,19,20, 9,17, etc.: nulleð, will not, 10,25, 12,18; walde, sg. pret. 6,8, 10,31, 16,35, etc.: nalde, would not, 11,37, 22,28, 25,37; naldest, 2 sg. pret. wouldst not, 21,36; walden, pl. pret. 18,8

wummon, n. woman, 5,4, 10,10 11,31, etc.; wummen, pl. 18,7

wunde, n. wound, 21,33

wunder, n. marvel, strange thing, 9,1, 18,9, 21,25, etc.; wundre, *preposit.*: (al) to wundre, (quite) outrageously, **17**,20n, **21**,38; **wundres**, *pl.* **3**,30, **21**,21

wundri, 3 *sg. pres. subj. reflex.*: ne wundri ha hire nawiht, let her not be at all surprised, **16**,5

i-wunet, *past part.* accustomed, **12**,36, **22**,8

wunne, *n.* joy, delight, **4**,15, **5**,31, 33, etc.

i-wunnen, *past part.* won, **29**,28

wununge, *n.* dwelling (place), **4**,6, **16**,17

wurche, 1 *sg. pres.* do, perform, make, **5**,11; **wurcheð**, 3 *sg. pres.*

19,21; **wrahte**, 3 *sg. pret.* wrought, **21**,21; **iwraht**, *past part.* **25**,28

wurpe, *see* warpen

wurð, *n.* worth: to lutel wurð, of little value, **19**,6

wurð, *adj.* of worth, precious, worth, **8**,37, **9**,19, **25**,39, etc.

wurðe, *adj.* worthy, **21**,25: wurðe to, fit for, **24**,13

i-wurðen, *infin.* become, **23**,19; wurðe, 2 *sg. pres. subj.* **26**,29; iwurðe, 3 *sg. pres subj.* **14**,1

zedual, *n.* zedoary, **13**,4n

INDEX OF PROPER NAMES

together with selected references to Introduction and Notes

TEXAS WOMAN'S UNIVERSITY LIBRARY